Great Lives

Great Lives

KAREN
FARRINGTON

BOOKS

This book is published to accompany the BBC Radio 4 series entitled *Great Lives*.

Series Producer: Miles Warde
Editor: Clare McGinn

1 3 5 7 9 10 8 6 4 2

Published in 2011 by BBC Books, an imprint of Ebury Publishing.
A Random House Group Company

Main Text by Karen Farrington

Copyright © Woodlands Books Ltd 2011
Foreword copyright © Matthew Parris 2011

The Random House Group Limited Reg. No. 954009

Addresses for companies within the Random House Group can be found at
www.randomhouse.co.uk

A CIP catalogue record for this book is available from the British Library.

ISBN 978 1849901093

The Random House Group Limited supports the Forest Stewardship Council® (FSC®), the leading international forest certification organisation. All our titles that are printed on Greenpeace approved FSC® certified paper carry the FSC® logo. Our paper procurement policy can be found at
www.randomhouse.co.uk/environment

Commissioning editor: Albert DePetrillo
Project editor: Nicholas Payne
Copy-editor: Steve Tribe
Designer: O'Leary & Cooper
Illustrations: Maria Raymondsdotter
Production: David Brimble

Printed and bound in the UK by CPI Mackays, Chatham, Kent, ME5 8TD

To buy books by your favourite authors and register for offers,
visit www.randomhouse.co.uk

Contents

Foreword

by Matthew Parris

D ID YOU KNOW that Dr (Samuel) Johnson liked rolling himself down a hillside until he was giddy? Or that America's *Battle Hymn of the Republic* was written by a pacifist and early feminist ('Let the hero, born of woman, crush the serpent with his heel / His truth is marching on')? Did you know that Sarah Bernhardt's first ambition was to be a nun?

Sometimes, someone comes up with an idea for a book or radio series that is so straightforward and compelling that you wonder whether it isn't… well, a bit pat. 'It's too obvious,' I thought, when BBC Radio 4 asked me to take over a series called *Great Lives*. The format was surely too simple. Inviting well-known people to choose a hero from the past, finding some archive material where possible, then turning it into a half-hour, three-cornered conversation between presenter, guest and an expert witness… Was that all? It was like (say) asking someone to imagine themselves on a desert island, choose their favourite music, talk about their lives… and, er, that's it. Oh, please! Couldn't they devise a cleverer framework than that?

Such were my doubts. But as I took the reins I quickly found that, far from being the flaw, simplicity was the key. In the years since I first took the presenter's chair, I've found there are almost no universal rules about what makes these stories sing. Does either the guest or the guest's choice have to be a celebrity whom most people will know all about? You might think so but I soon discovered otherwise when one of my first guests, Frances Cairncross (a distinguished economist and writer, and rector of an Oxford college, but best-known only among a fairly intellectual audience) chose as her great life an obscure 19th-century Hungarian doctor, Ignaz Semmelweis, working in a general hospital in Vienna. My heart sank. This programme, I thought, would be a tough one to bring to life.

It proved one of my most memorable. I hardly had to speak. Cairncross, who knew her subject backwards, raised the curtain on the amazing but forgotten story of the man who discovered, years before it was acknowledged, why millions of women worldwide had died or would die after childbirth of 'childbed' (or Puerperal) fever. It was so simple: bacteria on the hands of the examining doctor. The solution was simple too – wash the hands. Yet a mulishly arrogant male medical establishment refused to accept that they were causing rather than curing disease. Rejected, Semmelweis – who had proved his theory resoundingly by in-house trials at his hospital – ended his days, ignored, in a lunatic asylum.

So, any universal rules about what brings a Great Life to life? Actually there's only one. Somebody – guest or choice – has to be extraordinary. Frankly, I wouldn't care whom Nelson Mandela, Bob Dylan or Muammar Gaddafi (if we could get them into the guest's chair) selected. The very fact of their choosing a personal hero would arouse our interest; and in some ways the more obscure the individual, the more intriguing the choice. Likewise, if the hero is Darwin, or Churchill, Napoleon or (Christopher Hitchen's choice) Trotsky, then, however luminous or obscure my guest, the life itself will dazzle.

Many in these pages do dazzle. Others perplex. Some horrify. Some reveal as much about the chooser as the choice. Repeatedly I've asked myself two questions that will no doubt occur to you too as you read this book. First, must we approve of an individual or their achievements if we are to call the life great? Second, can a Great Life qualify on the basis of just one big thing: one supreme achievement or talent, even though the life itself – the human being as an individual – was a flop, a bore or a mess?

To the first question – must we approve? – I offer an emphatic No. Trotsky deserved the ice-pick in his skull – but what a life! Who would dare deny that Genghis Khan led a great life? I was disappointed that in his book *Courage – Eight Portraits*, Gordon Brown altogether avoided the debate about whether it is possible for the virtue of courage to be exhibited in an indifferent or even wicked cause. I have no doubt it is possible.

To the second question – is achievement all you need? – I give an emphatic Yes. What a mess Nina Simone made of her life; yet I remember sitting with my guests in a BBC studio, tears pricking our eyes as she sang 'Don't Smoke in Bed'. 'That talent,' I thought, 'that sound, that timing, outweighs in the balance all the mistakes it would be possible for a woman to make.'

It was Nietzsche (another of our great lives) who, to the remark that 'no man is a hero to his valet', replied: 'No. But that is not because the hero is not a hero, but because the valet is a valet.' Many of the choices herein have had feet of clay. Delicious among the studio pleasures of exploring their lives have been the valets'-eye views of great men and women, from the feet upwards. We should not exclude these views. We should wonder 'what were they really like?' We should be curious – even nosey – about their besetting sins, their sexual and emotional relationships, the way they treated their children, their butlers or their chambermaids.

But at the start, and in the end, we should ask only this: what did they achieve? What did they create? What did they bring? What did they leave behind? Every guest I've ever interviewed has chosen their hero not for a rounded life, not for a balanced life, not even for a virtuous life, but for the messy, awkward, troublesome, infinitely disputable quality of greatness.

Greatness resides not in being but in doing. Greatness resides in action. As someone whom none of my guests has yet had the audacity to choose as their Great Life, once said: 'By their fruits ye shall know them.'

Alexander the Great

(356–323 BC)

Alexander has to be at the top of the A list of any great figures. His greatness is suspect: the suspicions are what one enjoys. Alexander did install a civilisation but it didn't take altogether. In the present time the Middle East is in continuity with the mess of peoples and religions that Alexander stirred up. People began to define themselves by their religion rather than their nationality; this is still an element that is very difficult to resolve. The modern world is more like the Hellenistic world than we would care to admit.

Frederic Raphael (Screen writer and journalist)

Alexander was king of the Macedonians in Northern Greece and he came to the throne [in] 336 BC. In thirteen years he had managed to conquer what was then the largest territorial empire in the world, that of the Persians based in modern Iran, and at the time of his death aged 33 in circumstances still speculated over he had plans for further conquest which in his mind may well have meant world conquest.

Tony Smorforth (Professor Ancient History,
Newcastle University)

17

WORLD DOMINATION IS by its nature beset with heroic failures. Alexander the Great is arguably ensconced in the sparsely populated category that came closest to achieving it, forging a mighty empire that stretched between India and Europe and encompassed the Middle East.

Admittedly he found maintaining everything within his expanded borders a challenge similar to herding puppies. Nonetheless, in a rudimentary age, he could call the known world his playground and accordingly assumed the mantle of a god. Figuratively he was an immense figure although claims by the ancients that he was physically a giant have been dispelled by modern scholars.

However, Alexander continues to pose a problem for historians as there are two versions attached to almost every episode in his life. One is surely the work of professional flatterers who whitewash his ruthlessness and highlight his wisdom. Another ignores his military prowess to underline his vanity. The two schools of thought are usually irreconcilable.

Plutarch is one of Alexander's major apologists. Although he lived much later, he based his commentaries on existing texts, of which there were plenty, and he bequeathed a compelling description of the night of Alexander's conception. 'On the night before the marriage was consummated the bride dreamed that there was a crash of thunder, that her womb was struck by a thunderbolt and that there followed a blinding flash from which a great sheet of flame blazed up and spread far and wide before it finally died away.' Moreover he insisted that Alexander exuded a pleasing scent. Perhaps.

Callisthenes is another fan, a student alongside Alexander who accompanied him on campaigns as an historian. His accounts often reflected the events of Homer's *Iliad*, which had a great effect on Alexander. But there's no doubt that if Alexander was capable of great courage and extraordinary wisdom he was also accustomed to brutality, having prisoners of war put to the sword by the thousand and executing men who had served alongside him.

Alexander was born to the Macedonian king Philip II and his wife Olympia. As a child, Alexander was tutored by Aristotle, who gave him a grounding in philosophy, science, literature, medicine and rhetoric. After his father's assassination, Alexander took the throne, ordering the killing of court conspirators to safeguard his immediate future.

His first task was to bring the Greek states into line behind his rule. Although the Greeks were neighbours there was a traditional hatred between themselves and the Macedonians. Having made an example of Thebes, which was razed by Alexander and his men, the rest swiftly complied with his wishes. Afterwards he set his sights on the extensive Persian empire, under Darius III. With a helmet distinguished by two white plumes, Alexander led from the front and afforded himself no privileges that were not available to his men. He scythed through the Persian army, allegedly with few losses, in the first of several confrontations in which he attacked using a wedge formation to great effect.

He then went to Gordium, a city in what is now Turkey, where there was an intricately knotted rope. According to legend the man who unravelled it was supposedly assured of world power. In typically blunt fashion Alexander slashed the knot with his sword so it fell into pieces, content that this indicated he was destined to rule. Following another battle with the Persians, Alexander headed to Egypt where he was welcomed by a population tired of Persian rule. There was a third battle to finally subdue the Persians before Alexander was distracted by unrest in Greece. Within just three years he won himself a mighty domain reaching from Greece to Syria, encompassing Israel, Turkey and Egypt.

Alexandria in Egypt is one of many cities named for the conqueror. It was here he consulted with an oracle and began delusions of deity that bloomed in the remaining years of his life. Alexander also favoured eastern robes above those of Macedonia, spoke in Persian, and insisted those who approached him spread-eagled themselves on the floor as a sign of supplication. His former tutor, Aristotle, was among many in ancient Greece who felt those who were not Greek were barbarians and should be enslaved. Alexander disagreed, feeling it was his duty to civilise the world by incorporating the conquered nations within the empire rather than subjugating them. Alexander remained determined to blend eastern and western cultures, orchestrating numerous marriages between his Macedonian nobles and Persian women, including his own. But even those who supported him felt he had gone too far.

By now he was drinking heavily. Indeed, during one drunken evening he killed a close friend, Cleitus, with a spear. Mad with grief, Alexander contemplated suicide. His men were now wary of his wayward temper. And still his days of marching and fighting were not finished, although many Macedonians were now weary of these epic journeys. Alexander marched into India until his men would go no further. (He believed he was heading for an ocean that marked the edge of the world.) His death from a fever put an end to these global ambitions as, without a designated successor, the empire fractured into fiefdoms ruled with greater or lesser skill by his generals.

Although Alexander was without doubt ruthless, he clearly possessed an enlightened mind to some degree, as revealed by a story from Plutarch about a meeting between the warrior king and the philosopher Diogenes: 'When he saw so many people approaching him Diogenes raised himself a little on his elbow and fixed his gaze upon Alexander. The king greeted him and inquired whether he could do anything for him. "Yes," replied the philosopher. "You can stand a little to one side out of my sun." Alexander is said to have been greatly impressed by this answer and full of admiration for the hauteur and independence of mind of a man who could look down on him with such condescension. So much so that he remarked to his followers who were laughing and mocking the philosopher as they went away: "You may say what you like. But if I were not Alexander I would be Diogenes."'

Alfred the Great

(849–899)

He is the only English monarch ever to be given the title 'Great'. He made a difference to our history. But for his remarkable military, political and administrative skills England would have been a Scandinavian country in terms of its ethnicity, its language and its culture. And of course we remained an English country.

Norman Tebbit (Politician)

We can certainly call him great. Had Alfred lost, we would most certainly be speaking a dialect of Danish in this country, and it is hard to imagine what this society would be like without the great tradition of English literature. It was also a bit like the Churchillian era in that he had his back to the wall.

Professor Alfred Smyth
(Director of Research, Canterbury Christchurch)

HISTORY KNOWS HIM as the king who was challenged in cooking skills. But although King Alfred is best known for burning cakes, his reputation should lie in his extraordinary enlightenment in the Dark Ages. He was a warrior king, a scholar, a lawgiver and a Christian who saved his country from being overrun by Vikings. Beyond that he founded the British navy and became the first king of a united England.

Yet Alfred was not born to be king. He was the fourth or fifth son of Aethelwulf, the King of the West Saxons. One by one his brothers were killed in conflicts with the marauding Vikings. It was the same story in other English kingdoms as rulers were systematically murdered or fled. Alfred was England's last hope.

He succeeded to the throne in 872, a year after he and his brother Aethelred triumphed over the Danes in the battle of Ashdown in Berkshire. The invaders returned in numbers to Wessex from the south and east, however, and Alfred lost more battles than he won. He was chased into the Somerset levels where he lived as a fugitive. (It was while he was in Somerset that the cake-burning incident reputedly occurred, presumably as he pondered tactics.) He continued to plague the enemy with guerrilla-style attacks but failed to secure a decisive victory until 878 in the battle of Edington in Wiltshire, having called Saxons to arms from across the region. This final victory proved the most significant. At this point the Saxons and the Vikings made peace, with Alfred overseeing the Danish king Guthrum's baptism, which put an end to this Viking's pagan ways.

It didn't put an end to the Viking threat, though, and Alfred took steps to consolidate the victory and defend his realm. After negotiations he secured a border between Saxon and Viking territory stretching from the Thames to the Tees. This gave him control of Kent and West Mercia for the first time, while Viking law and customs were observed across the frontier in the Danelaw. Alfred also fortified towns near the border, realising Vikings were bold in open battle but less sure about siege-style strategies. Alfred further established a fleet of boats to counter the waterborne threat of Viking invasion, using expertise imported from the Low Countries to do so.

With his kingdom stable, Alfred turned his attention to law and order. For Saxons, justice was linked to a compensation scheme which he rationalised:

> In many synods they fixed the compensations for many human misdeeds and they wrote them in many synod books, here one law, there another. Then I King Alfred gathered them together and ordered to be written many of the ones that our forefathers observed, those that pleased me. And many of the ones that did not please me I rejected.
>
> For I dared not presume to set in writing at all many of my own, because it was unknown to me what would please those who should come after us.
>
> If any man pledges what it is right for him to carry out and leaves it unfulfilled he is with humility to hand over his weapons and his possessions to his friends for safekeeping and be 40 days in prison.

There were differing levels of compensation paid by men who slept with the wives of others. And there were other rules that he instituted to govern his people, the titles of which include 'on the penalty for bringing a nun out of nunnery without permission', 'on the compensation due when a pregnant woman is killed', 'on accidental death caused by a falling tree', 'on an owner's liability for offences committed by his dog', 'on a man's liability on crime committed with weapons lent to him by someone else' and 'on procedure when someone is wounded by a spear carried over a man's shoulder'. These are the roots of written government rules, records and procedures that largely survived the Norman invasion and have guided English society to the present day.

Thanks to Alfred there came a stable coinage and a taxation system that further secured the kingdom. Indeed, by the 890s coins were indicating that his title was King of the English, implying some hitherto unknown unity among the regions.

Then there was his love of learning that, combined with a pious faith, brought new texts to England when there was little education to be had after the sustained pillaging of monasteries. According to Alfred: 'Learning had declined so thoroughly in England that there were very few men on this side of the Humber who could understand their divine services in English or even translate a single letter from Latin into English. There were so few of them that I cannot recollect even a single one south of the Thames when I succeeded to the kingdom.'

Having learned Latin in his thirties, Alfred rescued books discarded since Roman times and translated them into the language of the West Saxons. He commissioned other translations as well. More importantly still he began the Anglo-Saxon Chronicles, ordering that they be kept in monasteries and regularly updated. It was a tradition of recording history that endured for several hundred years. Alfred became a romantic figure in written record, the tale of cake-burning appearing less than a century after his death.

There's little doubt that without him England would have fallen under Viking influence, changing the laws, the literature and the language that is so familiar to us today. While the Saxon influence might have remained, it would have been watered down beyond recognition. One chronicle records of Alfred after his death: 'In the year 899 the magnanimous Alfred passed from the world, king of the Saxons, unshakeable pillar of the western people, a man replete with justice, vigorous in warfare, learned in speech, above all instructed in divine learning for he had translated unknown numbers of books of rhetorical Latin speech into his own language, so variously and so richly that his book would arouse tearful emotions not only with those familiar with it but even in those hearing it for the first time. His body lies at peace in Winchester.'

Hannah Arendt

(1906–1975)

She is one of the most important public intellectuals of the twentieth century. Her writings on totalitarianism shaped a whole generation of thinkers and certainly influenced my own writing. She was a very brave woman in what she said and did. She always did what she thought was the right thing rather than what was popular, what was safe. She had integrity and I admire her a great deal for that.

Dr Munira Mirza (Mayor of London's arts adviser)

She was so magnetic, she is a good argument why women should not be concerned about ageing if they have character. She required no plastic surgery or cosmetics. She had a very distinctive voice, always a cigarette in her hand – truly a commanding presence.

Dr Leon Botstein (President of Bard College, New York and Arendt's personal friend)

FOR A RIGHT-WING writer, Hannah Arendt appeared to have some troublingly left-wing leanings. And as a socialist, she seemed uncomfortably close to conservatism. In fact, in a century that was dominated by political labels, Arendt neatly sidestepped being pigeonholed and ruffled many feathers by doing so. With Hannah Arendt, people had to expect the unexpected.

Born in Germany to middle-class Jewish parents, Arendt was cultured and widely read before the end of her teenage years. Her mother coached her to complain if teachers made anti-Semitic remarks in the classroom, and Arendt also tussled with antagonistic fellow pupils. As someone who was always passionate about politics, she was undoubtedly affected by the upheaval in the political landscape of Germany during her first quarter of a century. Still a child when imperialism held sway, she saw the German nation flirt with revolution at the end of the First World War and witnessed the faltering of the democratic Weimar Republic before the National Socialists emerged as the dominant political force.

In 1924, Arendt began to study theology in the University of Marburg, where she met philosopher Martin Heidegger. They were involved in a brief but passionate affair that ended when she went on to study at the University of Heidelberg. This relationship caused controversy that dogged her later life, not because he was married and a father, but because he later joined the Nazis. Indeed, he was a member of the Nazi party when the Second World War came to a close. Despite this, Arendt resumed a friendship with Heidegger after the conflict, even though he didn't renounce his extreme political opinions.

In September 1929, Arendt married Günther Stern, a fellow rising star on the academic circuit although the union didn't last. Initially it seemed Arendt would enjoy a glittering career as a writer and theorist, but her opportunities were dramatically halted in 1933 when Hitler came to power. She immediately became an activist against the government, helping the German Zionist Organisation to fight anti-Semitism and, on a practical level, engineering the rescue of Jewish children from the Third Reich. After being arrested for her efforts, she escaped and fled to Paris. There she met her second husband, Heinrich Blücher, and both escaped from internment after Germany invaded France in 1940.

It was obvious that Arendt would have to leave Europe in order to survive. In 1941, she went to America with her mother and Blücher, securing citizenship there a decade later. Arendt was a perfect fit with the lively intellectual community that already existed in New York. Soon after her arrival in America, she was writing for Jewish publications. Later she wrote for a left-wing journal in polished prose.

Her first book, *The Origins of Totalitarianism*, appeared in 1951 and compared the cults of Hitler and Stalin in a landmark work that influenced post-war thinking. Immediately there was evidence of some of the 'outside-the-box' thinking that characterised her thoughts and beliefs for the rest of her life. There was limited information about the machinery of the Soviet state at the time, and many people were resistant to the idea of drawing parallels between the two dictators. But, persuasively and with remarkable insight, she argued racism was embedded into European culture from the eighteenth century and that totalitarianism was the inevitable result. The book contained some ideas that recurred during the rest of her writing. Speech was the most valid form of political action in her view, so one could feel at home anywhere there was freedom to enjoy political debate.

Being a Jew was central to Arendt's identity, yet she was determinedly secular and refused to conform to any cultural stereotype. Indeed, she found identity politics obnoxious. Accordingly she refused to favour cultural entities, insisting she didn't love people as a whole but individuals. She believed in a Jewish homeland protected by its own army but felt strongly it should be achieved in cooperation with resident Palestinians. After Israel achieved independence, she was immensely disappointed with the way Arabs were treated. Despite the horrors of the Holocaust, she continued to celebrate the German culture to which she was fundamentally attached. 'It wasn't the language that went crazy,' she would remark when challenged. She remained a staunch defender of civil liberties and personal freedom.

She courted still more controversy when she covered the trial of escaped Nazi Adolf Eichmann in Israel for the *New Yorker*. Her reports were then published in book form. Eichmann had fled to Argentina after the war and lived there secretly until he was kidnapped and returned to Israel for trial. During proceedings, it became clear to Arendt that Eichmann had a disturbingly dispassionate and bureaucratic approach to the deportation and extermination of Jews. To reflect this, she coined the phrase 'the banality of evil'. Once again, she expounded her theory that with totalitarianism people lost the capacity to think cleverly and act conscientiously. She felt Eichmann was not the personification of evil but a pen pusher who exalted only in doing his job efficiently. He and others like him appeared to lack the imagination that would normally inform them about their victims' suffering. Under authoritarian government, people like Eichmann allow themselves to become a tool of the state. Critics felt her work permitted Nazis like Eichmann to be exonerated from guilt, despite the fact she publicly supported his death sentence.

Arendt also wrote other books of extraordinary stature, including *The Human Condition*, published in 1958, and *The Life of the Mind*, published posthumously in 1978. She was an ardent fan of the arts and believed that music, art and literature were more than merely window-dressing for civilisation.

Louis Armstrong

(1901–1971)

Other players … played blustery things that were quite effective. Louis turned them into perfect gems, works of art. He had a knack of making the perfect phrase and it was always right. He did something nobody else could ever do unless they imitated him.

Chris Barber (Jazz band leader)

He transformed the concept of the solo. When he started playing the trumpet or cornet, it was not the focus of a jazz orchestra. He made it the focus through sheer force of his personality and his musical brilliance. Over the eighty- or hundred-year history of jazz, Louis has inspired or launched more jazz musicians into their careers than any other figure. Young people now keep rediscovering him.

Laurence Bergreen (Biographer)

WITH A BROAD smile and languid style, it was no surprise to discover one of his biggest hits was called 'What A Wonderful World'. Yet Louis Armstrong was more than just a feel-good musician with a quirky voice. Thanks to him, jazz made substantial headway despite gross discrimination against black musicians in the USA. Many students of the subject believe there was no discernible jazz before Armstrong appeared on the scene, among them jazz clarinettist and bandleader Artie Shaw: 'I would say modern jazz as we know it almost stems from Louis Armstrong, I don't know where he got it from. He himself doesn't know where he got it. All he knows is that it sounded right to him.'

Armstrong grew up on the margins of New Orleans society, after his father ran off when he was an infant and a mother who sometimes turned to prostitution to make ends meet. After dropping out of school aged 11, he sold coal from a truck, cleaned gravestones, did almost anything in fact that would bring in some cash for the family. As he worked, he listened to the sounds of the city, which was at the time getting a feel for something known as 'hot jazz' that sounded improvised and rowdy.

After being confined to a 'Negro Waifs Home' for firing a gun on New Year's Eve, he learned to play the cornet and joined a band. As a teenager he was freed and immediately beat a path to the clubs where local, notable musicians like Joe 'King' Oliver, one of the finest trumpeters in the city, played. King became a mentor and later Armstrong admitted: 'Nobody inspired me like him.' King encouraged Armstrong with the words: 'Play more lead on that horn, you have a beautiful tone.' It is how Armstrong developed his distinctive approach to trumpet-playing.

Aged 21, Armstrong left New Orleans at King's invitation to work in Chicago. A pattern of touring and recording that he followed his entire life was set in train. In the recording studio equipment was put at a distance as Armstrong, thanks to his phenomenal lung power, could play louder and higher than anyone else. Two years later, after pressure from his second wife Lil, he moved to New York to play with the Fletcher

Henderson orchestra. Pianist Lil also had a significant impact on his career by her insistence on a practice regime. Armstrong called it 'wood-shedding' because those lonely hours of rehearsal were spent in the wood shed. But life on the road was punishing on a marriage and Armstrong was ultimately wed four times. A hectic studio and stage schedule, coupled with a Broadway appearance in 1929 singing 'Ain't Misbehavin'', finally established him as a star.

Artie Shaw, born in 1910, was quick to point up Armstrong's influence. 'I happened to put on a record called "Savoy Blues", I remember it vividly because it made an enormous impression. I heard this trumpet player, I can still sing you note for note that whole record. I couldn't quite decide what it was, it was so far away from anything I knew about. It was so much of an influence on me aged 17 or 18 I got in the car and went from Cleveland all the way to Chicago. I went to the south side, to the Savoy Ballroom where Louis was playing and sat right at the foot of the bandstand and listened to him play "West End Blues". It was one of the most astonishing musical experiences of my life. Later I talked to him and, like any young kid, my eyes must have been shining. I looked up at him and I said, "Mr Armstrong." Imagine, in those days a white kid calling a black man "mister". He took it very calmly. There was a man with real assurance.'

Largely Armstrong kept antipathy towards racism locked up inside. He was for years restricted from returning to New Orleans because it was against the law to have black and white band members play together in public. Often he and his band played in hotels where they were unable to stay or even eat a meal. At some venues, black and white elements of the audience were separated with barbed wire. His anger erupted in 1957 when he saw black schoolchildren being spat on by whites in Little Rock, Arkansas, and he dashed off telegrams to the President and the State Governor articulating his fury. For this, he was called a firebrand. Yet by others he was criticised for being an 'Uncle Tom' figure, who happily conformed to a stereotype using black vernacular to accommodate whites.

Artie Shaw believed he was more a happy maverick: 'Louis wasn't so much a bandleader. Louis was an individualist. He played and he sang, he was a kind of shining soul. There he stood smiling and grinning. It was a real smile. Louis didn't do that to kowtow to the white man. He was no Uncle Tom. Louis had his own view. Truly his smile was genuine. He was a very natural human being. How did he keep it that way? It was a rather remarkable thing for a man to stay himself through all the things he went through.'

What is certain is that the popularity of jazz promoted by people like Armstrong helped to break down segregation in the USA.

In the 1930s, he toured the world, getting marvellous receptions wherever he went. From 1935, he employed a manager, Joe Glaser, who reputedly had links to gangster Al Capone, to take care of business so Armstrong could concentrate on music. Glaser was a mover behind the 1947 formation of the Louis Armstrong All Stars, an enduring ensemble that flourished in the mainstream. At this time, he emerged as an ambassador for the USA, travelling the world. He was known as Satchmo, short for Satchelmouth, or Pop.

Although Armstrong never had children he adopted Clarence, the brain-damaged son of a cousin. Armstrong was a keen and lifelong user of marijuana which may well have contributed to his death. But it is widely believed he worked himself into a relatively early grave. Before his death, he insisted he had stayed true to himself throughout his career: 'All we play is good music. We never did worry about styles. There ain't no such thing as styles; there's but two kinds, good or bad, that is all. I get my applause from playing good. In any language a note's a note.'

Clement Attlee

(1883–1967)

In its range and its boldness and the whole scale of achievement of that [post-war] government, it is the most effective Britain has had, certainly in the twentieth century. For all his modesty, his shyness and his pragmatism – and with no huge commanding intellect – Attlee was the leader of it. What I find in him is a determination to achieve [and] to make the country a better place to live in. He got to power in 1945 and, good heavens, how he used it.

Tim Waterstone (Bookshop founder)

He was somebody who had greatness thrust upon him. He was created by history rather than somebody who made waves in determining his own success and victory.

Ben Pimlott (Historian)

CRITICS HAVE LINED up to lambast Clement Attlee. Staid, uninteres-ting or Clem the Clam are just a few of the uncomplimentary remarks made about him. Winston Churchill famously called him 'A modest man with a lot to be modest about.' It was, however, Attlee at the helm when the post-war Labour government steered an astonishing array of social reforms into legislation, including national insurance, the National Health Service and nationalisation. He led the Labour party for twenty years, surviving numerous internal plots to oust him. He remained a socialist and a patriot until his death.

Attlee was born in Putney, London, into a family of city solicitors. He went to Haileybury school and Oxford University, following the same route as many boys in the upper middle class. When he went to East London to help in a boys' club sponsored by his old school, however, he witnessed immense and widespread hardship at a time when poverty was often perceived a weakness of character. In response he gave up a lucrative job in law and became a social worker. His political views changed from Conservative to Labour.

In 1912, he started lecturing at the London School of Economics but gave up the job to apply for a commission upon the outbreak of the First World War. This caused problems between him and a brother, Tom, who was a staunch pacifist and spent much of the conflict in jail. After serving in the disastrous Gallipoli campaign, Attlee was severely injured but still returned to the Western Front in the final months of the war.

It was the plight of people in inter-war Britain that further shaped Attlee's politics. He became Mayor of Stepney in 1919, then stood for Parliament in 1922 in Limehouse, where he gave this moving speech:

'Like many of you I took part in the Great War in the hope of securing lasting peace and a better life for all. We were promised that the men who fought in the war should be cared for and unemployment, slums and poverty would be abolished. All these promises have been broken. In every way the condition of the workers are worse than before. Wars and threat of war continue.

'Your wages are still falling and many of you are unemployed. You pay high rents and live in overcrowded hovels. Ex soldiers are found lining up for unemployment pay or outdoor relief. The wounded and widows have to struggle on a starvation dole. Men made insane in the war are sent to pauper lunatic asylums. If you return me to Parliament to represent people among which I have lived and worked for the last 17 years I shall carry the message that they are sick and tired of the injustice that condemns them to toil long hours for low wages. To live in poverty and squalor without the certainty of where the next meal is going to come from and to see their children doomed to endure the same conditions.'

Attlee served in the Labour government led by Ramsay MacDonald, a man he initially admired but grew to despise. Attlee remained at the heart of Labour activities when the party was decimated by MacDonald's politicking as he tried to hold on to power in the face of an unpopular programme of public service cuts linked to the Depression. The brief experience Attlee garnered in office in the 1920s made him an ideal candidate for the party leadership in 1935. He then joined Winston Churchill's wartime coalition, in roles that dealt with civil aspects of the conflict. Throughout, he deputised for Churchill.

In the 1945 election, Labour won a surprise landslide victory after running a crusade under the banner 'Let Us Face the Future'. By contrast Churchill's Conservative campaign was poor. Finally, Attlee would have the opportunity to ensure the post-war chaos that engulfed the country in 1918 could be sidestepped.

There is plenty about his administration that is remarkable. Its policies were largely rooted in the 1942 report by William Beveridge, an economist and social reformer, that aimed to eradicate five infamous public enemies: want, disease, ignorance, squalor and idleness. The way forward, said Beveridge, was cradle-to-grave welfare run by the state and available to all. In 1946, the National Health Service Act was introduced despite across-the-board opposition in the medical profession. There were acts that dealt with family allowance, rent controls, roads, new towns, fairer elections and even the creation of national parks. It was all carried out while about ten million people involved in the war effort were found new jobs. Attlee's government also oversaw Indian independence, when the colony was severed from the British Empire and the world's largest democracy was created. Although there was considerable unrest and bloodshed in the subcontinent at the time, the violence would have been worse if the process had dragged out any longer.

Diffident, determined and hardworking, Attlee had little time to revel in these accomplishments. As Labour's leader, he was the target of many ambitious colleagues who wanted the top job. He dealt with these threats with reasonable equanimity and continued to rule his cabinet by consensus. He was returned to office in the 1950 election but with a substantially reduced majority. An election forced the following year resulted in a Labour defeat, and Attlee returned to the opposition benches. He remained Labour leader until 1955 when he resigned after a second election defeat, to be succeeded by Hugh Gaitskell. Attlee went to the House of Lords where one of his notable battles was to reform the laws governing homosexuality.

Attlee was devoted to his wife Violet and their four children. As for religion he professed to believe in the ethics of commonly held faith but couldn't stand 'the mumbo jumbo'. After his death from pneumonia he was buried in Westminster Abbey.

In his spare time, Attlee wrote verse, perhaps the most telling of which was a limerick that perhaps ideally sums up his understated personality.

> *Few thought that he was even a starter,*
> *There were many who thought themselves smarter,*
> *But he ended pm, ch and om*
> *An earl and a knight of the garter.*

Joseph Banks

(1743–1820)

Here is a person in an early phase of this particular science who came back [on the Endeavour*] with 1,300 new species. His house in 22 Soho Square was centre of both social and scientific circles in Georgian London, where ideas were exchanged. It is that kind of influence, in reshaping the way people went about things, that is every bit as big a contribution as counting academic papers today.*

Lord (Robert) May (President of the Royal Society)

Science now is such a major component of our society that it is very hard to imagine back into a time when science wasn't important. For me, one of the brilliant things about Joseph Banks is that he persuaded the government that science should be funded. After Banks, the government came to recognise that science could be valuable for extending the British Empire and consolidating trade routes.

Patricia Fara (Biographer)

DURING THE EIGHTEENTH century, most around-the-world adventurers were seeking to make their fortunes by reaping gold and jewels. Already in receipt of his family's immense wealth, Sir Joseph Banks gathered instead a treasure trove of plants and animals that propelled natural science to new levels. And thanks to his investigations into the world's flora and fauna, there were associated boosts in medicine and commerce. He also worked hard to unite the international scientific community at a time of numerous conflicts and revolutions.

Officially, Banks was President of the Royal Society for a record-breaking forty-two years, and director of Kew's burgeoning botanical gardens for almost as long. Unofficially, he was an adviser to king and country about science and its range of possibilities. It is not a bad record for a boy who was notoriously unscholarly until he happened across a book about herbs on his mother's bedside table. After that, he was hooked into the life of plants.

Banks inherited his father's fortune while he was studying at Oxford University. Five years afterwards, he organised a trip to Newfoundland and Labrador to collect plant specimens. On his return he was elected as a fellow of the Royal Society, but he didn't become famous until he paired up with Captain James Cook on the Pacific voyage that began in 1768.

Fired by the possibilities, Banks offered to pay his own way but insisted on bringing four servants, a secretary, two artists, a botanist, two dogs and a large amount of luggage. However, without this retinue, the results of the voyage would have been the poorer. The artists' stunning work set a high benchmark for future expeditions.

The stated aim of the voyage was to observe the transit of Venus, a rarely occurring astronomical marvel in which the planet passed across the face of the sun, from Tahiti. In the warm embrace of the southern seas, the men aboard *Endeavour* discovered Tahitian women were unusually accommodating. Banks wrote:

[Here] Love is the Chief Occupation ... both the bodies and souls of the women are modeled into the utmost perfection for that soft science. Idleness the father of Love reigns here in almost unmolested ease, while we inhabitants of a changeable climate are oblig'd to Plow, Sow, Harrow, reap, Thrash, Grind, knead and bake our daily bread ...

In fact, the Tahitians were furnishing themselves with guns and iron, two items to which they had no access. The ship's carpenter was ordered not to issue any more nails – used by sailors to win favours with islanders – as the ship was at risk of disintegrating.

Cook was then told by the Admiralty to claim as much Pacific land for England as he could. As a consequence, in 1770, Banks became one of the first people to see Australia – and he was not impressed:

The countrey tho in general well enough clothd appear'd in some places bare; it resembled in my imagination the back of a lean Cow, cover'd in general with long hair, but nevertheless where her scraggy hip bones have stuck out farther than they ought accidental rubbs and knocks have intirely bard them of their share of covering.

Perhaps it is only fitting that an early suggestion to name the new land 'Banksia' was dismissed.

When he returned with an impressive collection of vegetation, rocks and insects in 1771, he immediately set about organising a trip to Iceland, with similar intentions. It was the last expedition he went on, as plans to join Cook's second voyage were thwarted when an extra deck demanded by Banks to accommodate himself, his staff and his specimens made the ship impossibly hard to handle. It was duly ripped out, and the voyage departed without him.

It wasn't the end of his influence, however. Already he had persuaded King George III to invest in such expeditions, having proved their scientific worth. His home in Soho Square was transformed by exotic foliage imported from overseas. It was also a repository for samples collected by other overseas travellers. In 1778, he became President of the Royal Society, initially admired but later mocked for grimly holding on to the post until his death.

Banks financed more expeditions, including an ill-fated voyage by Captain Bligh on HMS *Bounty*, which is better remembered for its mutiny. He was also alive to the opportunities presented by experimenting with commercial crops worldwide. He ensured breadfruit from Tahiti was transplanted to the West Indies. Tea, he realised, could be grown in India not just in China. Sheep would fare well in Australia, he decided. Using his expertise in this way, the seeds of the British Empire were sown, with the trade winds blowing favourably for England.

Ultimately, the Banks collection included 110 new genera and 1,300 new species. About seventy-five species bear evidence of his name, along with islands off New Zealand. Although he moved in exalted circles, he was determined that the wealth of knowledge he had corralled should be open to as many people as possible. One of his biographers said he was very keen that science should not be cordoned off from the public by 'abstruse terminology and overspecialisation'. He was a founder member of numerous august bodies, including the Linnean Society, the Royal Institution and the Horticultural Society.

One blot on his landscape was his suggestion that English prisoners could be transported to Botany Bay, Australia, to both alleviate overcrowding in Britain and create a new colony – although arguably it was his interest in the trading opportunities that would then ensue that guided his thoughts. In the end, officers on the First Fleet bypassed his suggested site in favour of Port Jackson.

More than 30,000 of his letters survived him, offering extraordinary insight into the explorations and politics of the era. An early exponent of networking, his abiding aim was to spread the word regarding botany and natural sciences to as many people as he could. In clunky terms, he explained as much when he talked about why he adopted the lizard on his heraldic crest:

> I have taken the lizard, an animal said to be endowed by nature with an instinctive love of mankind, as my device and have caused it to be engraved as my seal, as a perpetual remembrance that a man is never so well employ'd as when he is laboring for the advantage of the public; without the Expectation, the Hope, or even a wish to derive advantage of any kind from the result of his exertions.

Thomas Beecham

(1879–1961)

The world of British music was changed for ever by Thomas Beecham, and basically for the better. He could make a second-class piece of music sound first class. Music wasn't well organised in Britain [and] Beecham spent the family money from the Beecham's pills empire putting on operas.

David Mellor (Former politician)

He does have a very good rhythmic vitality and the dynamism in the shaping of a phrase was so different to what anyone else could do.

Leanne Langley (Music historian)

S IR THOMAS BEECHAM had a weakness for women, a rapier wit and a predilection to spend other people's money. With all the perils on the home front after Britain became embroiled in the Second World War, Beecham left for America on a lucrative four-year tour and later became a tax exile. He was largely forgiven for all his vagaries, however, thanks to his extraordinary musical talent. Not only was he an excellent conductor, he was also responsible for reviving Mozart's operas in Edwardian England.

Beecham was the grandson of the founder of a pharmaceutical company that bore the family name. Also called Thomas, his grandfather was a chemist who learned his trade working as a boy shepherd in Lancashire. Remedies he made from herbs to treat the sheep were also beneficial to people, he discovered. By the time of his death in 1907, business was booming.

But conductor Thomas didn't always have access to the family's fortune. In 1899, father Joseph committed his mother Josephine to an asylum, although her mental state was sound. Together with an elder sister, Thomas liberated his mother and was subsequently disinherited by an outraged Joseph. Only Thomas's continuing success in music, which attracted the attention of King Edward VII, convinced Joseph to seek a reconciliation.

When he could, Thomas used his family's money to stage concerts and especially operas for large audiences. It was long before the era of grants or sponsorship, so ambitious arts projects could not take place without patronage. By spending this money and whatever else he could extract from wealthy friends, Beecham was therefore contributing significantly to the country's cultural landscape.

Beecham first began conducting in his home town of St Helen's, Lancashire. However, most of his early professional life was spent in London, initially with the New Symphony Orchestra and later with the Beecham Symphony Orchestra.

At the time, musicians were at liberty to send deputies to play on their behalf if a better offer arrived. Sometimes the deputies would find replacements themselves and this had a disastrous effect on the overall quality of the assembled orchestra. Beecham chose to recruit from music schools, concert halls and among existing musicians on the strict understanding that no deputies were employed. At a stroke, he improved the standard of performances immeasurably.

He was more likely to stage his own personal favourites rather than pander to public taste. And he had firm views on music of the day: 'Brass bands are all very well in their place – outdoors and several miles away.' One of Beethoven's movements he likened to 'a herd of yaks jumping about'. He felt Wagner pieces were too long, and Verdi barely moved him. His favourite composers were Berlioz, Sibelius and the relatively unknown Frederick Delius.

With the London Philharmonic Orchestra, which he created in 1932, and the Royal Philharmonic Orchestra formed in 1946, he was lauded for his inspired leadership. He believed he got great results because he let the musicians play without perpetually giving direction, which he deemed unnecessary for adult professionals.

Nonetheless there was an imperceptible understanding between conductor and orchestra member that elicited superb results. One man who played in the BBC Symphony Orchestra under Beecham's direction wrote: '[He] started with his baton under his left armpit and swung it until it was high in the heavens to the right of him. The whole orchestra just came in with this extraordinary gesture. But it wasn't just the big gestures, it was the little ones. He could wag his finger at you and get a marvellous effect.' Beecham was also known for the way his penetrating gaze locked on to different sections or musicians. Part of his success was inevitably because the most able young players were keen to join his enterprises.

While he exhibited considerable respect for musicians, he was swift with damning criticism, often couched in cruel terms. To a cellist he memorably chided: 'Madam, you have between your legs an instrument capable of giving pleasure to thousands – and all you can do is scratch it.' One performance featured a live horse on stage during the finale. As if on cue, the horse raised its tail and deposited a mound on the stage. 'Ah, gentlemen,' cooed Beecham. 'Not just an artist but a critic as well.'

Beecham married three times. With his first wife, Utica Celestina Welles, he had two sons. But he lost interest in the marriage within a handful of years and conducted numerous affairs, including a longstanding liaison with Lady Cunard, who helped finance some of his musical ventures. He wasn't divorced until 1943, when he married concert pianist Betty Humby, some 29 years his junior. A year after her death and two years before his own, he married for a third time, to former secretary Shirley Hudson.

He was suspected of chauvinism thanks to his marked lack of inclusion of women in his orchestras. He was, though, happy to employ Betty Humby, so perhaps his attitude was more a sign of the times rather than a principled stance.

Beecham risked public antipathy not only through his well-publicised affairs but also by visiting Nazi Germany before the outbreak of war, performing before Hitler on one occasion. Germany was central to European musical life at this stage, however, in a way that England simply wasn't.

During the war, Beecham left England to live and work in America and, when he returned, he found the cultural life of the British capital had changed, leaving him an outsider. He was curiously unsuited to state-funded programmes staged in times of national austerity due to his tendency towards extravagance.

Although he twice narrowly avoided bankruptcy, Beecham was knighted in 1916 and succeeded his father as baronet later the same year. He was presented with the Légion d'Honneur, France's highest decoration, in 1938, and in 1957 he was made a Companion of Honour, an award founded by King George V that recognises achievement in the arts.

Sarah Bernhardt

(1844–1923)

She never gave up, she just kept going, I like that in a woman. She sounds like a nightmare – which is good.

Jenny Eclair (Comedian)

She had terrific energy and terrific pace. She could captivate audiences. At the start of her career, she tried to do everything straight and by the book with Comédie-Française. It was never really going to be her but she had several goes at it, was fired several times. So she set up on her own, mixed the classics with her own style of roles that would really suit her. What made her exceptional is that she was risqué, alluring, eccentric and at the same time a consummate performer, someone who was immensely skilled and a talented performer.

Professor Elaine Aston (Writer and historian in performance arts)

WHEN IT CAME to late-nineteenth-century celebrities, there was really only one standout candidate for the A list. Actress Sarah Bernhardt was a star in France, England and America. She became the poster girl during a golden age of photography and made silent cinema popular in its early days. The Divine Sarah, as she was known, was passionate, edgy and loved to outrage. Her reputation for unconventionality was confirmed when she played Hamlet, earning some reasonable notices although the show was five hours long. 'I have often been asked why I am so fond of playing male parts,' she once said. 'As a matter of fact, it is not male parts, but male brains that I prefer.'

She flourished during an age in which audiences demanded melodrama and all its associated exaggerations, leaving some critics including George Bernard Shaw unimpressed at what he considered stagey affectation. But her mantra for success permitted a touch of 'over the top' behaviour: 'To be a good actor it is necessary to have a firmly tempered soul, to be surprised at nothing, to resume each minute the boring task that has barely just been finished. He who is incapable of feeling strong passions, of being shaken by anger, of living in every sense of the word, will never be a good actor.'

Bernhardt was the daughter of a French courtesan of Dutch/Jewish descent, who might be known today as a high-class hooker. Her French father played little part in her upbringing other than apparently to send her to a convent in her early teens.

Initial instincts to become a nun were set aside in favour of a career in the theatre. (According to her memoirs, her godfather suggested the stage because she was an unruly child; however, there's scant evidence to back up some of the claims she made in the book, *My Double Life*.)

She trained at the Conservatoire then joined Comédie-Française, but hopes of instant acclaim were soon dashed. She fared little better in burlesque. In 1866, she joined the Odeon Theatre in Paris where she began to make her mark, pausing only to help wounded soldiers during the Franco-Prussian War. Her commitment to the tragic roles that made her name was so wholehearted she bought herself a silk-lined coffin to sleep in instead of a bed, so as better to feel the pain and despair of the doomed heroines she portrayed.

Her distinctive voice was often described as 'silvery'. Physically, she was striking with a thin frame, a seventeen-inch waist and unruly hair. At the height of her fame, she was lampooned in newspapers as either a skeleton or a mop. A vegetarian who abhorred the taste of meat, her memoirs reveal a possibly unhealthy obsession with food and weight.

Although she was slight, Bernhardt developed the art of filling a stage. She was known for making grand gesticulations during her performances and considered herself ideally formed to do so: 'For the theatre one needs long arms. It is better to have them too long than too short. An artist with short arms can never, never make a fine gesture. The truth, the absolute truth, is that the chief beauty for the theatre consists in fine bodily proportions.'

Her sexual conquests are rumoured to have included the Prince of Wales, who later became Edward VII, author Victor Hugo, and a number of women. She had a son, Maurice, fathered by a Belgian nobleman in 1864, but his family discouraged the relationship. Bernhardt finally married in 1882, but her relationship with the Greek actor Aristides Damala broke down because of his dependency on morphine.

While there were numerous affairs, there's no doubt her son remained central in her affections. She wrote this when they were reunited on her return from her first trip to America in 1880: 'All at once I notice masses of little white flags being waved on the small steamer. I got my glasses then let them fall with a joyous cry that left me without any strength. Without breath, I wanted to speak, I could not. My face it appears became so pale that it frightened the people who were about me. They wanted to make me sit down. I would not. Hanging on to the bulwarks I smell the salts that are thrust under my nose. I allow friendly hands to wipe my temples but I am gazing over there whence the vessel is coming. Over there lies my happiness, my joy, my life, my everything, dearer than everything.'

Her talents were not restricted to the stage. Bernhardt also painted, sculpted and wrote – claiming to have kept a diary of her colourful life. 'Life engenders life,' she would say. 'Energy creates energy. It is by spending oneself that one becomes rich.'

Despite increasing age, she continued to perform as a leading lady across the world before moving into theatre management. Indeed, she was 60 when she hurt her leg, jumping from stage ramparts. The injury caused her pain for years until, a decade later, it resulted in amputation above the knee when she was 70. Yet nothing stopped her from either performing or travelling. Refusing a prosthetic leg, she took her place on stage discreetly shielded by blankets or furniture. When Bernhardt visited troops during the First World War she was carried on a sedan chair. An American writer who visited her in Paris after the operation described her existence: 'Madame Sarah, as she is called by the members of her household, spends her days in a sunlit room on the second floor. She never leaves her big chair. On leaving the house she is carried to the motor and carried up the broad flight of steps when she returns.'

On 27 March 1923, *The Times* carried this obituary:

> We regret to announce that Mademoiselle Sarah Bernhardt died at 8 p.m. last evening at her Paris residence. She died in the arms of her son Maurice. Immediately after Mademoiselle Bernhardt passed away those present brought in masses of roses and lilac and dressed the chamber with them.
>
> No temperament more histrionic than Mademoiselle Bernhardt's has perhaps ever existed. To read her memoir or her biographies is to live in a whirl of passions and adventures, floods of tears, tornadoes of rage, deathly sicknesses and incomparable health and energy, deeds of reckless bravado, caprices indescribable.

William Beveridge

(1879–1963)

He seemed to be the great hero in our family. He was of course, among other things, the man who brought in family allowance books. My mother's family allowance book was the most valuable possession she had. I saw a photograph of him taken in 1944 and he is surrounded by women as if he was a pop star. And they all look like my mother. He is everything I am not, and he is everything I admire.

Anne Fine (Author)

I admire him because he has shaped the world that we live in. Beveridge was brilliant at spinning it ... and managed to get [his] report into flight. He thought it impossible to run the new world on the lines of the old, and he was certainly bolder in planning terms than the 1945 Labour government was.

Frank Field (Former welfare minister)

IT WAS A title that he despised as a 'horrible advertising slogan', but 'father of the welfare state' neatly sums up the contribution made by William Beveridge to British society. At the outset, he was an unlikely warrior for social justice. But after seeing poverty and squalor rampant in London's East End, he modified his previously reactionary views.

Part capitalist, part socialist, he made a personal pledge to eradicate what he saw as the country's worst evils: want, disease, ignorance, squalor and idleness. His 1942 report – with the unprepossessing title of *Social Insurance and Allied Services* – presented a plan that put a safety net in place for those who found themselves on the lower rungs of life's greasy ladder. On publication, *The Times* hailed it as 'a momentous document, which should and must exercise a profound and immediate influence on the direction of social change in Britain'.

Yet despite his colossal achievements, Beveridge was not universally appreciated. Politicians ranging from Ernest Bevin to Winston Churchill were known to dislike him. According to biographer Jose Harris: 'To some, he seemed wise and lovable, to others overbearing and vain. To some, he was a man of dazzling intellect, to others a tedious bore. To some, he was endlessly generous and sympathetic, to others he was harsh and self-centred to the point of complete insensitivity. He has been described to me personally as a man who wouldn't give a penny to a blind beggar and as one of the kindest men who ever walked the Earth.'

As a consequence, it's a challenge to locate the real Beveridge. He was born in Bengal, the son of a judge in the Indian civil service. His schooling was traditional, Charterhouse followed by Oxford, after which he became a barrister. However, his interest in social campaigns led him to study the issue of unemployment insurance. In 1908, he joined the Board of Trade, and he was the main mover behind newly launched labour exchanges, helping the jobless back to work.

At around the same time, he wrote leader columns for the famously Conservative *Morning Post* with what must have seemed a surprising radical tone: 'I never wrote a word I didn't believe and I never had a word crossed out except once when … the editor was away and the deputy was a little frightened of something I said. My suspicion is that none of the people who ever took the *Morning Post* ever read the leaders.'

His organisational abilities came to the fore during the First World War, when he planned the mobilisation of men and food. In 1919, he joined the London School of Economics, siding strongly with the Fabian elements of the university. Yet still his views were not strictly socialist. Beatrice Webb, from the Fabian Society, recalled a conversation with him from 1938:

> His conclusion is that the major if not the only remedy for unemployment is lower wages. If this does not happen the capitalist will take his money and his brains to other countries where labour is cheap. He admitted almost defiantly that he was not personally concerned with the condition of the common people. He declared that he had no living philosophy. He was a thorough going materialistic agnostic about man's relation to the universe and he had no particular credo or ideal as to man's relation to man.

Indeed, he only reluctantly accepted the brief as architect of social change in the Second World War, painfully aware he was being sidelined. It was encouragement from his wife Jessy that convinced him to stick with it. During his endeavours he was assisted by Frank Pakenham, later Lord Longford.

When Beveridge announced that, in return for a weekly national insurance contribution, people would be paid a small sum if they were sick, unemployed, widowed or retired, he said emphatically: 'I believe this plan, or something rather like it, is what we need.' His findings received a cool reception from the Conservative Party, but luck was on his side when it came to announcing the plans. Prior to the outbreak of war, the country had been seized by economic depression. Anything that remedied the hardships people experienced then was going to have broad appeal.

In 1942, Britain had just triumphed over Germany at El Alamein, signalling for the first time that the war might be won. Instantly, people were more receptive to ideas that in a different mood might have fallen flat, and it gave them a glimpse of a fairer future, something for which to continue the fight. To ensure he captured their attention, Beveridge sought maximum radio coverage and travelled the country to attend meetings explaining its principles. His words achieved bestseller status. In 1944, he wrote *Full Employment in a Free Society*, arguing that government should provide sufficient jobs to keep unemployment to a rate of just a few per cent.

Before the conflict ended, Beveridge was a Liberal MP. When he was ousted in Labour's landslide election victory of 1945, he was made a Lord. His report was then adopted by the new Labour government as a blueprint for change. It went hand in hand with proposals for a National Health Service and, together with other ground-breaking measures, provided the 'cradle-to-grave' care that Beveridge had envisaged.

Yet Beveridge himself was left unhappy with the fruit of his labours. He put special emphasis on the importance of individual responsibility alongside government duty. As the welfare state manifested itself, he thought it increased rather than undermined the evil of idleness as politicians sought popularity rather than genuine life improvements. In 1959 he declared: 'I take every possible opportunity of denying authorship of the welfare state. I believe in welfare, but the welfare state suggests that all you have to do to get welfare is vote the right way at an election and get it from the state. To me, welfare depends upon a right division of the responsibilities of the state and of the individual, and therefore I never use the term welfare state.' On another occasion he said: 'It chills my heart to think that people will get their sickness benefit through the post.'

He moved away from government to organisations including the Abbeyfield Society, which cares for the elderly, and wrote an opus on the history of pricing. He was apparently still penning this masterpiece when he died, after uttering the words 'I have a thousand things to do.'

Ernest Bevin

(1881–1951)

[He is] the most important figure in the British trades union movement who has ever existed. He was Britain's greatest foreign secretary and indeed the only world statesman you would really compare him to is [Franklin D] Roosevelt. He did as much as anyone to create modern Europe and the Atlantic community with his support for the Marshall Plan and the creation of NATO.

Lord Healey
(Former Chancellor of the Exchequer)

He is the greatest British statesman of the twentieth century. As a person, he may not be everyone's cup of tea now, but as a political figure he deserves a huge amount of attention and a much bigger place in our national story.

Dr Brian Brivati
(Professor and author)

FROM HUMBLE CIRCUMSTANCES, Ernest Bevin emerged to play not one but three pivotal roles in Britain's history. With immense energy and perception, he helped to found the Transport and General Workers' Union, the biggest in the world. His talents were so glaringly apparent he was later co-opted into Churchill's war cabinet when he wasn't even an MP to mobilise the country's workforce. Finally, as foreign secretary, he helped fashion the structure of the post-war world, welding Europe and America together as a bulwark against totalitarianism. All this from a man who was orphaned aged 6, left school aged 11 and was 29 before he held any significant union role.

There was nothing in his unremarkable childhood in Somerset to signal that Bevin was a man with special qualities. First as an agricultural worker on notoriously low wages, then as a delivery man and tram driver in Bristol, Bevin was one of millions struggling to make ends meet at a time when the economy was sluggish or poor, long before the advent of the welfare state.

Although his education was meagre, he was a voracious reader and studied politics from the pages of a newspaper. He joined the Dockers' Union, which was sorely weakened by a perpetual lack of unity. After the Baptist Church was superseded by the Socialists' Society in Bevin's books, he won a union job and revealed his organisational talents.

In 1920, he represented dockers in a court of inquiry set up by the government to settle a rumbling pay dispute. While Bevin had no legal training, he tied his opponents in knots throughout the twenty-one-day hearing with a practical and powerful argument. He brought to court the food that dockers were supposed to exist on to prove theirs was not a living wage. By comparison, he also brought a menu from the Savoy Hotel where bosses sometimes ate. His arguments were so persuasive he won a wage increase for dockers and with it a glittering reputation among working people. In 1922, after wide-ranging negotiations, he engineered the formation of the Transport and General Workers' Union, giving workers the best chance they'd ever had to win rights from company owners and the government. As general secretary, he was at its head.

Bevin had no appetite for the disastrous 1926 General Strike and tried hard to avert it. His support for the Soviet Union was also rapidly diminishing. But his passion for social change was undimmed and his comments often reflected Labour Party policy.

'The school leaving age of working class children should be raised. And if the wage of the parents is not of a standard to enable them adequately to feed, clothe and house them then they are entitled to be supported by the state. You cannot now find full employment for all these children. And many of those who do find employment are taken to industry at the age of 14 and discharged at 18 and their lives are wasted and ruined. On the grounds of equality and justice this nation should face up to this problem immediately.'

With so many union votes at his disposal, Bevin was courted by the Labour Party, which had formed at the turn of the century. In 1931, Labour was left reeling when its leader Ramsay MacDonald deserted to form a coalition government. Bevin was one of the figures that rebuilt the party before the outbreak of the Second World War, putting his curious blend of idealism and pragmatism to good use. He was doggedly opposed to Hitler, although he initially tempered his remarks during appeasement. It was perhaps the only common ground he shared with Winston Churchill, who invited Bevin into his government in 1940 as one of only seven war cabinet ministers, before he had a parliamentary seat. A month afterwards, Bevin was duly elected to Parliament.

He was arguably the only man in Britain at that time capable of encouraging and coercing the nation's workers to produce armaments at the phenomenal rate that was necessary. His opposite number in Germany had slave labour at his disposal, while Bevin could only utilise goodwill and common cause. Nonetheless, Britain matched or even exceeded Germany's output. It was a tribute to Bevin's compelling personality too, that he succeeded in recruiting young men to work in Britain's mines in order to fuel the factories at a time when service life seemed more glamorous. With a distinctive West Country burr, he would give morale-boosting talks around the country. In Bristol he told a crowd: 'I just come to wish you good luck in all these great efforts and to tell you to keep your pecker up and victory won't be far off.'

In 1945, there was a Labour landslide in the election and Clement Attlee, the new Prime Minister, appointed Bevin as Foreign Secretary. By now Bevin was almost at retirement age. So he was not about to change the fundamentals of his personality to fit in with the expectations of the middle- or upper-class civil servants who worked alongside him. His manners were questionable and he was famous for talking and eating at the same time. Throughout his life he was a heavy drinker and smoker. Yet government officials who could boast a far greater education than his grew to respect him. He went to the Potsdam Conference in 1945 to resolve how Germany would be punished for its fascist adventure, alongside Attlee, Stalin and Harry S Truman. Further, he approved the Marshall Plan, devised in America to help Europe rebuild and funnelling billions of American dollars to the war-ravaged continent. Soviet Russia turned down the aid.

Critics argue that Bevin was out of touch with his opposition to Indian independence and the doubts he freely expressed that countries incorporated into the British Empire were capable of ruling themselves. Nor was he convinced in the wisdom of creating Israel, believing it would expand at the expense of its Arab neighbours. His supporters believe he was merely accurately predicting the violence that would paralyse those countries or regions following British withdrawal. As Foreign Secretary, he supported Britain's nuclear programme, engineered close ties with the USA and championed the system of collective security that would manifest itself as NATO.

Bevin resigned because of ill health in 1951 and became Lord Privy Seal, a prestigious but functionless role in government. He died a month after celebrating his 70th birthday, having been right-hand man to prime ministers Churchill and Attlee while remaining the voice of the working man.

Dietrich Bonhoeffer

(1906–1945)

This guy goes right to the nub of what faith is all about. [He was] a man who stood for others. He dealt with reality like no one I have ever known. He had a battle between hubris and humility. And he admitted it.

David Soul (Actor and singer)

There's no theologian better qualified [than Bonhoeffer] to be a patron saint of getting your hands dirty. That is one of the finest things about him. At the end of the day, speaking, preaching, talking is not enough.

Dr Peter Selby
(Retired bishop and President of the National Council for
Independent Monitoring Boards in Britain's jails)

O N 9 APRIL 1945, four men convicted of plotting against Hitler were stripped naked and hanged with piano wire. For years they had trodden a treacherous path as part of the small but determined German resistance who pledged to overthrow Nazi tyranny. Two weeks later, the concentration camp where they died was liberated by the Allies. Among the ill-fated quartet was Dietrich Bonhoeffer, something of a modern martyr. Unlike the others, he wasn't a military man or a diplomat. Bonhoeffer was a pastor who was confronted with questions of conscience about how pacifist men of God should respond to institutionalised evil. In the end he found the ambivalence of faith wanting and he remained true to his personal ethical code. At the gallows, a camp doctor who watched his demise wrote: 'I have hardly ever seen a man die so entirely submissive to the will of God.'

Bonhoeffer was one of twins born to his parents Paula and Karl in Breslau when it was part of Germany. They were among eight children who were taught at home by Paula, fearing the 'sausage factory' approach of state schooling. With their father an eminent professor of psychiatry at the University of Berlin, all the children were brought up in a privileged and intellectual home to have lively, inquiring minds. When Bonhoeffer announced his intention to join the church it wasn't welcome news. His family believed it to be 'a poor, feeble, petit bourgeois institution'. Bonhoeffer's response was to declare: 'Then I shall reform it.'

Graduating with distinction from Berlin University, Bonhoeffer then worked in Spain before travelling extensively. He became painfully aware that the edicts of the church meant little to people suffering widespread privations. After a spell in New York, Bonhoeffer was ordained a Lutheran pastor in 1931, just as Fascism was unleashed on Germany. The politics that levered Hitler into power were despised by the Bonhoeffers. At her funeral, Bonhoeffer recalled how his grandmother customarily marched through rows of stormtroopers to shop at Jewish stores.

But for Bonhoeffer it wasn't merely an affront to civil liberty that perplexed him about the rise of Nazism. His opposition was theological, as he saw the church in Germany being fundamentally subverted by unfolding events, with congregations holding the Führer in higher esteem than God. Many German Christians were supporters of Hitler, being steeped in nationalism and civil obedience, and it was they who controlled the church's governing body.

As early as 1933, after witnessing the persecution of Jews, Bonhoeffer said the church must not simply 'bandage the victims under the wheel but jam a spoke in the wheel itself'. His was an isolated voice. The same year the church agreed that only Aryan candidates could apply for church appointments. A long-held mission to convert Jews to Christianity was abandoned by some church leaders who subscribed to the idea that Jewish people were a different race and had no place in a European congregation. Inevitably, like-minded Lutherans formed the Confessing Church as an alternative to the submissive mainstream one, with Bonhoeffer at the head of its seminary in Finkenwalde. Although it fell a long way short of open resistance it was shut down by the government in 1937. Bonhoeffer was subject to numerous government controls.

With Europe on the brink of war, Bonhoeffer went to America for a job contrived for him by friends. Within weeks, however, he was on the boat back to Germany. Although initially it seemed an ideal way to avoid conscription and the accompanying dilemma of swearing an oath to Hitler, he was troubled by the consequences of his absence: 'I will have no right to participate in the reconstruction of Christian life in Germany after the war if I do not share the trials of this time with my people ... Christians in Germany will have to face the terrible alternative of either willing the defeat of their nation in order that Christian civilisation may survive or willing the victory of their nation and thereby destroying civilisation. I know which of these alternatives I must choose but I cannot make that choice from security.'

In 1940, he became an unlikely double agent in Germany, working for Abwehr, the German intelligence unit that was controlled by anti-Nazis. With his brother-in-law, Hans von Dahnanyi, he helped some Jews escape to

Switzerland. He was also a courier, running messages to the British government on behalf of the resistance. As a leading light in world ecumenism, he used contacts he had developed during a dozen years. Attempts to negotiate with the British government were always met with a demand for unconditional surrender, which the resistance was unable to deliver.

In 1943 he was implicated when Abwehr offices were raided by the rival SS. The extent of his work was hidden through some fast talking by Abwehr officers. Nonetheless, he was jailed – just three months after becoming engaged to Maria von Wedemeyer, twenty years his junior. When the plot to assassinate Hitler in July 1944 failed, the resistance largely unravelled and Bonhoeffer was finally revealed as a major player. In February 1945, he was moved to Buchenwald concentration camp and later to Flossenburg, where he died. Stoically, Maria followed him between prisons and received 150 letters from him before his death.

Fortunately his writings survived him. Bonhoeffer had alighted on the notion of 'religionless Christianity'. By this he meant the dogma, privilege and history attached to the church should be stripped away so the message of Christ could emerge untainted. He urged Christians to take the right path rather than the easy path. He also discussed the ethics of being a man of peace and yet campaigning to kill. Indeed, his significance was not so much what he achieved in practice but in his intellectual contribution which has become his legacy. His words have often been quoted since his death as the church seeks to plot a new path in secular times.

Hermann Buhl

(1924–1957)

As a mountaineer, he is my hero because of the way he lived his life, the things he did, the style in which he climbed. He epitomised to me what modern mountaineering is really about. To me, the definition of a hero is somebody who does something that has a lasting impression on future generations, who points the way, who is inspirational. To be able to make the impossible possible is an extraordinary thing to do, and I think Buhl did that.

Joe Simpson (Mountaineer)

Nanga Parbat was over the magical mark of 8,000 metres. There are only fourteen of these peaks in the world, and they can only be climbed for the first time once. There was a great deal of kudos to be gained. In one of the expeditions, sixteen people died in a single avalanche. By the time Buhl climbed it, thirty-one climbers and porters had died. Buhl was an arch individualist. He wanted to do it on his own terms, under his own steam.

Ed Douglas (Climber and writer)

'*IN CLIMBING THERE are no spectators, no prizes, no medals. Why climb? For the natural experience, for the danger that draws us ever on, for the feeling of total freedom and for the monstrous drop beneath you.*'

Eloquently, mountaineer Hermann Buhl tackled the question that plagues the majority of the population who are 'flat earthers', to whom crampons and ice picks are alien objects. Elegantly, he conquered two mighty peaks in Pakistan's Karakoram mountain range before dying during a whiteout on a third. The embodiment of the sheer mental and physical stamina needed for mountaineering, he made his exhausting climbs with the minimum of equipment to ensure maximum speed.

Born in Innsbruck, Austria, Buhl was 4 years old when his mother died and he was placed in an orphanage. A sickly, lonely child, he found solace in the mountains as a teenager and joined an Alpine rescue team near his home. During the Second World War, he enlisted in Hitler's army and worked as a medical orderly as German forces were pushed back through Italy. He was captured at Monte Cassino by American forces. An anecdote from this era reveals his abiding passion for the mountains. Alongside other prisoners, he was being paraded at a hotel in Innsbruck before being released, with arms raised and torsos bare as the Americans searched for SS tattoos. Halfway through, he spotted a fellow climber and shouted, 'Great forecast for the weekend. We are going climbing. Can you get any transport?'

Back home, he worked as an odd-job man to finance his trips into the mountains, tackling some of the most challenging Alpine ridges and rock faces for the first time ever. He married in 1951 and would father three children. Two years later, he joined an expedition heading for Nanga Parbat, a mountain in the Karakoram as yet unconquered. It was an old-style expedition, with numerous base camps and dependent on heavy equipment.

Although only the ninth highest mountain in the world, Nanga Parbat is considered one of the toughest climbs. Mount Everest in the Himalayas, the world's highest mountain at 8,848 metres, had been climbed by New Zealander Edmund Hillary and Nepalese Sherpa Tenzing Norgay in May 1953. This news was fresh in the minds of the climbers who set off with Nanga Parbat in their sights. (K2, the world's second highest mountain at 8,600 metres, wasn't achieved until the following year, when an Italian expedition breached the summit.)

Always poor at taking orders, Buhl was among four men in an advance party who refused to return to base camp at the command of the expedition leader. Instead he ventured forth, dumping the backpack he perceived to be slowing his progress before tackling the final ascent. When he reached the summit, it was 6 p.m. Now he had the tricky descent ahead of him with nightfall racing in and no kit at hand. Consequently, he stood awake between 9 p.m. and 4 a.m. in the lee of a rock in what mountaineers call 'the death zone'. As soon as the snow was dappled with the first morning rays, he began his treacherous journey again, powered only by stimulant pills that helped him ignore the agony of frostbitten feet, and plagued by hallucinations:

> The sun is burning down mercilessly and I fall into a half slumber. Thirst and hunger soon wake me. I'm totally dehydrated and can think of nothing but getting something to drink. Here and there I hear voices above me, possibly my friends with a flask of tea. But no, nothing. It takes all my strength to pull myself together and continue the descent. Everywhere I can see signs of human presence but I know full well that I'm the first person to be here. It is all new land.

Exhausted, he was finally reunited with his colleagues. He had achieved the mountain summit without equipment or oxygen in a forty-one-hour turbo charge, pioneering a new manner of climbing in the process.

At home, his welcome was rapturous. He became Austria's best known sportsman and did much to rebuild the nation's shattered esteem after the Second World War. Once he got over his frostbite, he was back to his climbing best.

Afterwards, his reputation for excellence became well known. Like all climbers, he was a curious combination of team ethic and self-reliance, of respect for the peak and almost reckless rule-breaking. Always conscious of the risks involved after seeing a solo climber die before his eyes in the Alps, he made perpetual safety assessments, while trying to push back the boundaries. He possessed singular drive. 'Hermann climbs totally without compromise,' one colleague noted.

His aim was now to climb in small tight groups on high mountains without fixed ropes and extensive camps. In 1957, he was part of a group that climbed Broad Peak in the Karakoram for the first time, when he was once again struck by the stark beauty of nature's palette on the mountain peaks:

'It is a solemn moment. The sun is glowing red and hanging just above the horizon, the [mountains] are lit up in the dying light and from minute to minute the dark shadows wander higher and higher, gradually extinguishing the light over the surrounding summits. As this happens the really high ones begin to burn, the whole horizon has turned red.'

From Broad Peak, he and colleague Kurt Diemberger could see the ridges of Chogolisa, which fell below the magical 8,000-metre mark but was still virgin territory in mountaineering terms. Although Buhl had only achieved Broad Peak thanks to Diemberger's help, he was undaunted. Together they set off towards Chogolisa that same year, climbing Alpine-style with minimum equipment.

Before they reached the summit, they were enveloped by a snowstorm that slashed visibility to nothing. They took off the ropes that joined them and edged along a narrow path. Diemberger felt a vibration under his feet at one point as a cornice of snow collapsed but forged ahead. Soon afterwards, he waited for his companion but Buhl failed to appear. As he tracked back, Diemberger saw his own footprints veer close to the precipice – and saw a second set which went over the edge into oblivion. Numb with loss, he nonetheless photographed the eerie scene and returned alone to the mountain bottom. Buhl's body was never found.

Robert Burns

(1759–1796)

What's important about 'Auld Lang Syne' for me is that it makes everybody hold each other at New Year, and there's not another song in the world that does that. It is a massive achievement for a songwriter.
Eddi Reader (Singer)

A glossary for Burns is as helpful for most Scots as for most English people. But if you go to a Burns event where 'Tam o' Shanter' is being recited, ninety per cent of it is intelligible. Burns is certainly no more difficult, and probably less difficult, than Shakespeare. Times change, things move on, but what continues is the communication of emotion and humanity, which Burns had in spades.
Dr Gerard Carruthers (Biographer)

TODAY, BURNS NIGHT is as much a fixture on the calendar as Bonfire Night and May Day, and it is celebrated worldwide. Tartan-clad attendees are regaled with Robert Burns's poetry as they enjoy a dish of haggis and a slug or three of whisky. After the haggis is beckoned by the call of the bagpipes, it is welcomed to the table with the following lines:

> Fair fa' your honest, sonsie face,
> Great chieftain o' the puddin'-race!
> Aboon them a' ye tak your place,
> Painch, tripe, or thairm:
> Weel are ye wordy of a grace
> As lang's my arm.

There's no doubt that Burns, a notorious womaniser and heavy drinker, would have been the life and soul of the party if he'd been around for a Burns Night supper. (The tradition didn't begin until 1801, five years after Burns's premature death.) But what's remarkable about him is not the quantity he drank or the number of children he fathered but the dexterity of his diction and its broad appeal. Burns pitched his poetry and lyrics at a Scottish population watching in despair as native culture slipped through its fingers. By reviving Scots dialect and embracing everything that Scotland had to offer, Burns instilled a new national pride and patriotism that continued long after his demise.

Burns was brought up in relative poverty. He learned the hardship of farm life at the head of the plough, under the uncertain skies of southern Scotland. His family became virtually bankrupt because of an overbearing landlord. At the same time, a typically Presbyterian love of education meant his father insisted on him reading books from an early age and even paid for a tutor. From his mother he learned the folklore and supernatural tales that fed the Scottish imagination during the era.

From the age of 15, Burns began writing verse, although he maintained a day job on the family farm for years. Upon the death of his father in 1784, his responsibilities expanded. The family moved to a new farm but found the living equally as hard. His domestic problems were compounded because his mistress was pregnant but her family refused to let them marry.

Two years later, aged 27, he sold the copyright for his first book, *Poems Chiefly in the Scottish Dialect*, for 100 guineas, hoping to flee the farm in favour of the warmer climate of the West Indies. But the book's runaway popularity persuaded him to stay. Soon he went to Edinburgh where he was fêted in literary circles. There he met fellow writer Walter Scott, who left this description of Burns:

> He was strong and robust, his manners rustic not clownish. He had a sort of dignified plainness and simplicity that made me think of a very sagacious country farmer of the old Scotch school. His conversation expressed perfect self-confidence without the slightest presumption. Among the men who were the most learned of their time and country, he expressed himself with perfect firmness and without the least intrusive forwardness and when he differed in opinion he did not hesitate to express it firmly yet at the same time with modesty. He was like a farmer dressed in his best to dine with a laird. His address to females was extremely deferential and always with a turn towards either the bathetic or humorous.

At this time, Burns behaved shrewdly, collaborating in the view that he was a ploughman poet which wrongly implied a lack of education. It won him a niche in a world where he was painfully aware of the need to earn money, although high-born Scots were slow in coming forward with adequate patronage. A rich vein of radical politics evident in his poems was not lost on agitators in subsequent generations, though.

Despite rubbing shoulders with the aristocracy, Burns remained an edgy, unorthodox character. He was outspoken in his criticism of the men of the Kirk who he suspected of double standards. More than that, he dallied with the Catholic church, the faith that had inspired the Jacobite rebellion that ended just 14 years before he was born. It was the failure of the Jacobites in 1745 that motivated English-led repression of Scottish culture. Burns was among the first to unpick this, fired as he was by the principles of the Enlightenment. He wrote both in Scottish dialect and in commonly used English as he cared less for narrow boundaries in terms of Scottish life, more the broad picture.

A competent fiddle player, he toured Scotland collecting songs as well as penning verse and it is now that he dusted down 'Auld Lang Syne', sung every Hogmanay – although there's a suspicion among students of folk music that it is actually an English rather than a Scottish song. Still, he needed a more regular income to support his growing family – he fathered more than a dozen children – and became an excise man, with a brief to rein in the activities of smugglers. It meant riding on horseback for miles in foul weather, when his health was already frail. He was also subject to the ravages of depression. Perhaps his early death was far from surprising.

He died of something that resembled rheumatic fever although there have been many groundless rumours that he was suffering from a sexually transmitted disease. Among rich and poor alike, Burns had been held in great affection and his death was greeted with an outpouring of grief that was repeated upon the death of his wife, Jean Armour, forty years later. In 1844 the first ever Burns festival held in Ayr attracted at least 50,000 people.

Almost immediately following his death, pilgrims began flocking to places associated with Burns, including his birthplace in Ayrshire and Alloway Kirk, where 'Tam o' Shanter' is set. His mausoleum in St Michael's churchyard in Dumfries was visited by thousands of fans. Statues of Burns appeared across the Lowlands paid for by subscriptions raised among

Scottish workers. At the same time, Scottish nobility were castigated for their meanness towards a national bard who had died in poverty. Attempts by the aristocracy to reclaim Burns after his death were sharply repelled by radicals who strongly felt him the voice of the working man.

In fact, his universal appeal probably lies in the fact that his work is informed by a pastoral existence that died around the same time he did, as the industrial revolution changed the lives of working people and eliminated the romantic idyll after which the sentimental still yearn.

Julius Caesar

(c.100 BC–44 BC)

The more I get to know about him, the more sympathetic to him I become. He was responding to his own chemistry and using that and all his unbelievable energies and abilities to what he thought was the good of the state. To me that is pretty virtuous.

Barry Cunliffe, CBE (Professor, writer and broadcaster)

We cannot reach a definitive conclusion on him because there are elements of his life where we lack the basic information to know what he was doing and what he was thinking. He did so much and a lot is extremely controversial. He slaughters enormous numbers of people and he carries out reforms that benefit everybody. He is a very odd mixture. There are some terrific things about him and some really terrible things.

Dr Adrian Goldsworthy (Biographer)

THINK OF ANCIENT Rome and one man stands out from the crowd. Julius Caesar was a seasoned soldier, a canny politician, a lover and a fighter. Centuries after he was treacherously stabbed to death in the forum, his name remains as familiar in modern parlance as Winston Churchill or John F. Kennedy. Facts about his life are well worn and sometimes patchy. They have been embellished by fiction provided by William Shakespeare and assorted creative writers keen to underscore his importance. Nonetheless, his pivotal role in pushing forward the boundaries of the Roman Empire is beyond doubt. And for a while he was the acknowledged leader of the known world.

Caesar was born in or around 100 BC. Contrary to popular belief, he did not lend his name to Caesarean sections. At the time, if babies were cut out of their mother's stomach, the woman inevitably perished. Caesar's mother did not die in childbirth and indeed was a forceful figure in his adult life. (He did bestow his name to autocratic leaders down the ages, for Caesar is the root of Kaiser and Czar.)

The star of the Caesar family had recently fallen in Rome and, after his father died, his mother was keen her only son would bring it to prominence once more. As he grew up, Rome was a dangerous place. Alleged traitors' heads were frequently nailed to the speaker's platform, and bodies of murdered men were often spotted floating down the Tiber. The ruthless Sulla was already a dictator in the Roman Republic. Caesar was shown how to achieve immense power by use of force. In fact, Sulla told the teenage Caesar to divorce his wife Cornelia as she belonged to a proscribed family. Risking everything, Caesar refused to obey and lived in hiding until Sulla retracted the order following pressure from influential family members linked to his mother.

Caesar used his enforced absence from Rome for study and also went on a mission to the Black Sea province of Bithynia to forge an alliance with its king, Nicomedes, a known homosexual. Rumours that Caesar had enjoyed a relationship with the king dogged him for much of his career, prompting him on one occasion to swear a public oath to convince people it wasn't true. He was famously captured by pirates who asked for a ransom of twenty talents. Outraged, Caesar insisted they demanded more. Apparently he developed a cordial relationship with his captors, while saying he would come back to crucify them for their temerity. Ultimately, Caesar was freed after his friends raised the ransom and he did pursue the pirates, crucifying them as he had promised. But, as a nod to the hospitality they had shown him, he had their throats slit so they wouldn't suffer unduly. On reflection it seems only Caesar himself can have propagated this story, and this tallies with the sense of showmanship that is evident throughout his life.

For the first forty years of his life, Caesar seems to have kept his ambitions to the confines of Roman convention, taking on some public positions while heading up a few low-profile campaigns. Recurring financial problems might also have played a part in curbing his aspirations. However, having allegedly pondered on a statue of Alexander the Great who achieved much more than he had at a younger age, he decided to accelerate his career believing himself to be the most capable man of the era. And, like other Romans, he was in the happy position of being able to combine military and political occupations.

He was elected consul and, with some swift manoeuvring, was part of the first triumvirate to rule Rome, alongside Pompey and Crassus. Caesar was an accomplished leader of men, being charismatic, disciplined, merciful and determined. He moved quickly in battle and made bold campaign decisions. In order to improve his finances and to keep the problematic Germanic tribes at bay, he embarked on the conquest of Gaul. It was during the invasion of what is now modern France that Caesar came to Britain, at the time considered a risky venture to the world's end.

Married three times, he frequently bedded other people's wives, including those of Pompey and Crassus, as well as the mother and sister of Brutus, the man who would eventually murder him. It was not these infidelities that led to civil war in Rome, however, but an attempt by Pompey to sideline

Caesar. Fearful that he would be arrested if he entered Rome as a private citizen as Pompey proposed, Caesar came with an army – and Pompey fled. It was pursuit of Pompey that led Caesar to Egypt where he found his adversary had been beheaded.

Instead of waging war, Caesar met Cleopatra, the cultured young co-ruler of Egypt, and the two began an affair. At this point he was 53, balding and exhausted, having come to the end of a ten-year campaign. He was sufficiently beguiled to stay in Egypt when perhaps he should have returned to rule in Rome. According to Roman historian Suetonius, Caesar and Cleopatra 'often feasted until first light and he would have sailed through Egypt on her royal barge almost to Ethiopia if his army had not refused to follow him.'

When he finally went back to Rome it was as dictator, realising the chaotic Republic would otherwise unravel. His agenda was not unpopular, but the notion that Caesar was adopting imperial fetishes did raise concerns when the bedrock of the Republic was nominal equality for all men. There was a programme of reforms, but observers looked on in concern as Caesar increased his own powers at the expense of other political institutions.

The motive of his killers isn't necessarily clear. Brutus, one of the main protagonists, was also named as second in line to Caesar in his will. Having ignored warnings, Caesar was killed on the Ides of March, three days before a planned campaign. In the final analysis, his insistence that enemies should be pardoned rather than killed did not induce sufficient loyalty to save his life.

Andrew Carnegie

(1835–1919)

For me what marked his greatness was that he was a self-made man. He came from a poor Scottish family that emigrated to the United States. When he got there they had very little and when he came back, he did so with the greatest fortune ever amassed. But it wasn't just about the money. It was what he did with the fortune that impressed me. He didn't just make this vast pile of cash, he gave most of it away. It is an extraordinary story.

Jeff Randall (Journalist)

He changed American thinking. He gave Americans an idea of what wealth is for; not simply for piling up, not for social aggrandisement but for betterment, and that was a powerful meaning to introduce to a society that frankly needed that kind of direction. Also, he was a traitor to his class of the super rich. He was a profound supporter of graduated death duties. He thought that rich people should be taxed until the pips started to squeak. That made him an outsider in the world he should have belonged to and connected him directly to that Scottish radical tradition that was so important to him. So he remained consistent and true at that level of his life.

Professor Eric Homberger (Author)

WHEN HE SOLD his steel company at the turn of the twentieth century for $500 million, Andrew Carnegie was in cash terms probably the richest man on the planet. Today the sum equates to untold billions. Carnegie had it all at his fingertips, but he was a man of high principle, as unbending as any of the steel girders he used to manufacture. At the core of his being was a belief that 'the man who dies rich, dies disgraced'. Accordingly, he set about giving away his fortune, taking special care that libraries and schools got the lion's share. His agenda was to promote education which he saw as the way out of poverty – and more effective than any hand-out. Before his death he gave away $350 million dollars, and then donated a further wedge of his fortune to the charitable foundation that bears his name, with the express intention that it should 'promote the advancement and diffusion of knowledge and understanding'. Consequently his good works continue today, almost a century after his death.

Carnegie had a rags-to-riches story that began in Dunfermline, Scotland. When he was 12, his father, a weaver, fell on hard times and the Carnegie family moved to America to escape the effects of Britain's economic collapse. Although he had left Scotland, Carnegie carried with him the family values of radicalism, application, endurance and the desire to win a fair deal for the working man. His father struggled to find a job while Carnegie became a bobbin boy in a cotton factory near Pittsburgh, continuing his education at night classes. 'It was burned into my heart that my father had had to beg for work. Then and there came the resolve I would cure that when I got to be a man,' he recalled later.

Two years later, Carnegie began work for the local telegraph office and his quick wits and ability were spotted by a company superintendent. Carnegie began work as his secretary and later succeeded to his job. His progress was noticeably swift, not least because he was a consummate networker. Soon he'd saved enough money to become an investor in other businesses, too, including small iron mills, and a manufacturer of bedded train carriages. During a visit to Britain, he recognised the next big thing emerging in industry: a converter that turned pig iron into steel, invented by Henry Bessemer. In 1870, Carnegie opened his own furnace on the same lines and the groundwork for his mammoth fortune was laid.

Although he was only 35, Carnegie was already thinking of abandoning industry in favour of philanthropy. He believed that 'Simply making more money must degrade me beyond hope of permanent recovery.' In fact, hopes of an early retirement spent dispensing his largesse were misplaced. But his words serve as an indication of how, even as a young man, he was determined to distribute his wealth for the common good.

Carnegie spent considerable time in Britain and was swift to criticise the monarchy, the upper classes and a system of inherited wealth. Meanwhile he supported Irish home rule, and thus was generally seen as a troublemaker. After a strike in one of his American's plants which ended in the death of ten men, however, he was branded a hypocrite for spouting liberal values but not living by them. The incident happened when he was out of the country and after he instructed his partner not to use strike-breakers – the flashpoint of the dispute – but he never publicly stepped back from taking responsibility, although he knew his reputation was tarnished by it.

He married and had a daughter, although none in the family were familiar figures on the social circuit that defined the wealthy on America's east coast. Indeed, Carnegie preferred the company of writers, thinkers and artists. His daughter Margaret recollected that 'My father was a kindly, friendly man. He liked people, he liked to make them happy. He always wanted to be remembered as one who loved his fellow men. He was a great optimist, incurably so. All is well since all goes better, that was his motto. He lived by it and believed in it firmly.'

It might be a misconception to believe he was kindly to those in business, either working alongside him or as rivals. He expected hard work and commitment and could seem ruthless if he didn't get it. But his business creed was no secret. Carnegie's beliefs are outlined in 'The Gospel of

Wealth', written in 1889 before the sale of his steelworks. In it he calls the rich trustees of wealth who are obliged to dispose of it before their death so it can be recycled for public benefit:

> The surplus wealth of the few will become, in the best sense the property of the many, because administered for the common good, and this wealth, passing through the hands of the few, can be made a much more potent force for the elevation of our race than if it had been distributed in small sums to the people themselves. Even the poorest can be made to see this, and to agree that great sums gathered by some of their fellow-citizens and spent for public purposes, from which the masses reap the principal benefit, are more valuable to them than if scattered among them through the course of many years in trifling amounts.

His role in the spread of education particularly among low-income families enabling them to move towards a brighter future remains unquantifiable.

Rachel Carson

(1907–1964)

She has emerged out of the Second World War alongside the exponential development of science in the service of corporate America; extraordinarily ambitious, audacious science and careless science. And to stand up against that in the name of the creatures with whom we share the planet and ordinary citizens, she becomes a very important figure. She translates that science into the language of everyday life, like a poet.

Bea Campbell (Author, playwright, journalist
and green campaigner)

Before Rachel Carson, Americans really didn't know that pesticides were toxic. Probably the world didn't know that. Now we know what we are doing when we put chemicals on our lawn or in our landscapes. Now we question our government officials about the long-term effects of the technology and the science they are putting out there. Now we demand the right to know.

Linda Lear (Biographer)

'THEN A STRANGE *blight crept over the area and everything began to change. Some evil spell had settled on the community; mysterious maladies swept over the flocks of chickens, the cattle and sheep sickened and died. Everywhere was a shadow of death. The farmers spoke of much illness among their families … No witchcraft, no enemy action had silenced the rebirth of new life in this stricken world. The people had done it themselves.'*

This pen portrait of a dismal, doomed future came from the authoritative hand of Rachel Carson, who combined her talents for writing and science to produce one of the landmark books of the twentieth century. *Silent Spring* was a dire warning about the fate of the world if indiscriminate chemical use continued unabated. It still sells 25,000 copies a year in Britain alone. The book is credited with kick-starting a green movement that's flourishing today, having changed public perception about the agro-chemical industry.

For taking a stand, she was branded 'a commie', 'a health quack', 'a peace nut' and 'an hysterical spinster'. Perhaps a more measured epitaph comes in the words of David Brower, a conservationist and founder of Friends of the Earth: 'She did her homework, she minded her English and she cared.'

Carson was born in Springdale, Pennsylvania, the youngest of three daughters. Her mother Maria shared with the young Rachel a love of the natural world that grew stronger still during adulthood. By the time she left Johns Hopkins University in 1932, she was already an accomplished writer and a marine biologist. A twenty-year career was primarily spent in government service, writing and editing publications for the US Fish and Wildlife Service.

In 1952, she came to public attention with a book called *The Sea Around Us*, which swiftly became a bestseller. A sequel followed three years later, *The Edge of the Sea*. Already, her contention that mankind was only one component of nature was an evident theme. There followed a book called

Help Your Child to Wonder – in which she sought to pass on her passion for nature and underscored again her belief that all life on Earth was linked – and then a third book about sea life.

But she had growing concerns about the way pesticides were being used with abandon as powerful chemical companies overhauled the food industry after the Second World War. She regarded the science which was blinding America at the time with its capacity to destroy bugs and blights as Neanderthal: 'It is our alarming misfortune that so primitive a science has armed itself with the most modern and terrible weapons, and that in turning them against the insects it has also turned them against the Earth.'

Initially reluctant to delve into this mire, she realised she was the best-qualified person for the job and that she would know no peace until it was done. She saw that American society was affluent and complacent. Her challenge was to ignite a curiosity and a clamour that would change the path of ecological history away from an impending disaster.

She was scholarly and scrupulous in her approach. Yet her words gave extraordinary clarity to a complex issue, translating science into the easily digestible language of everyday life. In fact, her greatest fear was not the criticism the book would engender but a lawsuit that would break her financially. Although her text was devastating to the giant corporations funding pesticides and the like, no legal restraints were forthcoming.

There were disparaging comments, however. One scientist declared: 'The modern scientist believes that man is steadily controlling nature. If man were to faithfully follow the teachings of Miss Carson, we would return to the Dark Ages, and the insects and disease and vermin would once again inherit the Earth.'

It wasn't, though, attacks from scientists that exercised Carson as she wrote. A woman of strong family values, she cared for her mother, nieces and great nephew Roger while fighting the effects of an aggressive breast cancer. Although she had many friends she did not have a partner. Later she said: 'There is quite a story behind *Silent Spring*, isn't there? Such a catalogue of illnesses, if one were superstitious it would be easy to believe in some malevolent influence at work determined by some means to keep the book from being finished.'

After reading *Silent Spring*, President John F. Kennedy launched a commission to investigate the effect of chemicals like DDT on the landscape. In 1963, Carson gave evidence before Congress about the best way to protect human health and the environment. Ultimately, chemicals were restricted and an environmental movement and the organic food principles were spawned. She died the following year, knowing her book had turned a tide which had risked engulfing North America.

Carson did not reject science outright but felt it should take its rightful place in harmony with the world rather than being the boss of it. When we respected nature, she felt, we became better people:

> I believe that natural beauty has a necessary place in the development of any individual or society. I believe that whenever we destroy beauty, whenever we substitute something manmade and artificial for a natural feature of this Earth, we have retarded some part of man's spiritual growth. In contemplating the exceeding beauty of this Earth, I have found a calmness and courage. For there is symbolic as well as actual beauty in the migration of birds, in the ebb and flow of tides, in the folded bud ready for the spring. There is something infinitely healing in the repeated refrains of nature.

Brian Clough

(1935–2004)

He led an unfashionable club to two European Cups – unheard of today. He rebuilt two teams that were down on their luck in not a particularly thriving part of the country. But most [outstanding] of all was his wonderful personality; the way he could command a room, the way he could talk to you in such a direct manner that you were almost transfixed listening to him. When I went to do my first interview with [the] BBC, I said to my editor: 'What sort of things do you want me to get him to say?' And the editor looked at me and said: 'Listen, if Brian Clough read the telephone directory people would still listen.'

John Motson (Sports commentator)

It was a very poor childhood. In Middlesbrough in the 1940s and 1950s, just like everywhere in post-war Britain, life was incredibly difficult. And he had a slight fear of not wanting to go back to that, ever. And yet the other element of him was that he gave away money incredibly generously. He certainly gave of his time. But the amount of money that he must have given to various charities without any coverage at all shows what a complex Chinese box of a man he was.

Duncan Hamilton (Biographer)

HE IS WIDELY acknowledged as the best manager the England team never had. Eccentric, overbearing, and a loudmouth who was both big-headed and big-hearted, Brian Clough was the people's choice for the top job. But Clough was loved and feared in equal measure. The Football Association sensed his mercurial ways would spell disaster for the national team and calls for Cloughie to take the helm were rejected. Still, even without the post of England manager Brian Clough became the best-known football manager in Britain. He was among the first wave brought to prominence through television during the 1970s, and his no-nonsense approach to football and TV interviewers won him fans across the board. Clough was not universally successful, however. His golden touch worked at Derby County and later in Nottingham, but there were two disastrous stints at Brighton and Leeds between the triumphs. There were other contradictions too. He was an avowed socialist with a weak spot for wealth.

Certainly, a hard-knock childhood in a north-eastern city – which he nonetheless regarded as a little piece of paradise – affected his outlook. He was the sixth of nine children who remained exceptionally close to his mother, Sally. Indeed, it was she who engendered in him a passion for football. Although he was bright, he failed his 11-plus examination and left school aged 15 to work as an office clerk.

But it was soccer rather than work which was central to his existence. At 16 he signed for Middlesbrough Football Club for a brief but impressive spell as centre forward. He then transferred to Sunderland to continue his goal-scoring habit. In 274 appearances as a player for the two clubs, he scored 251 goals, a post-war record, and was twice capped for England. But his playing days ended abruptly on Boxing Day 1962 when he sustained a serious injury playing for Sunderland against Bury in a clash with the goalkeeper, when he was aged just 27.

Unable or unwilling to break the bond with the sport he loved, he went into management and when he took over at Fourth Division Hartlepool aged 30 he was the youngest manager in the football league. Two years later he arrived at Derby County, once a high-flying club but by then a longstanding fixture of the Second Division. He brought in Peter Taylor as his assistant manager, the start of a highly fruitful partnership that would endure for many years. Almost immediately the pair established themselves with a League Cup run that took 'the Rams' to the semi-final. After two years, Derby were seven points clear at the top of the Second Division and preparing for a return to top-flight football in what was then known as the First Division.

In 1972, they were champions, with a squad of only 16 players. Just a year later Clough and Taylor fell out with the board and left the club, prompting protest marches in Derby. By this time Clough was a favourite on chat shows and a popular although controversial pundit whose gamut of emotions constantly bubbled close to the surface. Soon Clough found himself at Brighton and then the bright lights of Leeds United, one of the country's most successful outfits at the time, beckoned. However, Clough's reputation for caustic comments and abrasive banter preceded him. Despite the abundant charms in his locker, Clough failed to win around guarded players and after only forty-four days he left the club.

It was undoubtedly a bruising episode for Clough, although he found solace in the immense payoff he received from Leeds. Fortunately, the best was yet to come with a move to Nottingham Forest in 1975. Like Derby, it was languishing in the Second Division when he arrived. After winning promotion in 1977, Nottingham Forest went on to win two European Cup titles, a League Championship and the League Cup four times. All his trophy cabinet lacked was the FA Cup. For his part, Clough regarded his greatest achievement as Forest going undefeated in all competitions for more than a year.

He continued to manage in tandem with Peter Taylor, freely acknowledging his partner's role: 'Football management is a very lonely job on occasions. No matter how many people you are surrounded with there are times when you sit down and – unless you have a right-hand man like I had with Peter Taylor – it is a lonely job and you are on your own.' But in 1980 the partnership ended and the pair were ultimately estranged by a schism that was never bridged.

One constant in his life was his childhood sweetheart Barbara with whom he had three children, Nigel, Simon and Elizabeth. Sadly, the other was alcohol and his reliance on drink grew until it badly affected his health.

By 1991, he was the longest-serving manager in the league. When he received the OBE in the birthday honours list he joked that is stood for 'old big 'ead'. But two years later, with Nottingham Forest teetering towards relegation from what was now the Premiership, he retired. His last match was marred by a defeat on the field and emotionally charged scenes among devastated fans off it. After undergoing a liver transplant and then suffering stomach cancer, Clough died and was mourned by thousands of fans who put the age-old rivalries between Derby and Nottingham Forest behind them for a day to attend a memorial service at Derby's Pride Park ground. At the service Clough's widow read out a poem written especially for her shrewd, uncompromising, affectionate, unpredictable husband:

> *What made him so endearing is elusive to explain,*
> *This tyrant in a sweatshirt barking orders in the rain.*
> *Today he offered vitriol, tomorrow marzipan,*
> *A paradox, a puzzle but a diamond of a man.*
>
> *When the Gods apportioned modesty, one youngster wasn't there,*
> *He was in the queue marked confidence, receiving twice his share.*
> *With two good feet beneath him he considered it enough,*
> *And so was born the character we know as Brian Clough.*

Samuel Coleridge-Taylor

(1875–1912)

I feel that Coleridge-Taylor's contribution and his courage is what you hear in his music. I find it both moving and immensely inspirational to think that this amazingly brave person existed and wrote that music in my country and I'm very proud that he was British.

Howard Goodall (Award-winning composer)

It was an amazing experience for him to go to the USA and be so lionised. But at the same time he was not willing to relinquish what he saw as his musical standards in the interests of being racially iconic. He would not allow Hiawatha *to be performed with piano. The problem was there were not enough black musicians to form an orchestra at that time in Washington. The solution was to hire the US Marines Band and augment it with some string players. Here were white federal employees playing under a black conductor. That must have been quite a coup.*

Stephen Banfield (Professor of music, Bristol University)

BLACK, BRITISH AND a leading international composer of the Victorian age, there was nothing about Samuel Coleridge-Taylor that was textbook. He was a man fellow musicians called 'genius'. As one of the few black faces in London society, he attracted everyone's attention – sometimes in the form of vile racism. But his natural talents combined with dignity and humility, and he became a beacon for the worldwide black community.

Coleridge-Taylor was born in Holborn, London, the son of an African medical student and an Englishwoman. It seems unlikely his father knew of his existence. His mother Alice moved to Croydon and married a railway worker. Coleridge-Taylor, with his younger half-siblings, was brought up in close proximity to her musical family.

Singing in two church choirs, he attracted the attention of one Colonel Herbert A. Walters, who steered Coleridge-Taylor towards the Royal College of Music. From the age of 15, Coleridge-Taylor had violin and later composition tuition at the RCM during the five years he was a pupil there. Along with Ralph Vaughan Williams and Gustav Holst, Coleridge-Taylor was taught to write music by Irish-born composer Sir Charles Villiers Stanford – and was reputed to be Stanford's favourite. If he found racism on the streets of London, there's little to suggest Coleridge-Taylor encountered it in musical circles as, thanks to his prodigious early talent, he was nurtured by Stanford and others.

After his first concert, held in a public hall in Croydon, Coleridge-Taylor was too shy to take a curtain call. However, he was nonetheless described in a local newspaper as 'plucky, persevering and painstaking'. The salon pieces he produced at the time were influenced by admiration of Czech composer Antonin Dvořák (1841–1904). After hearing Coleridge-Taylor's early work, August Jaeger of the music publisher Novello & Co wrote, 'That boy will do great things. He is a genius I feel sure if ever an English composer was.'

When Edward Elgar (1857–1934) was too busy to take on a prestigious commission, he passed it on to the young Coleridge-Taylor, which resulted in the popular 'Ballade in A Minor' that premiered in 1898. In the same year, he wrote perhaps his most enduring composition, 'Hiawatha's Wedding Feast'.

But by now he was exploring new musical directions. In 1896, he had met the black American poet Paul Dunbar and begun to read work by Booker T. Washington and W. E. B. Du Bois, both activists in the USA. With his hitherto dormant black consciousness stirred, Coleridge-Taylor turned his musical attention to the sounds of Africa in America. He was further enlightened by the visiting Fisk Singers, children of freed slaves who sang to raise money to build a college in Nashville, Tennessee.

Although Coleridge-Taylor had undoubtedly met bigotry on a regular basis, it fell far short of the institutionalised racism experienced daily by black people in America at the time where segregation was the norm. In 1900, he found time to attend the first Pan African Conference. By now, he was married with children in prospect and he was compelled to work wherever he could, so he not only wrote but also taught, lectured and conducted across Britain in a punishing schedule. In 1904, he embarked on one of three tours of America, where he was both entranced by the music and appalled by race politics.

The following year, Booker T. Washington wrote biographical notes for Coleridge-Taylor's 24 *Negro Melodies*, one of several works that was popular in America but little known in Britain. 'He is the foremost musician of his race, an inspiration to the negroes since he himself, the child of an African father, is the embodiment of what are the possibilities of the Negro under favourable environment,' said Washington. He went on to praise Coleridge-Taylor for giving folk songs associated with America's black community 'a new interpretation and an added dignity'.

Washington later wrote to Coleridge-Taylor to reiterate the importance of his role in the black community in the USA. 'In composing *Hiawatha* you have done the coloured people of the United States a service which I am sure you never dreamed of. It acts as a source of inspiration to us, not only musically but in other types of endeavour.'

But Coleridge-Taylor's fight was not confined to across the Atlantic. His dignified response to a debating group in Purley, presided over by a vicar, that hosted a barrister talking about 'the negro problem' in North America, appeared in the *Croydon Guardian*:

> No one realises more than I that coloured people have not yet taken their place in the scheme of things but to say they never will is arrogant rubbish and an insult to the God in whom they profess to believe. The fact is that there is an appalling amount of ignorance amongst English people regarding the negro and his doings as expressed by the clergyman in the Purley lecture ... personally I consider myself the equal of any white man who ever lived and no one could ever change me in that respect ... Really great people always look for the best in others. It is the little man who always looks for the worst – and finds it.

In 1912, Coleridge-Taylor wrote a violin concerto for a client in New York and dispatched it on the *Titanic*. After the ship sank, he had to write it again. In August he collapsed at West Croydon railway station suffering from double pneumonia and died a few days later deliriously conducting the problematic concerto. (It was finally recorded in 2004.) Overwork no doubt contributed to his premature demise. He had sold the rights to his greatest work, 'Hiawatha's Wedding Feast', for just a few pounds, thus inflicting upon himself a perpetual workload. So appalled were people that the system of royalties was changed so it became fairer for composers.

A poignant epitaph was inscribed on Coleridge-Taylor's gravestone: 'Too young to die, his great simplicity, his happy courage in an alien world, his gentleness made all that knew him, love him.'

Michael Collins

(1890–1922)

What Collins offers for me is a window through which one can begin to look at the nature of self justification that takes place in an individual who looks at the landscape of their lives, looks at their attitude to their country's future and decides, rightly or wrongly, only through violence will they achieve what they believe to be their specific ends. It is a really important lesson. We have got to start looking at problems in Africa and the Middle East in terms of the people who believe themselves to be repressed and suppressed.

Lord David Puttnam (Filmmaker and University Chancellor)

Collins had come to prominence by contemptuously setting himself against what he called the politicians in the movement, as the advocate of war. He turns to politics with a great appetite even while the war is being waged. It may be a sign of maturity or opportunism but he is beginning to shift his position.

Professor Roy Foster (Oxford University)

FROM RUTHLESS REBEL leader to democracy enforcer, Michael Collins lived and died by a series of twentieth-century political realities.

Collins was the youngest of eight children, whose father was 76 when he was born in the rural west of Ireland, where British rule was fiercely resented. Later Collins said: 'I was a reverential kid. Reverence was not only instilled into me by my father, it seemed a natural trait. Great age held something for me that was awesome. I was much fonder of old people in the darkness than I was of young people in the day time. It is at night you are able to get the value of old people and it was listening to the old people that I got my ideas of nationality.'

Despite nationalistic stirrings, Collins moved to London aged 15 to work for four years in a post office savings bank in London. Entrenched in the capital's Irish community, his passion for an independent Ireland heightened and he joined the Gaelic League. Soon he was a member of the Irish Republican Brotherhood, a group committed to securing independence by force. It was not a universally popular group, however, as it seemed home rule was likely to be won by peaceful means if only the British government would stop dragging its heels.

It was the IRB, with Collins among its ranks, that ignited the Easter Uprising in 1916. Collins had returned to Dublin to help occupy the post office in Sackville Street. Although the aim was to capitalise on British preoccupation with the First World War, the uprising is generally thought of as a chance missed. There were 450 deaths at the time, including a sizeable number of Dublin's civilians, while a further fifteen men were executed. Later, Collins rued the lost opportunity: 'The actions of the leaders should not pass without comment. They have died nobly at the hands of the firing squad, so much I grant. But on the whole I think the rising was bungled terribly, costing many a good life.'

Some Dubliners booed the revolutionaries as they were led away from the post office. But the harsh penalties handed down by a vengeful British government helped to unite the Irish behind a call to arms.

As for Collins, he was interned in Wales where he revealed his leadership potential by teaching guerrilla warfare and organising a spy network to fellow inmates. Many people have testified to his qualities:

> He had such tremendous energy. In any meeting he was in he was always the dominant personality.

> He had all the qualities that men loved. He was a wonderful leader, a wonderful man to get everything he wanted done. He wouldn't take no for an answer from anybody.

> He was boyish, enthusiastic, would crack jokes.

> He was a very ruthless kind of person who would never give you a second chance.

> I loved him. I would have willingly laid down my life for Collins at any time.

After 1916, British rule in Ireland was characterised by extreme cruelty, carried out by the army's Black and Tans and the Auxies, who were paramilitary police. Collins busied himself with organising subversive activities, which he preferred to static warfare. The political scene shifted in 1918 with an election. Collins was one of seventy-three Sinn Fein MPs elected to the British Parliament who preferred to sit in a newly founded Irish institution. By the following year, he was minister of finance, head of the Irish Republican Brotherhood, director of intelligence in the Irish Republican Army and embroiled in the Irish war of independence.

Collins was at the heart of the orchestrated assassinations of fourteen people thought to be British spies on 21 November 1920. British forces retaliated by entering Croke Park stadium during a Gaelic football match and turning guns on the crowds, killing a similar number. However, the Irish killers fondly sheltered by their community were also guilty of settling old disputes in their community in the name of nationalism.

By now Collins was being increasingly lured into the political arena not least by Éamon de Valera, who was both an ally and a rival. De Valera dispatched a reluctant Collins to London in 1921 in a delegation to negotiate an end to the war. The resulting Anglo-Irish Treaty established the Irish Free State, albeit with dominion status. An oath to it still mentioned the British King, and the six counties of the north, with a Protestant majority, were divided from the rest. It was a vast improvement on other Home Rule proposals previously on the table but was not the outright victory most had hoped for.

When he signed the Treaty – before achieving consensus from Dublin – Collins knew it would be poorly received in some quarters. 'Early this morning I signed my own death warrant,' he wrote. 'I thought at the time, how odd, how ridiculous. A bullet might just as well have done the job five years ago.' But he felt sure it was a firm foundation and he had enormous confidence in the fledgling country:

> Our poets and artists will be inspired in this stimulating air of freedom to be something more than mere producers of verse and painters of pictures. They will teach us by their vision the noble race we may become. They will inspire us to live as noble Irish men and Irish women should. Our civilisation will be glorious – or the reverse – according to the character of the people and the work we produce will be the expression of what we are.

Although Sinn Fein was split by the Treaty it was passed by the Irish Parliament by 64 votes to 57. Collins was now compelled to bring recalcitrant former colleagues into line. Furious, many Sinn Fein supporters took arms against the new provisional government established by the treaty.

By the middle of 1922, Collins, as commander-in-chief of the new national army, was in the uncomfortable position of having to attack those who had stood at his shoulder in previous battles against the British. Perhaps worse, he needed British assistance to do so. For many, he had gone from hero to public enemy. But he felt he was asking the anti-Treaty protestors to surrender their arms rather than their principles, in line with the will of the electorate.

It was perhaps no surprise that on 22 August 1922 he was shot in an ambush during a tour of his native Cork. He was the only man to die that day, and mystery has traditionally surrounded the identity of the killer. With the perspective of history, Collins was a founding father of terrorism, a democrat and, above all, a patriot.

Captain James Cook

(1728–1779)

How did someone from that background whose first job was delivering coal from the north of England to London actually end up sailing around the world and [becoming] the best cartographer of his day, with very little education?

Greg Dyke (Former BBC Controller)

Cook today has several personalities. There is the Cook who is one of the great, supreme navigators, and that part of his reputation remains. But there is uneasiness among many, particularly among Pacific peoples, about the legacy of Cook. Most white Australians and New Zealanders would still see Cook as a kind of founding father, almost an iconic figure. But the Maori aborigines and Hawaiians see a very different Cook; a despoiler, a destructive force.

Glyn Williams (Professor of History)

EXPLORER CAPTAIN JAMES Cook became living proof that one man could go far with the appliance of science. Figuratively, he left his humble rural roots far behind when he was made a Royal Navy captain, after revealing his seafaring expertise. Physically, he departed the shores of England and used cutting-edge navigational technology to travel further than any man before.

Cook had the skills of a cartographer at his fingertips and did more than anyone previously to chart the coast of Newfoundland, New Zealand, eastern Australia, numerous Pacific Islands and both the Arctic and Antarctic frontiers. He also possessed abundant courage, which enabled him to set off into the unknown. A quotation from Cook himself reveals how he embraced personal and physical challenges after becoming mired in ice off the Canadian coast:

> I will not say it was impossible to get in among this ice but I will assert the bare attempting of it would be a very dangerous enterprise and what I believe no man in my situation would have thought of.
>
> I whose ambition leads me not only farther than any other man has before me but as far as I think it is possible for any man to go was not sorry at meeting with this interruption.

He was a symbol of the Enlightenment, treating indigenous tribes that he encountered with respect and understanding in the context of the era. Ultimately it was an uncharacteristically heavy-handed approach with the Hawaiians that cost him his life.

Few would have predicted this astonishing life story lay ahead when young James was born to a farm labourer and his wife on the outskirts of Middlesbrough. Unsuited to farm and shop work, young James decided his true calling was at sea. After joining the merchant navy, he ferried coal from Newcastle to London and sometimes to the Baltic in a stout Whitby collier. The aspirational Cook spent his spare time studying hydrology, cartography and astronomy. Not content with a secure future as a captain in the mercantile fleet, he enlisted in the Royal Navy in 1755 as an able seaman and spent a dozen years working his way through the ranks.

There's no evidence as to why Cook took this extraordinary and demanding path. After he died, his wife Elizabeth burnt all his letters. But testimony still remains from men who worked alongside him. Lt James King wrote: 'The constitution of his body was robust, inured to labour and capable of undergoing the severest hardships. His stomach bore without difficulty the coarsest and most ungrateful food ... The qualities of his mind were the same hardy and vigorous kind with those of his body. ... His temper might perhaps have been justly blamed as subject to hastiness and passion had not these been disarmed by a disposition the most benevolent and humane.'

In 1767, he was chosen to lead an expedition to the Pacific that would chart the course of the planet Venus across the sun. Its subtext was to find the southern continent that many thought lay undiscovered in the southern oceans. For the task he selected a Whitby collier, which was duly renamed HMS *Endeavour*. From England he sailed around Cape Horn to Tahiti, where he forged an enduring relationship with islanders. Then it was on to New Zealand, which he charted, the unknown Botany Bay in Australia and home via Indonesia. Cook's journals and the work of accompanying scientist Joseph Banks created a major stir on their return.

The second voyage, in HMS *Resolution*, began in 1772 and lasted for three years. He headed to Antarctica in another fruitless search for Terra Australis, the mythical continent which was still the object of considerable debate in London. Afterwards he explored numerous Pacific Islands.

Back in London he once again found himself propelled into high society. There was a chance now to work as an administrator in Greenwich Hospital, near his East London home, and experience the joys of family life. But three of his six children had already died and Cook, still beset by pangs of wanderlust, became intrigued by the possibility of discovering a north-west passage that would improve links between England and North America. After the expedition began in 1776, however, his failure to find the fabled route frustrated him. Usually considerate of his crew, having been among the rank and file himself, Cook was unusually harsh. There were twice as many floggings on the third voyage as there had been on the first two.

Previously recorded observations by Cook indicate he bore none of the European superiority that many travellers of the time displayed. Having met Aborigines in Australia he wrote: 'they may appear to some to be the most wretched people upon Earth, but in reality they are far more happier than we Europeans ... They live in a Tranquillity which is not disturb'd by the Inequality of Condition ... [T]hey live in a warm and fine Climate and enjoy a very wholesome Air, so that they have very little need of Clothing and this they seem to be fully sencible of ... In short they seem'd to set no Value upon any thing we gave them ... this in my opinion argues that they think themselves provided with all the necessarys of Life.'

Yet when relations broke down with the Hawaiians during the final voyage following the theft of a boat, Cook risked their wrath by trying to kidnap a king. David Samuel, a surgeon on the trip, described what happened next:

> Captain Cook was now the only Man on the Rock, he was seen walking down towards the Pinnace, holding his left hand against the Back of his head to guard it from the Stones & carrying his Musket under the other Arm. An Indian came running behind him, stopping once or twice as he advanced, as if he was afraid that he should turn round, then taking him unaware he sprung to him, knocked him on the back of his head with a large Club taken out of a fence, & instantly fled with the greatest precipitation; the blow made Captain Cook stagger two or three paces, he then fell on his hand & one knee & dropped his Musket, as

he was rising another Indian came running to him & before he could recover himself from the Fall drew out an iron Dagger he concealed under his feathered Cloak & stuck it with all his force into the back of his Neck, which made Capt. Cook tumble into the Water in a kind of a bite by the side of the rock where the water is about knee deep.

Perhaps Cook himself provides the most suitably worded eulogy. 'The public will I hope consider me as a plain man zealously exerting himself in the service of his country.'

Tommy Cooper

(1921–1984)

I thought he was such a God-given man for humour. Everything was unlikely, and it all fell into place. He would keep people waiting and then come in backwards and say, 'There you are.' All the constituent parts in Tommy Cooper – his huge height, his amazing face, the podgy hands which were actually incredibly deft when it came to work, his bad feet about which he complained a lot – together they made one of the most startlingly effective comedians I have ever heard. Tommy loved an audience beyond all else, and he loved to laugh at his own humour, which normally you wouldn't give a lot of money for but in his case it was wholly endearing.

Clement Freud

He was a perfectionist in making you believe he was a buffoon. Everything he did was timed to perfection, everything was precise. You can't take it apart, you can't say why did that work. It was a combination of his physicality, the way he moved, his face, and his essence. It made you want to like him.

Jeremy Novick (Biographer)

WITH A TRADEMARK fez crammed over his tufty hair, two surprised eyes and a throaty guffaw, even a glimpse of comedian Tommy Cooper was enough to induce fits of laughter among British audiences. A doomed magic show peppered with timeless one-liners propelled him to the top of the variety bill on stage and television for two decades. A comedian's comedian, nearly thirty years after his death, he remains one of the most impersonated stars ever. Yet still no one can work out why he is so side-achingly funny.

Magician Paul Daniels recalled an appearance by Cooper at a function: 'This great big man just stood up. That is all he did. He just stood up, and the place was in absolute hysterics at a man standing up. Now, I don't care how much you study comedy, you can't define that, that ability to fill a room with laughter because you are emanating humour. After several minutes of laughter, he turned to his wife and said, "I haven't said anything yet." And the whole place went up again.'

In retrospect, it is fortunate he used something more than jokes to win over an audience as, in isolation, they could make you wince:

So I rang up a local building firm. I said, 'I want a skip outside my house.' He said, 'I'm not stopping you.'

I went to buy some camouflage trousers the other day but I couldn't find any.

I bought some HP sauce the other day. It is costing me 6p a month for the next two years.

I went to a paper shop the other day – it had blown away.

He said 'I'm going to chop off the bottom of one of your trouser legs and put it in a library.' I thought, 'That's a turn-up for the books.'

Frequently, he wooed audiences with his highly individual delivery. The intangible effect that he wrought brought poignant heartbreak with his untimely demise.

When the curtain came down on comedian Tommy Cooper for the last time during a show called *Live From Her Majesty's*, he left the live audience and TV viewers at home laughing. Only when his amplified rasps for breath echoed around the theatre did the laughter subside.

Cooper, who had been plagued with health problems, fell into the back curtain after suffering a heart attack. The manner of his collapse looked for all the world like it was another bit of priceless Cooper comedy. Helplessly, his wife Gwen watched saying, 'You may think this is funny, but I know he is finished.'

Born in Caerphilly, Cooper arrived two months prematurely and his survival was often attributed to his grandmother who fed him brandy and condensed milk. He spent his boyhood in Devon, as his family moved to find less polluted air, and he spoke with a West Country twang for the rest of his life. His most formative moment was when his aunt, Lucy, gave him the gift of a magic set, which kept the young Cooper intrigued for hours on end.

As a teenager, he joined a shipyard in Hythe, Kent, as an apprentice and used to entertain his colleagues in his spare time. One show went dramatically awry, with hidden cards falling from a sleeve and bunting remaining stubbornly stuck in a canister. He fled in tears but, as he heard the laughter continuing, he realised the mucked-up magic raised more laughs than when tricks were perfectly executed.

In 1940, he joined the Horse Guards and went to Africa. After being injured in the arm, he found a new role as an entertainer. He would wear a pith helmet for his act but, having forgotten the helmet on one occasion, he liberated a fez from the head of a passing Egyptian waiter, and it remained his signature prop for the rest of his career.

By 1947, he had become a professional comic, subjugating his other skills in the process. Although he realised failure was funny, he was in fact an expert magician and member of the Magic Circle.

He was one of a generation of entertainers who rode the first wave of television celebrity, although he retained a love of theatre work, not least because gags could be repeated from one city venue to the next. A concept tried once on television was soon worn out, he discovered.

His wife Gwen, known to Cooper as Dove, helped him time his routines. Indeed, it was perhaps the timing that made his comedy such compulsive viewing. Actor Trevor Howard believed Cooper to be a genius of timing and thought every actor could learn from his delivery.

Cooper's reputation was for being a kind, industrious, decent and inventive man. But among his colleagues stories circulated about his meanness with money. Often, his good humour got him off the hook, though. Few taxi drivers took offence when Cooper thrust a teabag in their pockets and said, 'Here, have a drink with me.'

Later in his career he became a heavy drinker, having relied for years on a tipple to overcome chronic stage fright. His timing was less perfect after a drink and he was apt to leave the stage before his slot was finished, but his infectious laugh remained the same.

His marriage survived some legendary alcohol-fuelled rages. His wife said, 'He was the nicest, kindest – and most awkward – man in the world.'

Ostensibly happily married for thirty-seven years and a father of two, he had a mistress, who worked alongside him for a number of years, although her existence was only revealed after his death.

Marie Curie

(1867–1934)

From childhood I still remember reading children's comics about Marie Curie. She and her husband shovelled tons of pitchblende into a furnace. How hard they worked, day after day, so much so they had callouses on their hands and eventually became ill. At the end of it they discovered radiation and radium which they held in their hands like some giant diamond. The more I've learned about her the more I feel the cartoon strip wasn't that far away from the truth. It was tabloid in its truest sense, it really got to the heart of what motivated her and made her important.

Pallab Ghosh (BBC Science correspondent)

Marie Curie along with her husband Pierre discovered two new chemical elements, the first polonium which she named for her native country Poland and the second radium.

Sarah Dry (Biographer)

THROUGHOUT THE TWENTIETH century, scientist Marie Curie was lionised for making discoveries that became the foundation stones for the radioactive age. In relative poverty, she laboured long hours to secure the scientific evidence she needed for the quest. Curie herself wrote, 'Sometimes I had to spend a whole day mixing a boiling mass with a heavy iron rod nearly as large as myself. I would be broken with fatigue at the day's end.' Nor was her life made easier by the fact that she was a Polish woman working in Paris in an age where gender and national identity could be pivotal. Yet nothing broke her stride in a career that kept scientific advance in sharp focus. 'One never notices what has been done,' she once admitted ruefully. 'One can only see what remains to be done.'

She was born Maria Skłodowska in Poland when it was under Russian rule, one of five siblings born to well-regarded teachers in Warsaw. As a child, she learned the fervour of Polish nationalism as her family railed against the bitterness and brutality of the occupying Tsarist forces. Her misery was further increased with the death of a sister and her mother, before Curie became a teenager.

As educational opportunities for girls evaporated in Poland, she headed to France and enrolled at the Sorbonne, one of only twenty-three women to attend, although she never lost her loyalty to Poland. She might have returned to her family if not for a meeting in 1894 with French scientist Pierre Curie, 'a tall young man with auburn hair and large, limpid eyes'.

'As I entered the room Pierre Curie was standing in the recess of a French window opening on a balcony. I was struck by the open expression of his face and by the slight suggestion of detachment in his whole attitude. His speech, rather slow and deliberate, his simplicity and his smile, at once grave and youthful, inspired confidence. He seemed to me a dreamer, absorbed in his reflections.'

After their marriage in 1895, they became a couple whose working life, pushing back the boundaries of science, was every bit as vital as their romantic liaison. In a love letter, Pierre wrote, 'It would be a fine thing in which I hardly dare believe to pass our lives near each other hypnotised by our dreams: your patriotic dream, our humanitarian dream and our scientific dream.' Both subscribed to one belief: 'Nothing in life is to be feared. It is only to be understood.'

As scientific research, Marie chose to investigate uranium, minute scraps of which were found in pitchblende, the waste material from mines. Already another scientist, Henri Becquerel, had pinpointed how uranium produced X-rays. Marie, working first alone then with her husband, worked out that its energy came as a result of an internal atomic reaction. Despite help from a local factory, the process of liberating one-tenth of a gram of radium took three long years of hard labour, by effectively boiling tar day and night. By 1898, they could announce the discovery of polonium, named for Marie's homeland, and radium, taken from the Latin word for rays. Ultimately, they also coined the phrase 'radioactivity'.

In 1903, the Curies together with Becquerel were awarded the Nobel Prize for Physics 'in recognition of the extraordinary services they have rendered by their joint researches on the radiation phenomena discovered by Professor Henri Becquerel'. Pierre had to fight for recognition for his wife with the Nobel committee, although most of the work had been hers. In the same year, he turned down a Légion d'Honneur, asking instead for a proper laboratory to replace what Marie called the 'miserable old shed' where they had made their compelling discoveries.

There was a flipside to their success, however. Both the Curies and the staff in their laboratory were faint with the effects of radiation sickness. Before its perils were fully understood, the Curies would take a nugget of radium to dinner parties around Paris and Pierre strapped some to his bare flesh to monitor how much it burned. There was also immense popular interest in the couple spearheaded by the press. Marie soon labelled press interest in her and her family an abomination.

In 1906, Pierre was run over and killed by a horse-drawn carriage, when their daughters were aged 9 and 2. Fortunately, his father babysat so Marie's work could continue. She took over her late husband's job at the Sorbonne, to become the first female professor there. In his memory, she founded the Radium Institute in Paris and later Poland to further research, although her dream that it would one day cure cancer was not realised.

Old prejudices erupted in 1910 when news of her affair with a married man hit the headlines. That she was trading off her (French) husband's name and wrecking a (French) marriage excited press and public. She was still recovering from the shock waves of this when she won the Nobel Prize for a second time in 1911, this time for Chemistry, specifically 'for her services in the advancement of chemistry by the discovery of the elements radium and polonium, by the isolation of radium and the study of the nature and compounds of this remarkable element'. She remains the only woman to have won twice, and in different disciplines.

The advent of the First World War gave her the opportunity to practically apply the benefits of radiology, pinpointing shrapnel and bullets in injured soldiers at the front line. She lobbied for sufficient cash to deck out vans with X-ray equipment, called 'petites Curies', which she and her eldest daughter drove to the Western Front.

Curie saw herself as an exception rather than the rule. 'It isn't necessary to lead such an anti-natural existence as mine, I have given a great deal of time to science, because I wanted to, because I loved research. What I want for women and young girls is a simple family life and some work that will interest them.' Her daughter Irene, however, followed in her mother's footsteps. With husband Frederic Joliot, she won the Nobel Prize for Chemistry in 1935. Sister Eve was a noted writer.

Marie Curie died from leukaemia, undoubtedly a side effect of her life's pursuit. Since 1995, her ashes, with her husband's, have been buried beneath the Pantheon in Paris.

Ian Curtis

(1956–1980)

He made a telling and lasting contribution ... to music. He is still somebody who is talked about and revered and missed as much as anybody I can think of by a particular generation. My passion and respect for Joy Division has only grown over the years. I think more about [the music] now than I ever did. For me, Joy Division at that time captured the soul of northern Britain and the way I felt as a young man.

Simon Armitage (Poet and writer)

Even though Ian died thirty years ago, I live with him every day. It is a strange feeling. It certainly wasn't a wretched life. I don't remember him like that at all. I still don't know why he committed suicide. He was too good at hiding his true feelings. He didn't want to let us down and he didn't want us to worry. He acted like we wanted him to act.

Peter Hook (Bass player, Joy Division)

IN A VOICE that was unusually low and mildly off key, Ian Curtis sang the anthems of alienation that lit a fuse for a generation. As the lead singer of the band Joy Division, he had trim hair, wore utilitarian clothes, possessed a psychotic stare and danced like he was having a seizure. And sometimes he was.

He was diagnosed with epilepsy at the age of 22, and fits were frequently induced by strobe lights and the stress of live performance. Fans apparently relished the sight, but the fits and the prevailing ignorance about the condition left Curtis exhausted. He was unable to pick up his baby daughter for fear of dropping her if he was gripped by a convulsion. Drugs he took to control epilepsy led to severe mood swings and, furthermore, Curtis was torn between the love of two women. On the eve of a tour to America, Curtis hanged himself in the family home.

Curtis was brought up in Macclesfield, the son of working-class parents with the potential to do well academically. But although he won a scholarship to a fee-paying school, he lost interest in education after O levels and gained a fervent passion for music. By day, he worked for the civil service. At night, he listened to the sounds of David Bowie, the Velvet Underground and Kraftwerk and thought up lyrics. Aged 19, he married wife Debbie and they lived near Oldham, saddled with a mortgage.

Soon after seeing punk idols the Sex Pistols perform in Manchester, Curtis met Bernard Sumner and Peter Hook, and they formed a band he called Warsaw, named after a Bowie track ('Warszawa') and reflecting the bleak landscape he saw both internally and on the streets. When drummer Stephen Morris completed the line-up, the band began experimenting. Music was already moving on from the raw indiscipline of punk to a new wave that featured different sounds. (Much later, Joy Division was credited with bridging the gap between The Beatles and Nirvana.) It wasn't long before the group was signed up by Tony Wilson, the guru of independent music in northern Britain at the time.

Curtis and Morris later told a Radio 1 interviewer about the benefits of developing their music in Manchester: 'In our terms it has been quite a good thing because we haven't been influenced by what's going on elsewhere really. We are apart from everything and we developed in our own particular way, in our own environment. ... At the time when we started in Manchester, there were only three or four other groups of the new wave type, yet in London there seemed to be a lot more. In Manchester, a lot of groups expanded and went their own different ways.'

The band name was changed to Joy Division because the original choice was deemed too close to an existing group's moniker. Joy Division referred to the prostitutes kept in concentration camps during the Nazi era, a literary allusion picked by the well-read Curtis for a group of lads whose lives were still overshadowed by the Second World War although the conflict ended a decade before they were born. Bomb-damaged Manchester was flailing in the wake of the post-industrial era, with a population that was largely poor and disaffected. They were also recording during the political pause between a failing Labour government and the extremes of Thatcherism. Their existence, like their music, was spare and incisive.

By the middle of 1978, the band had a manager, a promoter, a regular venue and a record label. The image, monochrome and melancholic, struck a chord with the young people who flocked to see them play. Later that year his fellow band members witnessed Curtis go into convulsions for the first time. Still the singer refused to slow down, embracing a hectic performance schedule and a punishing daily regime. Outwardly, his normally polite and sociable exterior gave way more often to explosive bouts of frenzy. During one recording, he confided to a band mate that he felt the words were writing themselves, while he was being dragged down in a whirlpool to claustrophobic depths.

On a trip to Belgium, he met and began an affair with journalist Annik Honoré. He became more remote from his wife Debbie, who later remarked, 'The marriage was over and he hadn't told me.' He was undoubtedly torn by self-loathing because of it, having fathered a daughter with his wife. Moreover, the controlling side of his nature was thwarted by a condition that refused to be controlled.

As it turned out, Joy Division reigned supreme on the music scene for just eighteen months before Curtis killed himself. He hanged himself barely a month after a failed suicide attempt using pills. Afterwards, it was fellow band members who felt guilty, realising the lyrics he had written were actually revealing the dark side of his soul. At the time, they believed there to be nothing sinister about his references to doomed love and shame, little realising Curtis had once told his sister he would die young like one of his idols, Jimi Hendrix. Curtis also determinedly batted away suggestions he should work less and rest more.

Since his death, Curtis has been the subject of a memoir written by his wife, two films and a documentary. The perpetual interest in Joy Division – which was reborn as New Order after his death – has kept his fan base at a healthy level. His live performances, captured on celluloid, seem as relevant today as they did thirty years ago.

Peter Cushing

(1913–1994)

He is an actor I have always admired, an actor I have always looked forward to seeing from a very early age and not just because of his appearances in horror films, which were my staple diet from childhood. He never gave a bad performance. He was an amazingly sincere actor, a very kind personality who nevertheless made his name playing monsters.

Mark Gatiss (Actor and writer)

He admitted he wasn't a very good actor to start off with. He learned his craft. He did three years in repertory theatre where he was playing a different part every week, which enabled him to try out just about everything. Because of television he had learned how to use very subtle inclinations of his eyes, maybe just widening his eyes fractionally which made all the difference. He had a wonderful trick of turning out of camera and then suddenly shooting back in. He does it in almost every film. It is a very theatrical trick, but he learned it and used it and the director knew it would work.

David Miller (Biographer)

HIS SCULPTED FEATURES and piercing eyes became hallmarks of the Hammer horror films that struck fear into the hearts of a generation of filmgoers. Yet, off screen, actor Peter Cushing was an archetypal English gentleman, whose talents extended far beyond that of monster-maker and vampire slayer.

Cushing was born in Surrey, the son of a quantity surveyor, and was still a schoolboy when he resolved to become an actor. He wrote to numerous repertory companies, finally finding work at a theatre in Worthing, Sussex, which paid 15 shillings a week. It was an excellent training ground for actors who had a demanding schedule of roles to learn for a busy cycle of performances. However, Cushing had serious ambition. He saved his wages until he had sufficient for a one-way fare to Hollywood.

He enjoyed some limited success there, including being a body-double in the acclaimed 1939 version of *The Man in the Iron Mask*, for which he was uncredited. In addition to some Broadway work, there was a role alongside comedians Laurel and Hardy in *A Chump at Oxford* in 1940. But by then Britain was at war and Cushing was torn by a painful mix of unfulfilled patriotism and homesickness. By a circuitous route he began a journey home.

He stopped in Canada en route, making cinema props to pay for the next leg of his journey. These included small flags with the Nazi emblem, like those pushed across maps in films featuring British wartime command centres. When his landlady saw the flags, she called the police and Cushing was nearly arrested as a German sympathiser.

He returned to the UK and, after hopes of joining the services were dashed due to a longstanding ear complaint, he joined ENSA, the Entertainments National Service Association. It was through this work that he met his wife Helen, to whom he was devoted. They encountered each other for the first time in 1942, at the stage door of the Drury Lane Theatre Royal in London, waiting for a bus to take them to the ENSA engagement in which they were both performing.

After the war, Cushing was noted for his stage work with Lawrence Olivier's company. But work became sparse in the post-war economy and Cushing, at the suggestion of his wife, turned to television. With this accidental foresight, he became one of the country's first television stars. After he had distinguished himself in productions of *Pride and Prejudice* as Mr Darcy and George Orwell's *1984* as Winston Smith, he was contracted to the BBC just before the advent of commercial television in 1955.

Yet the most defining part of his career had yet to begin. In the mid 1950s, Cushing joined the Hammer horror crew alongside actor and fast friend Christopher Lee for the first of its films in the grandiose gothic genre. In *The Curse of Frankenstein*, produced on a £65,000 budget, Cushing was Baron Victor von Frankenstein while Lee was the Creature. When it was released in 1957 it was a hit in the UK and America.

He went on to star in nineteen Hammer productions, and his performances include the roles of Van Helsing, the Dracula killer, and Victorian detective Sherlock Holmes. All his performances were marked by the potency of his expression on the screen as well as his precise diction.

In 1971, his life was marked by tragedy with the death of his wife, who had been suffering from cancer. Before she died, she wrote him a letter begging him not to commit suicide. In shock and trauma, he ran up and down the stairs of their home repeatedly hoping to induce a heart attack. As a committed Christian he was unable to further contemplate suicide. But he often spoke in terms of welcoming a reunion with Helen after his own death.

To distract himself from grief, he threw himself into work, making four films a year. In one, *Tales from the Crypt*, released in 1972, in which he played a recently bereaved man, he poignantly added a line: 'She was christened Mary, but I called her Helen.' And the set included a framed photo of his wife.

The demise of the Hammer studio did not signal an end to Cushing's film career. In 1976, he filmed the part of Grand Moff Tarkin, the boss of bad guy Darth Vader, in George Lucas's first *Star Wars* film. Boots supplied with the costume were so tight that Cushing was allowed to play the part in slippers. As a consequence, there were no full-length shots of him in the phenomenally successful movie. By the time of his death at his seafront home in Whitstable, Kent, he had appeared in more than fifty films.

His best-remembered television work was alongside comedians Eric Morecambe and Ernie Wise. He made regular appearances in their shows between 1969 and 1980 – made for both the BBC and ITV – apparently fruitlessly pursuing a £5 fee owed to him for a previous appearance. Neither his bit-parts with the comedy duo – who attracted record-breaking audiences at the time – nor the sinister characters he played in films reflected the real Peter Cushing. In an interview given in 1972 he revealed himself to be a man of simple pleasures:

> I used to go for many walks, and when I'm studying a part I always take the part out on long walks into the country and along the seashore. Study I find the hardest part of my work. It is getting the words learned so you can get rid of the script and get on with the more important part of acting it naturally.
>
> Before [I met my wife] when I was in America, I was desperately homesick. The noise that was most nostalgic for me and still is to me the most British noise – rooks cawing in a rookery.

Elizabeth David

(1913–1992)

No cook can ignore Elizabeth David. She lived a most amazing life and she was our greatest modern cookery writer. I so worshipped her and I would bring her tribute from my garden. I would pod all the peas and top and tail all the beans. What Elizabeth David has given the British cook is that backbone of authenticity. If there is still a real desire for good ingredients, not messed around and perfectly cooked, a lot goes back to Elizabeth David. She knew what mattered.

Prue Leith (Cook, restaurateur and novelist)

Although she was such a good journalist, extremely professional, copy always in on time, woe betide the sub editor who took away so much as a comma.

Artemis Cooper (Biographer)

WITH NURTURING WORDS, creative cook Elizabeth David awoke the dormant taste buds of a nation. She found herself in the right place at the right time after coming to austere Britain following the Second World War – although at first it didn't seem that way with her senses assaulted by the miserable cuisine that she found. Having travelled in Europe, Africa and Asia she was now confronted with a society of nose-wrinklers at the mere mention of garlic. Vegetables were boiled to within an inch of their existence and lard rather than olive oil was the cooking fat of choice. In desperation, she wielded pan and pen, spatula and typewriter, to sear through the shortcomings of the British kitchen. Later she recorded a mission statement:

> I was finding it very difficult indeed to swallow the food provided in the hotel. It was worse than unpardonable even in those days of desperation, and produced a kind of bleak triumph which amounted to a hatred of humanity and humanity's needs. There was flour and water soup, seasoned only with pepper, bread and gristle rissoles, dehydrated onions and carrot, corned beef toad in the hole. I need not go on. We all know that kind of cooking.
>
> Hardly knowing what I was doing, who scarcely ever put pen to paper except to write memos to heads of departments in the Ministry which employed me during the war, I sat down and started to work out an agonised craving for the sun and a furious revolt for that terrible cheerless, heartless food. By writing down descriptions of Mediterranean and eastern cooking, even to write words like apricot, olives and butter, rice and lemons, oil and almonds, produced assuagement. Later I came to realise that in the England of 1947, those were dirty words.

Before she died, she saw courgettes, aubergine, saffron and basil commonly used in meals that would be dished up on pine tables like the one she popularised, in houses where kitchens became the heart of the home. (Her own table was bought at auction after her death by Prue Leith.)

Born Elizabeth Gwynne, she had a privileged upbringing as the daughter of a Conservative MP. Her mother was remote and the household staff old fashioned, as David's childhood memories reveal:

> Probably some of everyone's most dismal nursery memories are connected with food. One might come to accept the stewed prunes, the hateful greens, even the tapioca pudding, as part of nanny's mysterious laws about what it was necessary to eat to survive the perils of childhood but the miseries of fish days were harder to overcome because food looked so terrifying even before it was on your plate. Egg sauce didn't do much to compensate for the black skin and monstrous head of boiled cod, fish pudding, a few spiteful bones inevitably lying in wait in that viscous mass, and whitings biting their own tails were frightening dishes for children and often painful too.

From the age of 11, she went to boarding school and then at 16 was sent to the Sorbonne in Paris, where for the first time she tasted the delights of fine cuisine. She ate 'lovely food' with the family she boarded with that was 'neither rich nor grand':

> What emerges from those days is not the memory of elaborate sauces or sensational hors d'œuvres but rather of beautifully prepared vegetables like salsify a la crème, puree of sorrel and pomme mousseline, many eggs dishes and soups delicately coloured like summer dresses, coral, ivory or pale green, a salad of rice and tomatoes, another of cold beef and especially, of course, [the cook's] chocolate and apricot soufflés.

Afterwards, she became an actress and stage manager back in London until she grew restless with London life. With a married lover, Charles Gibson-Cowan, she set off in a boat – the *Evelyn Hope* – in the summer of 1939, heading for Greece via the French canal system.

In the south of France, she met libertine and writer Norman Douglas, who discussed food and ethics with her, imploring her to recognise when something was second rate and not to accept it. She and Gibson-Cowan continued, only to arrive in Italian waters as Mussolini joined the Second World War. After a spell of detention as suspected spies, the pair were released but had to make their way to Greece by rail. They lived on a Greek island, with David making the most of local ingredients, until German invasion threatened. Then they were evacuated to Egypt and parted. David found herself once more immersed in the local cuisine, this time assisted by her house servant Suleiman. Among the young men she met at the time was a lieutenant-colonel in the Indian Army, Tony David, who became her husband. Eventually the marriage meant a move to India, where she became bored, bilious and homesick. With the marriage at an end, she returned to England where she discovered the paucity of decent fare.

In 1950, *A Book of Mediterranean Food* was published, ushering in a long-term love affair with French food among British people. There followed other books about French and Italian cooking in which she continually expounded her twin messages of simplicity and authenticity. More than just recipe books, they were a palate-cleanser for British minds mired in stodgy or fussy foods. Disaster struck in 1963 when David suffered a stroke that impaired her own taste buds. Although she continued to work and even opened a shop in London, life became more arduous for her.

She was a notoriously frosty and waspish character, with one eminent magazine editor admitting that when she dealt with David she was 'careful never to overstep the mark'. Loathing her celebrity status, David only rarely appeared on television or radio and declined many more magazine interviews than she granted. Much later, she was criticised for exaggerating the benefits of Mediterranean cooking at the expense of British cuisine. Nonetheless, on her death one obituary called her: 'The woman who changed the face of middle class kitchens'.

She worded her own legacy like this: 'A lot of people do think a bit more, what they are buying, what they are choosing and what they are cooking and how. I know it doesn't prevent them shoving somebody's packet of chicken curry into the microwave but still, there is always at least two parallel things going on. One's improving and the other is deteriorating. This is happening all the time in most spheres of life. It is bound to, it is history.'

Robin Day

(1923–2000)

He was this larger-than-life, very charismatic figure who made politics seem like it was about cut and thrust and sharp debate in a way that a lot of politicians didn't. He is the founder, the godfather, of the political interview. It is not going too far to say that without Robin Day there would be no Jeremy Paxman or John Humphrys. He set the tone and the trend in a way that was amazingly ground-breaking in the 1950s and the 1960s. Until he came along, the political interview was: 'And what would you like to tell us, minister?'

Krishnan Guru-Murthy (Journalist)

I remember once having a conversation with Robin at a party conference in Blackpool when he said, 'However hard a time I'm giving a minister, I always try to remember that they are doing something very difficult, which is to govern the country.' I thought that was rather wonderful and admirable. He himself became very dissatisfied with what his gifts had brought him. The rest of us should not allow his limitations to diminish in our eyes our admiration for what he achieved.

Sir Max Hastings (Journalist and historian)

FOR AT LEAST three generations, the sight of a polka-dot tie and a pair of horn-rimmed glasses was enough to strike fear into the heart of any publicity-hungry politician. These were the trademarks of broadcaster Robin Day, also known as the Grand Inquisitor, who hosted the most robust and rigorous interviews on television.

His bite-hard approach found him some friends. When he was in hospital recovering from a heart bypass operation in 1985, Prime Minister Margaret Thatcher wrote, 'Your absence from broadcasting makes us all feel a little uneasy. I prefer your presence despite the occasional pungent comments.' Much later, Thatcher admitted she always enjoyed the 'joust' with Day and claimed he was 'fair, witty and gracious'.

It also won him enemies. During the Falklands conflict in 1982, Defence Secretary John Nott stormed out of an interview after Day quizzed him about Royal Navy budget cuts after concerns voiced by senior officers. (At the time, Nott had already announced his intention to stand down at the next election.) 'But why should the public, on this issue, as regards the future of the Royal Navy, believe you, a transient, here-today and, if I may say so, gone-tomorrow politician, rather than a senior officer of many years?' Thereafter Nott was the object of derision for his walkout, while Day's reputation was further celebrated.

One of his earliest interviewees was the chair of the Independent Television Authority, Sir Kenneth Clark, later known for hosting a TV series called *Civilisation*. Although Clark was effectively his boss, Day conducted a relentless grilling about proposed cuts in the news budget, taking the concept of independent journalism to new levels. Day even asked US ex-President Harry Truman whether or not he regretted dropping the atomic bomb.

He was the youngest of four children born to a telephone engineer in London but was mostly brought up in Gloucestershire. He joined the army during the Second World War and went to Africa. After reaching the rank of captain, Day even considered making a career of the armed forces.

Instead he returned to civilian life and went to Oxford University, where he became President of the Oxford Union. Although he trained in law and was called to the Bar, he didn't enjoy working as a barrister. Consequently, he quit and went to America to work in the media for British Information Services. His year in the US coincided with the downfall of Senator Joe McCarthy, a rabid anti-communist, who thrived on smear campaigns. It was bold interrogation by reporters among others that unmasked McCarthy as a scaremonger, revealing to Day the value of scrupulous and meticulous journalism.

Day brought this forensic style back with him into a newscasting job with ITN at its launch, taking on politicians from all parties, who had previously enjoyed more deferential treatment at the hands of the press. This new approach caused something of a sensation as this early critic's account of Day revealed:

> So unequivocal is Mr Day's relish for his job that he seems at times to be daring you to contradict him. He treats the news with an air of what I can only describe as proprietorial, as if he had been out and got it all himself. He hunches forward, often into full close-up, narrowing his eyes meaningfully behind glinting spectacles, or withdrawing a foot or two he bites off some item of less than front page news with an unspoken hint of deeper significance. When a snippet of film shows him conducting an interview ... he is practically at the man's lapels. In the studio he puts his blunt, loaded questions with the air of a prosecuting counsel at a murder trial. As he swings back to face the cameras, metaphorically blowing on his knuckles, one detects the muffled disturbance as his shaken victim is led away.

Day was a formidable interrogator because he spent hours doing background research. Frequently, he was better acquainted with government white papers than the ministers he was interviewing.

In an interview in 1972 he explained why he favoured the bow tie. 'My father wore a bow tie, I think because Lord Salisbury, the Victorian statesman, wore one, but I'm not quite sure. But anyway, he taught me how to tie one, which has given me an advantage over people who can never tie one when they wear evening dress. ... I wore a bow tie one day when I started newscasting with Independent Television News in 1955 and this had never been done by a newscaster before and I stuck to it. Of course one of the main advantages of a bow tie is that it is a very economic form of apparel. You have two sides to each end of the tie and you can therefore tie it four ways which means it has a life four times as long.'

In 1959, Day moved to the BBC and worked on the eminent current affairs programme *Panorama*. He was most commonly on screen during elections. Arguably, it was after twenty years with the BBC that he finally found his niche with the launch of *Question Time*, featuring a panel of politicians who were questioned by members of the audience, and frequently by Day himself. On BBC Radio 4, he hosted a programme with a similar concept called *It's Your Line*, when listeners could call in to cross examine politicians. He also presented *The World at One* for eight years. His television celebrity coupled with a distinctive appearance and voice won him slots on entertainment programmes, and he relished doing sketches with comedians Morecambe and Wise and singer Des O'Connor. He was a wit and a womaniser.

Long before it came into being, he supported the case for televised Parliamentary debates in order that MPs activities should be under the spotlight. Having been an unsuccessful parliamentary candidate for the Liberal party in 1959, he believed at the end of his career that power and influence had eluded him. By then, though, he was much impersonated, both by comedians of the day and fellow journalists. His distinctive style had become the newsroom norm and his dream of politics at the hub of debate a reality.

Charles Dickens

(1812–1870)

I've always been an avid fan of Charles Dickens. It sounds desperately sad but while others were out I stayed in and read Dickens' novels. I found them very, very funny. Although his later novels get a bit broody, his instinctive comic take on the world is one that I immediately connected with.

Armando Iannucci (Comic)

At the middle of Dickens was this very sad, neglected, vulnerable person who had had a miserable period in his childhood which deeply affected him. He was a very funny person, there was a lot of actor in him. [But] the older he got the more pained he got [although] the wit, the charm was certainly still there.

Professor Andrew Sanders (Biographer)

'A NNUAL INCOME TWENTY *pounds, annual expenditure nineteen nineteen and six, result happiness. Annual income twenty pounds, annual expenditure twenty pounds ought and six, result misery.*'

Written 160 years ago yet still pertinent today, the world might be a wealthier place if only the architects of the twenty-first-century banking crisis had taken notice of the wise words of Wilkins Micawber in Charles Dickens's *David Copperfield*. In fact the homespun advice wasn't penned as an attack on greedy capitalists, more as a stark warning to those tempted to live beyond their means. Charles Dickens experienced the perils of poverty after his genial father John fell into debt and was imprisoned with his family, the usual punishment for debtors in Victorian England.

Young Dickens was not just incarcerated. Having reached the age of 12, his schooling ended abruptly and, considered ready for the workplace, he was duly dispatched to Warren's Blacking factory at Charing Cross where he worked ten-hour days in squalid conditions to earn six shillings a week. The horror of working as a child in a vermin-infested, tumbledown factory was etched on his mind thereafter, and his heartfelt desire to see an end to child labour surfaces again and again in his novels. Indeed, *David Copperfield* is thought to be, loosely speaking, his life story, with Mr Micawber a dramatisation of his father.

After a few months in debtors' prison John Dickens and his family were released when he unexpectedly received a legacy. Yet Charles Dickens's mother Elizabeth insisted her eldest son kept the detested factory job. It created complications in their relationship. Even when his education finally resumed at the insistence of his father, the London school he attended was beset with cruelties and he ended his childhood a somewhat tormented soul.

At 15, he left school to become a clerk at a solicitor's office. He disliked the stodgy office environment so taught himself shorthand with a view to becoming a reporter. After an initial spell as a court reporter, his brief expanded and soon he was writing articles about Parliament that called for reforms. Dickens, with no love of the aristocracy and imbued with a special feeling for the lower ranks of the emerging middle class, was inclined to be a radical. It was about this time that the Liberal Party was forming to reflect the views of people like Dickens. Although the 1832 Reform Act which partially extended the vote from the landed gentry and got rid of some corruption did not go far enough in his view, it was at least a starting point. And he began to see that fiction rather than the autobiography he had been planning was a way to change the world.

In 1833 the first in a series of his short stories was published in the *Monthly Magazine*, under the pen name Boz. All were popular with readers and he was commissioned to write *The Pickwick Papers* in twenty instalments. This meant he could write each chapter after witnessing how the previous one was received. There followed a succession of novels, almost all of which have stood the test of time. He used to great effect his comic timing and his succinct observation of London life, mixing in some clever satire for good measure. His passion for social change was fuelled by the Poor Law Amendment Act in 1834, which condemned the impoverished of the population to a workhouse, where life was particularly brutal.

A remarkable and boundless energy kept him working, which one man, James T. Field, noted on Dickens's first arrival in the US in 1842: 'You ask me what was his appearance as he ran or rather flew up the steps of the hotel and ran into the hall. He seemed on fire with curiosity and alive as I never saw a mortal before. From top to toe every fibre of his body was unrestrained and alert. What vigour, what keenness, what freshness of spirit possessed him. He laughed all over and did not care who heard him. He seemed like the emperor of cheerfulness.' (Dickens was not universally popular in America for pursuing publishers who pirated his books and for speaking out against slavery and chewing tobacco.)

His investment in a radical newspaper, the *Daily News*, in 1846 was altogether less successful than his novel-writing and he resigned as editor in 1850. But it wasn't the end of his role in journalism – he found an outlet with *Household Words*, a successful weekly focusing on politics, science and history and including instalments of campaigning novels like *Hard Times*. After arguing with its publishers, he began a new journal called *All Year Round*, concentrating on political and literary issues, which he published until his death.

His success as a writer was not wholly mirrored by happiness in his personal life. In 1835 he met and became engaged to Catherine Hogarth. They married and had ten children but the relationship foundered, not least because Dickens met and fell in love with actress Ellen Ternan in 1857. His fractured domestic life was the cause of some angst to Dickens who was by this time, thanks to advances both in publishing and photography, the most well-known author in Britain. Domestic happiness was frequently pivotal to his characters yet he had none himself. It's thought to be the cause of the darker hues of his later novels.

Later in life he was known as much for public readings as for his journalism, and he embarked on numerous demanding tours around Britain and to America. Exhausted, he died following a stroke and was buried in Westminster Abbey. He is acknowledged as an influence on subsequent writers including Tolstoy, Proust and Dostoevsky. There was palpable public grief upon his death, reflected in the obituary that appeared in the *Sunday Observer*:

> No doubt something of Dickens's wide-spread popularity was due to the circumstances of his time. In our days the reading public has reached dimensions which our forefathers would have deemed impossible, while the faculties of communication between all parts of the globe enable the written word to circulate with a rapidity rivalling that of the telegraph itself. But still, the like facilities were open to all writers of our time; and yet it was Dickens, and Dickens only, who made his works quoted through the length and breadth of everyone of those vast regions where the English tongue rules supreme.

Benjamin Disraeli

(1804–1881)

If I've been asked to plump for a hero figure, Benjamin Disraeli is the one that's come instinctively into my mind since I started in politics. His legacy is to show that the right-of-centre party in Britain could have social conscience and could have broad appeal. He did prove politics can be fun and can be an adventure.

Ken Clarke (Politician)

He is a wonderfully dramatic, colourful figure. He wasn't just a politician but an excellent novelist. What is exciting about Disraeli for any biographer is the fact that he is constantly reinventing himself in his novels. And also he wrote all these wonderful letters. There's a mass of material about him. He is never, ever boring.

Jane Ridley (Biographer)

IN LIFE, BENJAMIN Disraeli found many obstacles reared up in his path. Fortunately, he was blessed with sufficient natural talents and good fortune to overcome them all in his pursuit of political celebrity.

He was born into the Jewish faith, which automatically barred him from a Parliamentary career at the time. But, after his father quarrelled with elders at his synagogue, Disraeli was baptised into the Anglican faith aged 13. This endowed him with the necessary eligibility – although anti-Semitic prejudice dogged the rest of his career.

At first, Disraeli trained to be a solicitor. Aged 20, he lost substantial amounts of money on the stock market which, coupled with losses from a doomed newspaper venture, left his accounts in a parlous state. Swiftly he wrote a successful novel, *Vivian Grey*, to avert a personal financial crisis. Without a university education or aristocratic connections, he could easily have been left an outsider looking in. Ultimately he arrived at the top of the 'greasy pole', as he saw it, and instituted wide-ranging social reforms that improved living standards for everyone in Victorian England.

Before he was 30, he was considering a career in politics and, not a natural Conservative, he tried the Whigs (Liberals), Radicals and being an Independent before joining their ranks. He was finally elected to Parliament as MP for Maidstone in 1837, to have his maiden speech on Ireland drowned out by barracking. 'The time will come when you will hear me,' he muttered prophetically as he sank into his seat.

After several affairs, Disraeli married Mary Anne Lewis, the wealthy widow of a colleague, in 1839. She was some twelve years his senior, and observers believed he married for money, but there's no doubt there was genuine fondness between the pair until her death in 1872, which left him devastated.

In 1841, he was returned as MP for Shrewsbury, confident he would find himself in a ministerial role under Prime Minister Sir Robert Peel. However, no offer was forthcoming and Disraeli never forgot the perceived snub.

At the time, the import of foreign grain was banned under the Corn Laws. With Ireland suffering a famine and England unable to fill the gap after a succession of poor harvests, Peel wanted to scrap the Corn Laws to increase the supply of food. Landowners, however, believed it an attack on their business, and Disraeli joined the vociferous opposition to the Corn Laws' repeal. Although Peel had his way in 1846, he was quickly undermined with another bill and resigned, leaving the Conservative Party in tatters.

When the Earl of Derby won the Conservative leadership and a general election, Disraeli finally had an opportunity in high office. Despite his woeful record with money, he was made Chancellor of the Exchequer and Leader of the Commons. However, his 1852 budget was ripped to shreds in Parliament by his long-time adversary William Ewart Gladstone, and the government fell.

Given the political see-saw of the era, it wasn't his last chance to be Chancellor, which was clearly a role he relished. In 1858 he wrote: 'My life has been passed in constant combat but I'm glad to add, with respect to all important matters, constant victory. The enemy, however, still keeps the field and I really have to carry on the campaign under a scorching sky. Morning sittings and evening sittings with the duties of my department, cabinet councils and the general conduct of affairs engross and absorb my life from the moment I wake until the hour of rest, which is normally three hours after midnight.'

Only upon Derby's eventual resignation did Disraeli achieve the top job, at the age of 63 and arguably less effective than he had been as a younger man. It was the first of two periods of office. There was still time to showcase one of his innate skills, which was the ability to charm women. Queen Victoria had been in mourning for her husband, Prince Albert, since his death in 1861 and had withdrawn from public life. Disraeli flattered and coaxed her back into the public eye, not least by having her proclaimed Empress of India in 1876. Disraeli had overseen the British crown taking control of India after the 1857 mutiny, and both he and the Queen shared a desire to see England at the head of an empire. Soon afterwards he was made Lord Beaconsfield by Queen Victoria.

Abroad, Disraeli secured British interests in the Suez Canal and closely monitored Russian expansion in Europe. At home, his two administrations made some bold inroads into Victorian inequality in acts partly designed to trump his Liberal rivals. The practice of sending small boys up chimneys was outlawed, public health was improved, there was new factory legislation and there was some provision for slum clearance.

It's amply clear from his novels that Disraeli was troubled by the condition of Britain's poor. In an extract from *Sybil*, one of a successful trilogy published in the 1840s, he wrote: '"Our queen," says Egremont, "reigns over the greatest nation that ever existed." "Which nation," asked the young stranger, "for she reigns over two." The stranger paused. Egremont was silent but looked enquiringly. "Yes," resumed the young stranger after a moment's interval. "Two nations between whom there is no intercourse and no sympathy, who are as ignorant of each other's habits, thoughts and feelings as if they were dwellers in different zones or inhabitants of different planets, who are formed by a different breeding, are fed by a different food, are ordered by different manners and are not governed by the same laws." "You speak of," said Egremont hesitatingly, "the rich and the poor."'

His entire time in government was marked by the animosity between himself and Gladstone. He once outlined the difference between a misfortune and a calamity. 'If Gladstone fell into the Thames it would be a misfortune. But if someone dragged him out again it would be a calamity.'

Although he was an Anglican, he was painfully aware of the cruel racist remarks that beset his career. In one retort to an anti-Semitic jibe he said: 'Yes, I am a Jew, and when the ancestors of the Right Honourable Gentleman were brutal savages in an unknown island, mine were priests in the Temple of Solomon.'

When he was on his deathbed, Queen Victoria was anxious to visit. He pleaded that she should be kept away, saying: 'She'll only want me to take a message to Albert.'

Albert Einstein

(1879–1955)

He cared so much about humanity and he acted incredibly bravely again and again throughout his life in order to do things to help humanity. I know some of the science seemed mind-scramblingly hard but he thought very clearly and very simply and, with some of the really tough stuff, he came up with remarkably clear insights that aren't as hard to understand as other areas of physics. He changed our views about the universe for ever. From that point onwards scientists have got stuck in.

Kathy Sykes (Professor and presenter)

Nobody [until Einstein] had anything like the idea of the general theory [of relativity]. From that he is able to develop a theory that explains how the entire universe works. Nobody would have done for a generation.

John Gribbin (Biographer)

'*ONE THING I have learned in a long life: that all our science, measured against reality, is primitive and childlike – and yet it is the most precious thing we have.*'

To understand the universe and everything within it was Albert Einstein's ultimate goal. It would have been no surprise to the scientist that he died before achieving his lofty ambition. 'Do not worry about your difficulties in Mathematics,' he said once. 'I can assure you mine are still greater.' But there's no doubt he did more than any person previously to illuminate unseen scientific phenomena, earning him the soubriquet 'the father of physics'. His legacy included comparatively straightforward equations that explained incredibly complex notions, like the theory of relativity for which he is best remembered.

Einstein was born into a secular Jewish family living in Germany and was noticeably slower than other children to talk. Then he spoke in considered sentences rather than random words. One of his earliest memories was pondering in fascination the movement of a compass needle.

He enjoyed a childhood full of intellectual challenge. His mother taught him music, his father threw out mathematical quizzes while Harry Talmud, a student who came for dinner every week, set down rigorous academic guidelines for the young Albert. His behaviour at school was far from conventional, though. When his parents were called in by the teacher they were told young Einstein was a disruptive influence. Having asked what that meant, the teacher said he sat at the back of the class and smiled. Einstein later revealed how he hated learning by rote, which was favoured by German schools at the time, and thrived only in the atmosphere of lively discussion. He wrote an essay in French, speculating on his future:

> I would go to Zurich. I would stay there for four years in order
> to study mathematics and physics. I imagine myself becoming
> a teacher in those branches of the natural sciences choosing

the theoretical part of them. Here are the reasons which led me to this plan. Above all, it is my disposition for abstract and mathematical thought, my lack of imagination and practical ability. My desires have also inspired in me the same resolve. That is quite natural. One always likes to do the things for which one has ability. Then there is also certain independence in the scientific profession which I like a great deal.

He received half marks.

When his electrical business failed, having backed DC over the more popular AC, Einstein's father took his family to Italy to find work. Only Einstein was left behind, to underachieve at college. He left as soon as he could to enjoy a 'gap' year in Italy before heading for school in Switzerland, where once again his marks were relatively poor.

By 1905 he was married with two children, living in Berne as a Swiss citizen and employed at the city's patent office, the only job his mediocre grades left open to him. As the work didn't unduly test him he found plenty of time to write scientific papers of extraordinary quality. He published four of these in just twelve months, which became known as his *annus mirablis* ('miracle year'). His reputation as eminent scientist and intellectual heavyweight was at last established, although he only regarded what he'd achieved so far as stepping stones in a strategy with a more far-reaching purpose.

In 1908 he began his academic career, swiftly climbing up the rungs until, in 1914, he became Director of the Kaiser Wilhelm Physical Institute and Professor in the University of Berlin – and a German citizen. During the First World War he was a pacifist but didn't let politics get in the way of scientific study. He was on the scent of the general theory of relativity, a way of understanding how the universe worked. In 1921 he was awarded the Nobel Prize for Physics for his work.

Despite the post-war chaos, he continued to work in Germany and supported the faltering Weimar Republic until the rise of Hitler. Recognising the grave and personal threat posed by the inexorable rise of fascism, he finally renounced German citizenship in 1933 and moved to America, one of numerous scientists who chose to flee the scourge of Nazism. In 1939 he put his name on a letter to US President Franklin D. Roosevelt warning that sophisticated new weaponry could fall into Hitler's hands:

> It may become possible to set up nuclear chain reactions in a large mass of uranium by which vast amounts of power and large quantities of new radium-like elements would be generated. Now it appears almost certain that this could be achieved in the immediate future. This new phenomenon could also lead to the construction of bombs and it is conceivable though much less certain that extremely powerful bombs of a new type may thus be constructed. In view of this situation you may think it desirable to have some permanent contact maintained between the administration and the group of physicists working on the chain reaction in America.

In fact Einstein may have provided the building blocks but he did not work directly on the atom bomb venture, known as the Manhattan Project. It aroused similar feelings of horror within him as militarism had in the First World War. 'I know not with what weapons World War III will be fought but World War IV will be fought with sticks and stones,' he warned. He was also considered too left-leaning by the American government.

In the USA he worked at Princeton University, where he attempted to codify the laws of physics for future generations. During the war he was also a consultant to the United States Navy's Bureau of Ordnance. His support for the newly founded state of Israel after the Second World War was such that he was offered the presidency in 1952, although he turned it down on the grounds he lacked the necessary experience even for this mostly ceremonial role. He continued working on scientific theories, constantly challenging his own and other people's ideas in a robust pursuit of evidence.

He died having refused treatment for internal bleeding but left behind not only scientific but also important philosophical contributions. In 1932 he described his beliefs:

> The most beautiful and deepest experience a man can have is the sense of the mysterious. It is the underlying principle of religion as well as all serious endeavour in art and science. He who has never had this experience seems to me if not dead then at least blind. To sense that behind anything that can be experienced there is a something that our mind cannot grasp, and whose beauty and sublimity reaches us only indirectly and as a feeble reflection, this is religiousness. In this sense I am religious. To me it suffices to wonder at these secrets and to attempt humbly to grasp with my mind a mere image of the lofty structure of all that there is.

Edward Elgar

(1857–1934)

His love of poetry resonated with me. But nothing came easily to Elgar. Everything was slow and hard-won. He was a very complicated person, and yet he faced his soul without flinching and his greatness lay in the way that he transformed conflicts and failings in himself into sublime music.

Majorie Wallace (Journalist and chief executive
of SANE, a leading mental health charity)

He was the only example I know of a composer who was completely self-taught. He literally never had a composition lesson in his life.

Jerrold Northrop Moore (Biographer)

ELGAR'S MAGNIFICENT 'POMP and Circumstance' marches sound like a series of compositions from a man at the beating heart of the British establishment. With the first of the military marches also known as 'Land of Hope of Glory', it is music run through with patriotism to the point of jingoism. Yet it gives a false impression of Elgar, who felt an outsider throughout his life and deplored the use of his music to rally troops during the First World War.

Elgar was a Catholic at a time when Britain was predominantly Protestant, although he had lost his faith by the time of his death. He lived in rural Worcestershire when the movers and shakers of the music world were centred in big cities, especially London. And he was the son of a tradesman rather than a country gentleman, which he felt acutely since Edwardian society was so class-obsessed.

Edward William Elgar was born in Lower Broadheath, Worcestershire, in a small house that has since been made into museum. His father was a music dealer and piano tuner, visiting some of the big country houses in the area with young Edward in tow. So he grew up in the nuts-and-bolts end of music-making, mastering the piano, violin, cello, bassoon and trombone.

A dreamy child, he finished school aged 15 to work in a solicitor's office. But after a year he left to become a music teacher in Malvern to better satisfy his soul. At 22, he became bandmaster at the local pauper's asylum, working for a superintendent who was convinced the sound of music would heal at least some of those suffering mental illness.

Although his hands-on experience with music was substantial when he was in his twenties, his output as a composer was limited, initially comprising only choral pieces and cantatas. His aim was to one day write a symphony, but he knew he lacked the necessary skills at that time.

He met his wife Caroline Alice when she became a pupil in piano accompaniment. Her family were opposed to the relationship on the grounds of Elgar's class and faith. Familiarly known as Alice, she was nine years older than Elgar and there's speculation they had something approaching a mother-son relationship. Certainly, she had unbreakable faith in his talent and provided the optimum environment to accommodate his writing, arranging his desk and keeping the surroundings in strict silence. For her, he wrote the popular 'Salut d'Amour'. Much later, when he heard a busker play the tune outside the Queen's Hall in London, he said he hoped the street musician made more money from the piece than he had. When he asked the man if he knew its title, the violinist replied: 'Yes, it's "Sally, Damn Her".'

For a while, the Elgars lived in London, certain that Edward would soon penetrate important musical circles. In fact, this period was disastrously unproductive and they returned to Worcestershire, where Elgar flourished in the spectacular scenery and radiant nature that surrounded him. For years he would take long walks and even longer cycle rides in search of inspiration. At least the Midlands had a significant choral tradition and his first major commercial success was *The Dream of Gerontius*, which premiered in Birmingham in 1900.

Yet already his most famous piece was in the bag. The *Enigma Variations* was completed by the time that *Gerontius* opened. It was a series of pieces revolving around a mysterious theme, that Elgar called 'a dark saying that must be left unguessed – a black hole, something out of which creation may come'. Each one depicts a friend or colleague, with 'Nimrod' associated with friend August Jaeger.

Then came 'Pomp and Circumstance', 'a tune that will knock 'em flat,' Elgar confided to a friend. Although he acknowledged the tune was a great one, over time he began to think of 'Land of Hope and Glory' as vulgar and wished the words were less nakedly nationalistic than they were. He would implore musicians to play it as if they had never heard it before. Perhaps his most appropriate response to it was the Cello Concerto, written after the First World War to translate the misery of the trenches into haunting music. Today 'Pomp and Circumstance' No. 1 is best known for its inevitable appearance at the BBC Proms in London and in graduation ceremonies across America.

If he could have done, Elgar would have incorporated the notes into a symphony. But he was still preparing to write his first. While there was a dedicated core of fans already around Britain and Europe, Elgar was still only producing concertos and the like for want of experience.

In 1904, he was knighted, reflecting the high profile he was already enjoying in Britain. Four years later, the first symphony appeared, followed by another in 1911. A third was unfinished when he died. He experienced moments of anguish and despair although it rarely revealed itself in his music. Moody, melancholic and assailed by largely imagined health concerns, Elgar found himself unhappily alone after the death of his wife in 1920 from lung cancer.

Yet perhaps one of his most pivotal contributions had yet to be made. After 1926, he was able to record almost all his major works for the age of the gramophone, the first composer to do so. It provides a remarkable musical heritage, all the more valuable as Elgar's music had begun to go out of style even in his lifetime.

His final months were plagued by the ravages of intestinal cancer. On his deathbed, his Roman Catholic faith was barely alive. His consulting doctor Sir Arthur Thompson revealed that the composer was expecting oblivion rather than heaven.

When he died, one fan, Lady Stuart of Wortley, declared, 'He was our Shakespeare of music.'

Elizabeth I

(1533–1603)

I have idolised Elizabeth I from the time I first learned about her at school. The visionary leader, the vacillating woman, the virgin who was so splendidly attired and gorgeously made-up. She was all woman at the same time as being a great monarch. She showed how well a woman could hold down the greatest job in the nation, how she could restore order out of chaos, how she could give the nation back its feeling of self-esteem. At the same time she fostered an age of art, literature and music which we haven't really rivalled since. Quite an achievement.

Esther Rantzen (Presenter)

She had the best spin machine in British history. What historians are now trying to do is cut that away and look at the real woman. She is an amazing figure in that she completely ignored the rules that said a woman monarch married and settled succession with an heir and spare. The great achievement of Elizabeth was to prevent a religious war in England and also to keep the Spanish out. In that she was greatly helped by the weather. She was incredibly lucky.

Dr John Guy (Historian)

'I AM COME amongst you, as you see, at this time, not for my recreation and disport, but being resolved, in the midst and heat of the battle, to live and die amongst you all; to lay down for my God, and for my kingdom, and my people, my honour and my blood, even in the dust. I know I have the body but of a weak and feeble woman; but I have the heart and stomach of a king, and of a king of England too, and think foul scorn that Parma or Spain, or any prince of Europe, should dare to invade the borders of my realm.'

The words of Queen Elizabeth I at Tilbury are credited with stirring the passions of England's Royal Navy sailors sufficiently to chase off the Spanish Armada. In fact, it was strong winds rather than English cannon that wreaked havoc on the 130 ships sent by Spain to mount an invasion. We can't even be sure these are the words uttered by the Queen. They are the recollection of a chaplain at Tilbury, relayed in writing some thirty-five years after the event. Nothing on record from 1588, when the Armada broached British shores, has survived.

But it is a soundbite that fits the image of Queen Elizabeth I, also known as Gloriana, the Virgin Queen and Good Queen Bess. History remembers her resplendent in sumptuous, bejewelled gowns with porcelain skin, auburn hair, a high hairline and a haughty bearing. She was known to be a master of rhetoric so there's no reason to doubt that she spoke powerfully. Victory over the Spanish was perhaps the pinnacle of her rule.

Her lengthy and successful reign is notable not least because it followed an inauspicious start in life. When she was born a girl, rather than the boy her father, King Henry VIII, craved, she was instantly a crushing disappointment to the entire court. When she was 2, her father dispatched her mother, Anne Boleyn, to the executioner's block on trumped-up infidelity charges. Hated by her older sister and vulnerable as the focus of plots, she lived in relative obscurity as a girl. Stepmother Katharine Parr – the last of Henry's six wives – took charge of Elizabeth's education and ensured she was tutored by the best scholars. Elizabeth's quick mind responded well. And she was dependent on all her education, diplomacy and intuition after the death of her father in 1547 when the crown passed first to a sickly younger brother, Edward VI, then her older sister, Mary I.

Edward, like Elizabeth, was a Protestant. But Mary was a Catholic and was determined to restore to England the faith largely dismantled by her father. The difficult relationship between the sisters was exacerbated by Mary's marital unhappiness, ill health and blind convictions. Elizabeth neatly sidestepped accusations of treason, although she found herself locked in the Tower of London for two months and under house arrest for a long time after that.

With the death of her sister, though, things changed. Elizabeth succeeded to the throne and took charge of her own destiny. The two major problems at the top of the agenda were religion and a royal marriage. Although she was a Protestant, she was no ideologue, so she toned down anti-Catholic fervour, aiming to return England to a period of domestic peace. It sounds nothing short of reasonable, but at the time the memory of Protestants being burned at the stake was still fresh in the vengeful minds of many.

She was surrounded with advisers who pressed her to marry. But they couldn't agree on an appropriate candidate and Elizabeth, who had no intention of being subordinate to a king/husband, used that as an excuse not to wed. (It is assumed that her father's matrimonial history also turned her against the institution.) The one man she genuinely cared for was Lord Dudley, who she met when they were both incarcerated in the Tower, but William Cecil, her chief adviser, was against a union. In 1559, she responded to a Parliamentary petition about her single status:

> I am already bound unto a husband which is the kingdom of England and that may suffice you. And reproach me so no more that I have no children for everyone of you and as many as are English are my children and my kinsfolk of whom so long as I

am not deprived and God shall preserve me you cannot charge me without offence to be destitute. Lastly this may be sufficient both for my memory and the honour of my name. If when I have expired my last breath this may be inscribed upon my tomb. Here lies interred Elizabeth, a virgin pure unto her death.

The darkest point of her reign was undoubtedly the execution of Mary, Queen of Scots. Mary, a Catholic, had sought help from Elizabeth after being turfed out of Scotland. But advisers to the English queen saw implicit threat in her presence. Mary was a rallying point for Catholics and even had a greater claim on the English throne, if the notion that Henry's marriage to Anne Boleyn was illegal had credibility. Elizabeth didn't share those fears but failed to stamp her authority on the issue. Mary was imprisoned for nineteen years before apparently indisputable proof that she was plotting against Elizabeth was produced. Reluctantly, Elizabeth signed the execution warrant and, when Mary was beheaded, she wept for several days. It was Mary's death and English piracy sanctioned by Elizabeth that moved Philip II of Spain to gather an invasion force. At the time Spain and France were the big players in Europe, with England ranked far behind them.

At her death at the beginning of the seventeenth century, England's stock was rising and its golden future assured. For the most part, England was at peace during her reign, religious differences had fallen into abeyance for the time being and trade was busy. The poor remained poor but landowners prospered as they responded to a huge demand for food from a booming population. Since she died childless, the crown passed to James VI of Scotland, son of the ill-fated Mary, who became James I of England.

Giovanni Falcone

(1939–1992)

It is important to say loudly that Giovanni Falcone did not die in vain. He persisted (in his work) for the greater good of Sicilian, Italian and in my view European society. He has not fully succeeded because Italy is still riddled with organised crime but he has shown all of us it is possible to do something about it.

Misha Glenny (Journalist)

The impact he had is down to his display of integrity, professionalism and endurance to a degree which is rare anywhere but it is particularly rare in Italy, especially Sicily, where people are more used to the opposite: corruption, incompetence, fickleness. Falcone looked like a rock among pebbles.

Diego Gambetta (Professor and writer)

ON 23 MAY 1992, a motorcade travelling at high speed from Palermo airport was blown up by a bomb detonated by a member of the Sicilian mafia. The explosion was so immense that one eyewitness said, 'All hell seemed to open up before us.' Among the five victims was Giovanni Falcone, a prominent crusader against the criminal underworld that controlled Sicily.

In trying to prise open the vice-like grip that the mafia had socially and politically in Italy, Falcone came up against not only the gangsters themselves but the establishment figures they had implicated through shadowy dealings. Although his untimely death cut short his campaign, Falcone succeeded in having several top bosses sent to jail. For this he was hailed a hero by fellow Palmeritans. And he takes credit for reversing an apparent public affection for the mafia into a tide of opposition as the mobsters' 'Robin Hood' image was systematically destroyed.

Falcone grew up in a part of Palermo that was flattened by Allied air raids during the Second World War. His father, the director of a chemical laboratory, and his mother were intensely patriotic. Tempted by a career in the navy, he finally decided on practising law after he graduated in 1961. Three years later he was appointed a judge.

By the 1970s he was specialising in organised crime and encountering the tentacles of the mafia on an almost daily basis. By now the mafia was entrenched in drug-trafficking, notably heroin. Money from the illicit trade would be laundered through a banking system into the stock market, property or investment in art. This was in addition to the traditionally lucrative schemes engineered by the mafia, especially control of construction and racketeering.

At the end of the decade, the first shots of the second mafia war were fired. It went on into the 1980s, with hundreds gunned down as mafia bosses fought for supremacy in an era known as 'the years of lead'. Anti-mafia campaigners were also killed. The ruthlessness of the mafia was never in doubt. Falcone was certain he would die at the hands of his foe, although he took elaborate security precautions in a bid to outwit them. He and his second wife, Francesca Morvillo, a magistrate who died with him, refused to have children for fear of leaving them orphans.

He was a man of conviction, though, and often quoted assassinated American President John F. Kennedy when he was questioned about his drive and motives: 'A man does what he must in spite of personal consequences, in spite of obstacles and dangers and pressures – and that is the basis of all human morality.'

At home, Falcone did much to pioneer the *pentiti* programme, which encouraged mafia members to give evidence for the state in return for reduced sentences or even freedom and protection. In effect, he was tapping into the vast reservoir of people whose lives had been ruined by mafia murder and mayhem. The most high-profile *pentito* was Tommasso Buscetta, who yielded vital information to the authorities about the inner workings of the mafia in Sicily. 'Before Buscetta we had only a superficial understanding of the mafia phenomenon,' said Falcone.

> With him we began to see inside it. He confirmed for us numerous ideas about the structure, recruitment techniques and the functions of Cosa Nostra but above all he gave us a broad, wide ranging global vision about the phenomenon. He gave us an interpretative key; a language and a code. He was like a language professor who allowed us to go among the Turks without having to try to communicate with our hands.

Abroad, Falcone was one of the Italian lynchpins in an American trial that focused on drugs distribution through pizzerias in the USA. Although it did little to stem the flow of drugs into America, the 'Pizza Connection' trial conducted between 1985 and 1987 did disrupt mafia activity throughout its duration.

At around the same time, the 'Maxi Trial' of 475 alleged mafiosa took place in Palermo, against all odds. Falcone's investigation was thorough, and the evidence he produced was rigorous. Although it attracted enormous attention, most of the 338 convicted criminals served shamefully short sentences.

After the assassination of several prominent colleagues, Falcone found himself in a quartet of prosecutors who remained willing to tackle the might of the mafia. That they refused to be intimidated amid unbridled bloodshed says volumes about their characters. Despite the unquestioned courage of all four, the government was still equivocal about its support for their campaign, almost certainly because of kickbacks routinely paid by the mafia to Italian politicians. Falcone and his immediate circle were soon portrayed as fanatics willing to damage the interests of Italy. The longstanding myth that the mafia didn't really exist was once again perpetuated. Nonetheless, Falcone remained clear where his duty lay. He had no hidden agenda, other than to rid Italy of the domestic dark forces that had the power to overshadow everyone's existence. Even within the judiciary, there was division about whether people like Falcone should be promoted on merit or whether timeservers were better suited to the top jobs.

If his death proved anything it was that the mafia no longer had huge social popular support. As his assassination was announced, the widow of one of the bodyguards who had died with him made an emotional plea to the gathered crowds that touched the hearts of many:

> I address the men of the mafia for I know they are present here. I know they are not Christians but even for you, forgiveness exists. I forgive you but you must go down on your knees and have the courage to change. But they never change, they never change.

Dame Millicent Fawcett

(1847–1929)

She was one of the main leaders of the women's suffrage campaign in this country and I can't see why someone like her is just not known. Nobody has heard of her.

Lesley Abdela (Equality campaigner)

The Pankhursts had such a high profile at the time. Millicent Fawcett relied on gradualism, pragmatism, the slow drip-drip of steady action and not something that would grab the headlines.

Elizabeth Crawford (Suffragette historian)

LATEST FIGURES REVEAL that, on average, women are paid less than men for doing similar jobs. It is a fact that puts fire into the heart of every equal rights campaigner, but it pales against the inequalities suffered in Victorian England when women could not vote, own property or sue. If they were educated at all, women usually learned nothing more than a little French and embroidery. If they worked, it was in a household job as a governess or maid.

Women's rights champion Millicent Garrett Fawcett spent a lifetime trying to win the legal right to vote. She began supporting the equal rights cause aged 18 after hearing far-sighted Liberal John Stuart Mill speak on the issue. Aged 81, she listened to the debate in Parliament that finally gave women the same voting rights as men.

Born and brought up in Suffolk, Fawcett was one of ten children. Initially, like many others, she was educated at home by a governess, who she called 'incompetent to the last degree'. Fortunately her father was enlightened enough to want formal education for his daughters, and she went with several sisters to a school in Blackheath, London. Her siblings included Elizabeth Garrett Anderson, Britain's first woman doctor, and Agnes Garrett who, with a cousin, began the nation's first female interior decor company.

Fawcett met her husband for the first time on the day news of Lincoln's assassination reached England. When he overheard her remarking it was a worse disaster than the killing of any crowned head, he knew this was the woman for him. Henry Fawcett was the radical Liberal MP for Brighton who had been blinded in a shooting accident aged 24. After their marriage in 1867, Millicent accompanied her husband to government meetings, read his papers and sat by him as he spoke in public. It was a political apprenticeship available to very few women at the time and stood her in good stead when she began campaigning for women's suffrage.

In 1868, Millicent had a daughter, saw her first article published in a magazine, joined the London Suffrage Committee and – against convention – spoke publicly, reading the words of her husband. For this she was denounced in Parliament and the first ugly rumours casting doubt on her abilities as a mother circulated. She was described in the *Brighton Herald* in 1870 like this: 'She is a lady of small stature and fragile but very pleasing appearance, perfectly collected in her manner and with a clear distinct, emphatic delivery not at times without a sense of humour.'

Despite the gossip she began speaking publicly in favour of women's rights regularly, although she was perhaps a better organiser than orator. She would regularly cite thirteen reasons given by men – and some women – why women should not vote, then demolish the logic of each in turn. She lent support to other causes that improved conditions for women but kept the vote firmly as her focus, believing it would bring universal benefits. Her opposition included British statesmen, among them William Gladstone, Winston Churchill and Henry Asquith. She rarely became downhearted, saved from despair by her ebullient spirits.

'I once overheard a conversation in the waiting room of Ipswich station between two clergyman's wives who were busy making small articles of lace which were to be sold for the benefit of the schools in their respective parishes,' she recalled in her memoirs. '"What do you find sells best?" says number one to number two, who instantly replied: "Oh things that are really useful, like butterflies for the hair." Of course, there was a comic aspect to this which I did not fail to appreciate but I hoped the time would come before very long when intelligent and active minded women would cease to regard butterflies for the hair as really useful.'

Her husband's promising career was cut short by illness and he finally died in 1888. Two years later, Fawcett became president of the National Union of Women's Suffrage Societies, where she sought to work within the political system to win her cause in a stance that reflected some establishment tendencies in her nature. But frustration was boiling over among some women who, in 1903, turned instead to the newly formed Women's Social and Political Union led by Emmeline Pankhurst. Members of this group often broke the law to advertise their equal rights message.

Fawcett was concerned that all women would be branded volatile and unfit for citizenship as a result, although she remained sympathetic too:

> Militancy is abhorred by me and the majority of suffragists. None of the great triumphs of the women's movement have been won by physical force. They have been triumphs of moral and spiritual force. But militancy has been brought into existence by the blind blundering of politicians who have not understood the women's movement. I cannot wonder that people of excitable, fiery temperament have been goaded almost to madness by the shuffling and delay with which our question has been treated in Parliament. If men had been treated by the House of Commons as women have been treated there would have been bloody reprisals all over the country.

Her cousin Edmund Garret believed her measured approach and conciliatory personality did more to beckon belligerent MPs onside than the militants. She was, he said, the leader of 'the strictly reasonable section ... Nothing annoys her more than the idea that she and her friends wish in some way to make out that men and women are not different. Women, she admits, have more to do with the home and it is the home which she wishes more considered in our political life.'

The advent of the First World War brought a halt to campaigning for the vote but also propelled women into numerous jobs for the first time to counter the shortage of men. In 1918, Fawcett accepted a compromise solution, a Parliamentary bill that permitted women over the age of 30 to vote, although the voting age for men was 21. This was partly agreed to soothe the fears of many men in Parliament that, following the carnage on the battlefields, there would be more women voters than men. It took another ten years to win parity. Typically, though, Fawcett was upbeat about the battle:

People used to talk about our 50 year struggle as 50 years in the wilderness and offer their sympathy upon the length of time we'd had to work for our cause. But there was no call for commiseration. We had had a joyful and happy time marked by victory in some phase or another of our movement all along. Women were no longer treated either socially or legally as if they were helpless children, 'the milk white lambs bleating for man's protection' as one of our poets had called them. A fair share of the responsibilities of capable citizenship was within their reach.

Her memorial in Westminster Abbey bears a simple truth: 'A wise, constant and courageous Englishwoman. She won citizenship for Women.'

Ella Fitzgerald

(1917–1996)

There are few people who could fail to love her for her music and her voice. When I listen to her, I listen to a woman who reached excellence and never became bitter and persevered against all the odds in an America that was deeply racist. She must have done an awful lot to change people's views, just by being great.

Ivan Massow (Financier and insurance broker)

Jazz broke down more barriers than any other kind of music in the world. She was an ambassador for America, let alone black people. She sang everywhere in the world and everyone, no matter what colour they were, no matter what language they spoke, what sex they were or what religion, they loved Ella Fitzgerald.

Dame Cleo Laine (Jazz singer and actress)

VOCAL PERFECTION IS hard to achieve. Yet Ella Fitzgerald was a singer's singer because her renditions were perpetually flawless no matter how complex the song. She could explore every corner of her extensive three-octave range in front of an audience numbering hundreds or even thousands without faltering. Like other black jazz singers of her generation, she quietly smashed racial barriers with consummate performances in a country riven with anti-black bias.

Born in Virginia, Ella Fitzgerald never knew her father, having moved as an infant with her mother Temperance to Yonkers, a city north of Manhattan in New York state. There Temperance married and Ella gained a half-sister. But life was tough for the family in a nation paralysed by the Depression. As an adult, Fitzgerald refused to disclose details of her background, but all the indicators are that she was often hungry, unwashed and wore an assortment of ill-fitting cast-off clothing. Her home life ended with the sudden death of her mother in 1932, after which she spent time with an aunt, in an orphanage, in reform school and on the streets.

The beacon of hope in the gloomy landscape for her and many others was regular talent contests held at venues like the Apollo Theater in Harlem, New York. Her ambition to become a dancer was dashed when the contestants before her pulled off a dazzling performance. Momentarily transfixed by the spotlight as she wondered what to do instead, she finally began singing and received a rapturous reception. Much later she recalled the occasion: 'I really went on to try to be a dancer. In Yonkers I was known as a tap dancer. When I got on stage I saw all these people and I lost my nerve. I tried to sing like Connee Boswell [a popular US singer in the 1920s and 1930s]. I sang "Judy, Object Of My Affection". At that time I didn't even know one key from the other, I just sang.'

Initially, it seemed likely her opportunity would be lost because she was gawky and ill-kempt. However, one band leader, Chick Webb, who saw her perform soon after her debut, gave her a chance. With his guidance, she forged a singing career that was sufficiently robust she was able to take over the role of band leader after his untimely death in 1939. At the time her songs were typified by her biggest hit, 'A-Tisket, A-Tasket' and barely challenged her vocal range.

In 1942, she began a solo career and landed a recording contract with Decca Records. As swing gave way to bebop, Fitzgerald experimented with scat singing, which is improvised sounds rather than words that fit with the abiding rhythm. Fitzgerald, recognised as one of the best scat singers ever, said she was trying to impersonate the horn section of the accompanying orchestra.

She collaborated with some of the iconic musicians of the time, including Louis Armstrong, Dizzy Gillespie and Count Basie. More crucially, she met Norman Granz, a jazz impresario who ultimately became her manager. The son of Russian Jewish immigrants, Granz showcased the talents of most of America's best musicians in a series of well-regarded concerts known as 'Jazz at the Philharmonic'.

Not only was Granz a music lover, he was a man of principle. He paid all musicians above the going rate and they received the same if they were black or white, men or women. This was an era when skin colour was a big issue. Granz insisted on the same hotel accommodation, transport and service for all his musicians, regardless of their colour. As a black woman, Fitzgerald would have been bottom of the pile in terms of wages at the time. But thanks to Granz – who would cancel concerts at immense cost to himself rather than tolerate discrimination – she was treated equally.

Still, he couldn't always shield her from racist behaviour. Once she was arrested after Granz insisted on a mixed audience at a venue in America's south. Sometimes she was asked to enter hotels or clubs through the kitchens. On another occasion, as an international star en route to Australia, she was put off a plane at Honolulu because a white passenger wanted her seat. This happened even though she was travelling first class. It involved a three-day delay and she wasn't allowed to retrieve her luggage.

She faced incidents like this with enormous dignity and grace, refusing to join any political debate. Anyone who saw her exuberance in performance might have believed her the ideal figurehead for the anti-racist campaign. But, out of the spotlight, she remained painfully shy. 'It is a funny thing. Around people at a party I'm very shy but the moment I hit that stage it is a different feeling. I get nerve from somewhere, maybe because it is something I love to do,' she once explained.

Despite the pressure of a gruelling performance schedule, Fitzgerald never resorted to drink or drugs. As such, she was an ambassador for black people in an often hostile white world, who changed hearts rather than laws.

By the mid 1950s she was recording with Granz's label Verve. She embarked on a career-defining series of recordings in which she devoted an album apiece to America's best loved composers and lyricists. The Songbook series, as it is known, is perhaps her greatest legacy.

Fitzgerald married twice. The first union was annulled and the second marriage ended in divorce, although she remained friends with ex-husband and bass player Ray Brown. They had adopted a son, Ray Jnr and, although the pair had some differences, she spent her final years with him when she was disabled by diabetes.

During her long career she won fourteen Grammy Awards and a host of other honours, having stayed at the top of her profession for about sixty years. Following her death, one columnist paid this telling tribute to the cross-border nature of a career that celebrated the essence of modern America: 'Here was a black woman popularising urban songs often written by immigrant Jews to a national audience of predominantly white Christians.'

Sigmund Freud

(1856–1939)

Some people think of him as depressing. They think he sees life as guided by trauma. But in fact it makes life much more interesting if you think that it is not banal, that there are these great forces driving one which can either be controlled or let loose.

Craig Brown (Satirist)

Freud isn't a religious figure so it would be misleading to 'believe' in psychoanalysis, although you can find it illuminating or amusing. He is a very contagious writer and figure. Even people who claim they are scientists can have a sort of conversion experience when they read it. People who hate it, really hate it. They are moved to take it on and disprove it. [But] Freud had a genuine engagement with what people were suffering from and what happened to people when they started talking about their suffering.

Adam Phillips (Author and psychiatrist)

BEFORE FREUD, DOCTORS had mostly been concerned with the anatomy and repair of the human body. He felt the medical world wasn't looking at the full picture and, as the 'father' of psychoanalysis, he shone a spotlight into the deep, dark recesses of human memory to discover more about the workings of the mind.

He came up with some controversial findings that frequently related to sex. Those findings struck a chord with some troubled souls and the term Freudian, linked to his work, became incorporated into the language. Others, especially in the scientific community, believed him a charlatan for the lack of evidence to substantiate his claims. Love or loathe him, he left us plenty to ponder.

Freud himself was aware that he was at the eye of a psycho-storm as he outlined the nub of the Freudian dilemma in this brief letter written in 1938, a matter of months before his death:

> I started my professional activity as a neurologist trying to bring relief to my neurotic patients. Under the influence of an older friend and by my own efforts I discovered some new and important facts about the unconscious in psychic life, the role of instinctual urges and so on. Out of these findings grew a new science, Psycho-Analysis, a part of psychology and a new method of treatment of the neuroses. I had to pay heavily for this bit of good luck. People did not believe in my facts and thought my theories unsavoury. Resistance was strong and unrelenting. In the end I succeeded in acquiring pupils and building up an International Psycho-Analytic Association. But this struggle is not yet over.

Freud was born in Moravia as the first son of his father's second marriage. He was, in his own words 'a godless Jew'. As a child he moved to Vienna, and it was the city he called home until Nazi persecution became so acute in 1937 that he left for England. In many ways it was remarkable that he survived the political storm as long as he did, as his books were being burned by the regime as early as 1933.

To some, he seems emotionally icy. Yet when he was engaged Freud wrote these passionate lines to his fiancée after climbing the Notre Dame Cathedral in Paris: 'One climbs up 300 steps, it is very dark and very lonely. On every step I could have given you a kiss if you had been with me and you would have reached the top quite out of breath and wild.'

Details about his life remain sketchy as Freud developed the habit of burning any notes or diaries at regular intervals. 'Let the biographers labour and toil,' he told his wife Martha. 'We won't make it easy for them.'

One story about his childhood lingers, in which he urinated in his parents' bedroom at the age of about 4. His father responded by saying he would never amount to anything and it was apparently this phrase that motivated Freud throughout his career.

Freud initially trained as a neurologist. Subsequently, there were two major influences on his work, that of Josef Breuer in Vienna, who treated nervous disorders through extended interviews, and Jean-Martin Charcot, who used hypnotherapy. After working in Paris with Charcot, Freud returned to Vienna to begin his own private practice.

What of his legacy still remains? Well, he used the concept of the reclining sofa, which was not new, but sat behind the patient, out of sight, which was. He publicised the notion of the unconscious mind, which was already widely in circulation. To it, he attached the new idea of repressive drives, which he said were parked here out of sight because they were difficult issues to confront and perhaps first loomed in childhood.

It was through his theories on the interpretation of dreams published in 1900 that he became famous. Throughout his career, his theories evolved and, from 1923, he talked of the unconscious mind being three departments: the id, the ego and the superego. This he published in a missive purporting to be science of the mind.

He was authoritative and ambitious, determined that his newly found science should survive and thrive. His purpose was clear: 'A man should not strive to eliminate his complexes but to get into accord with them: they are legitimately what directs his conduct in the world.'

Accordingly, his supporters say that psychoanalysis is not about finding a cure, more about finding the inner self. As everyone is different, and the nature of memories is vague and fragmentary, it is hardly surprising that there is only speculative clinical data to support the theories that Freud brought forth.

In opposition, detractors think he used examples from art and literature rather than real life to make his points and that psychoanalysis amounts to no more than a cathartic experience. Philosopher Frank Cioffi calls Freud a pseudo-scientist, saying that he made claims for which he had no adequate evidence: 'He tells you things, like the most profound trauma in the life of every male human being is his very early discovery, aged about 3 or 4, that castration is a possibility. If we ask what grounds Freud has for believing this, we find them so radically inadequate we can't say it is just a mistake. We are tempted to use words like "the greatest intellectual confidence trick of the twentieth century".' Even while he was alive, Freud's methods and declarations caused fallouts with fellow theorists, including Carl Jung, who went on to develop a different branch of analysis.

Since Freud's death from mouth cancer – inevitably exacerbated by incessant cigar smoking – the science of the mind has altered immensely. Today a pill will, as like as not, treat conditions where once psychoanalysis was considered the answer. Even unbelievers will find some common ground with Freud, though, about everything we don't know. This analogy of his will probably still be current in the next century: 'The mind is like an iceberg, it floats with one-seventh of its bulk above water.'

Marcus Garvey

(1887–1940)

In Marcus Garvey's philosophy, nothing is too great. If you apply yourself, if you work hard you will achieve. Far too often these days, people are put off by challenges and problems. Garvey said, put that to one side. Stand up on your own two feet, raise your back and get on with it. I really do share those views. His legacy is best encapsulated in one of his very famous sayings: up, you mighty race, you can accomplish what you will.

Yvonne Brown (Chair, Black Solicitor's Network
and mediating group Resolution)

Garvey is arguably the most powerful and important figure in the twentieth century among people of African descent. For one thing, he built a pan-African movement like no other. It united African people over forty countries. It had over 1,200 branches and an incredible number of the major political figures all over the African diaspora from the 1920s and 1930s all the way through to the 1960s owed their allegiance to Garvey.

Dr Tony Martin (Professor and biographer)

TO MARCUS GARVEY it seemed the twentieth century world cast black people onto the bottom rungs of life's ladder and kept them there under a white man's boot heel. Accordingly this charismatic orator made it his life's mission to change the face of the status quo and to usher in a new age of equality. Unfortunately, his vision wasn't universally shared and his dreams were shattered by an awkward alliance of the white American elite and greedy black colleagues.

Garvey was born in Jamaica into a poor family, but one that aspired to greater learning. His father was a stonemason and a descendant of the maroons, runaway or freed slaves living outside colonial jurisdiction. As a student and later a printer, Garvey had ready access to books and became widely read and politically active. Early travels to South and Central America also helped shape his outlook. He then went to England to work on the London docks, where he found the same story of black oppression continuing on a different continent. 'For the last ten years,' he noted in 1915, 'I have given my time to the study of the condition of the negro here, there and everywhere. And I have come to realise that he is still the object of degradation and pity the world over in the sense that he has no status socially, nationally or commercially.'

His concerns about the plight of black people were crystallised when he read black icon Booker T. Washington's book and then sought to address the key issue of low self-esteem among black people in order to raise them from the bottom of the pile. Garvey's solution was to form the United Negro Improvement Association in 1914, which advocated self-reliance and unity among black people worldwide. Its message resonated so strongly that, by 1920, the international membership numbered in the millions. His first wife Amy Ashwood was initially secretary of the movement. The marriage ended after a year, however.

In American the UNIA found particularly fertile ground among black soldiers who returned from the First World War believing the world would be a different place, only to find their lowly station in it much the same

– with segregation and lynchings still commonplace. Garvey's magnetic presence, used to great effect on a fundraising tour of thirty-eight American states, continued to draw support, while Rastafarians declared him a prophet. One observer remarked: 'When he speaks, his hearers listen.' His message was intended to boost the expectations of black people who, he said, should look to themselves for advancement.

His messages were not always welcome, and meetings with white supremacists from the Ku Klux Klan centring on racial purity (for both black and white people) attracted the condemnation of many. Intellectual W. E. B. Du Bois, who favoured integration above black nationalism, insisted Garvey was 'without doubt the most dangerous enemy to the negro race in America or in the world. He is either a traitor or a lunatic.'

Close to Garvey's heart was the notion that there should be a place in the world that black people could call home. The obvious location for this was Africa. Garvey established the Black Star Line, a shipping company that would ultimately transport willing immigrants to the home of their ancestors. At the time, black people were treated badly by existing shipping lines, served food after white passengers with the same ticket and inevitably housed in third-class accommodation no matter how much they paid. The Black Star Line would herald equality for passengers and improve commercial opportunities in a business world dominated by white interests. Garvey set about raising the money by subscription so that contributors had a stake in the company.

He also began negotiations with Liberia, an African state founded and colonised by freed American slaves from 1820. Liberia was torn in its response – Garvey was implicitly presenting a challenge to the ruling group there. Surrounded by French and British colonies, the government was also subject to US pressure as America exerted undue influence over Liberia's fragile economy. For Garvey had by now attracted the attention of a nervous US government, which pursued an agenda specially designed to curtail his activities. At the same time, his colleagues seized the opportunity to make fast money either as secret government agents or in illicit deals at the expense of the shipping line.

In 1925, the government laid a mail fraud charge against Garvey, who was jailed for five years. There was undoubtedly wrongdoing in the administration of Black Star, although Garvey's guilt was far from certain. After two and a half years behind bars, he was deported to Jamaica. Although other worthy self-help projects he launched had flourished, these were largely forgotten when the Black Star Line dramatically and publicly failed, leaving many poor black stakeholders out of pocket.

He'd married for a second time in the early 1920s and had two sons who recalled him as serious but kind. However, post-jail he struggled to keep his UNIA intact. He was criticised for wearing extravagant feathered hats and creating a black nobility, although for his part he saw no reason why invented aristocracy should be restricted to whites only. Eventually, he moved to London where he died in relative obscurity. It was in the era of black awareness some twenty years after his death that his name rose to prominence again.

Elizabeth Gaskell

(1810–1865)

She is a gripping writer, extraordinarily so. Her novels have the great power of fairy tale. At the same time they are full of psychological complexity, acuteness and great humanity. [And] what a wonderful woman she was; joyous, energetic, effervescent, engaged with the world and she achieved all she did in the context of a happy marriage and raising children.

Amanda Vickery (Historian)

She is very literary and she likes playing with different genres. She plays with thrillers, with fairy tales, with documentaries, with romance. She is a very cultivated writer but once she gets going it just flows. She is underestimated.

Jenny Uglow (Biographer)

THROUGHOUT HER ADULT life and since her death, she has been known as 'Mrs Gaskell'. Instantly there comes an image of home cooking and homilies, a neat house and a tidy mind, a domestic goddess for Victorian times. It seems Elizabeth Cleghorn Gaskell was all of these things and much more besides. As a writer she was bold in her choice of topics, caring little for the powerful enemies she made in her career, while her heroines all spoke with a sense of conviction that was less common for the era. Like Dickens, she believed that readers who could identify with a novel's heroine would better understand the difficulties that faced people in a different walk of life to their own. Her heroines were factory workers and unmarried mothers at a time when Victorian tastes tended towards the romantic and idealised. Her villains were factory owners who imposed shocking conditions on the workers. She challenged moral conventions after witnessing the wide-ranging effects of desperate poverty.

Gaskell was born in Chelsea but left London as an infant after the death of her mother. She was sent to live with an aunt in Cheshire, Hannah Lumb, who she later described as 'my more-than mother'. Lumb's husband, already declared insane, had fathered another family and the pair clearly meant everything to each other. Gaskell was educated both at home and at school in Warwickshire. Her childhood was idyllic until the death in 1828 of her brother John, a merchant seaman, during a trip to India. She returned to the capital to nurse her father William, who was laid low by the tragedy. When he died the following year, Gaskell went to Newcastle to visit a distant relative, William Turner, who was a Unitarian minister. During a visit to Liverpool she met another Unitarian minister, William Gaskell, and the pair eventually married in 1832. She was deeply influenced by the charity and kindness of both men. Then she moved to the heart of industrial Manchester where she was immediately thrust into the front line of a cholera epidemic among textile workers, distributing food and clothes and teaching at Sunday school.

Although there's evidence she was an avid writer throughout her life, it wasn't until she lost a child that she set about writing a novel, to help overcome feelings of loss. The result was *Mary Barton: A Tale of Manchester Life*, which was published anonymously in 1848. Soon she was identified as the writer, however, and she became a target for angry factory owners who were cruelly depicted in the book. Many objected to the literary elevation of violent activists:

> My poor Mary Barton is stirring up all sorts of angry feelings against me in Manchester but those best acquainted with the way of thinking and feeling among the poor acknowledge its truth, which is the acknowledgement I most of all desire because evils being once recognised are half way on towards their remedy.

Nor was she discouraged in her mission, publishing *Ruth* in 1853, about a 15-year-old seamstress seduced and later destitute, while she revisited the plight of working people in *North and South* two years later. Provoking more anger, she wrote: 'I think I must be a very dangerous woman without knowing it.'

Her initial success caught the eye of social writer Charles Dickens, who asked her to contribute to one of his magazines. It's here, in *Household Words*, that the public first encounters Cranford, a place drawn from her childhood. Although their relationship was one of mutual admiration, Dickens found her inability to deliver to a timetable infuriating.

While she was writing she received support from her husband, who was also busy with his ministry, and looked after four daughters. The Gaskells were polar opposites, with him tall and thin while she was short and chubby, but they remained affectionate throughout their marriage. It was he who helped fend off law suits threatened after she published a book about Charlotte Brontë in 1857. Brontë's father Patrick asked Gaskell to write the book after the creator of *Jane Eyre* died in childbirth. Although she left out Brontë's contentious love for a married man, she included several disputed facts that were omitted from later editions. Nonetheless Gaskell succeeded in taking the art of biography writing to new levels.

From the mid 1850s, Gaskell travelled around Britain, usually accompanied by a daughter, then abroad. In 1865, she bought a house in Alton, Hampshire, as a surprise for her husband as he approached retirement. As she prepared it for his arrival, she died suddenly of a heart attack. One obituary mourned the loss of 'the most powerful and finished female novelist of an epoch singularly rich in female novelists'. Not all critics were so generous. A generation later, novelist Virginia Woolf wrote:

> When she was a girl, Mrs Gaskell was famous for her ghost stories. A great story-teller she remained to the end, able always in the middle of the thickest book to make us ask 'What happens next?' Keeping a diary to catch the overflow of life, observing clouds and trees, moving about among numbers of very articulate men and women, high-spirited, observant, and free from bitterness and bigotry, it seems as though the art of writing came to her as easily as an instinct. She had only to let her pen run to shape a novel ... With all her humour she was seldom witty, and the lack of wit in her character-drawing leaves the edges blunt. These pure heroines, having no such foibles as she loved to draw, no coarseness and no violent passions, depress one like an old acquaintance. One will never get to know them; and that is profoundly sad. One reads her most perhaps because one wishes to have the run of her world. Melt them together and her books comprise a large, bright, country town, widely paved, with a great stir of life in the streets and a decorous row of old Georgian houses standing back from the road.

Fans would not agree. Frederick Greenwood, editor of the *Cornhill Magazine*, who completed her unfinished novel *Wives and Daughters*, declared: 'It is unnecessary to demonstrate to those who know what is and what is not true literature that Mrs Gaskell was gifted with some of the choicest faculties bestowed upon mankind; that these grew into greater strength and ripened into greater beauty in the decline of her days; and that she has gifted us with some, the truest, purest works of fiction in the language. And she was herself what her works show her to have been – a wise good woman.'

Marvin Gaye

(1939–1984)

I remember hearing What's Going On *and it made the hairs on the back of my neck stand on end. I can still get that sensation when I hear it now. It was produced at a time when black American politics was reaching a critical point. Marvin Gaye became attuned to all of that but at the same time preached this amazingly unsaccharine view of peacefulness, of anti-war. It is one of the best records that's ever been made. The music of the last two decades is infinitely poorer because Marvin Gaye wasn't around and there's not that many musicians you can say that about.*

Tim Marlow (Art historian)

For all of the young black kids both here and in the US of my generation, Marvin Gaye was basically the soundtrack to our lives. I first discovered him mid 1960s. Speaking personally, I've felt Marvin Gaye's loss almost like [he was an] uncle I never knew. Even to this day I always strive to maintain the musical legacy of Marvin Gaye. He was also a style icon for many of us.

Norman Jay MBE (DJ)

SOUL SINGER MARVIN Gaye had two failed marriages, a cocaine habit, suffered violent beatings as a child and spent a lifetime arguing with his father. Yet out of this troubled existence, he emerged with ground-breaking songs that changed the track of black music for ever.

He was born Marvin Pentz Gay and named for his father, a minister with the marginal House of God church. It was a blend of Judaism and Pentecostalism, characterised by joylessly strict moral codes. Discovering his wife and four children unable to live up to the church's high standards, Marvin senior was regularly enraged and Marvin and his siblings were beaten on an almost daily basis. Unsurprisingly Rev Gay also had shortcomings when it came to his personal conduct, frequently taking mistresses and, perhaps curiously, dressing as a woman.

So even in childhood, Gay Junior was an outsider on three fronts: his colour in segregated Washington; his faith, which fell outside mainstream Christianity; and the eccentric behaviour of his father, sufficient to alienate some school friends. Music proved to be a shelter from life's storms. From the age of 3, Gay sang in the church choir led by his father and before long he was performing solos. At 16, Gay left home to join the US Air Force but a resentment of authority quickly surfaced and he was given an honourable discharge after he feigned mental illness.

Back home, he neglected the church choir in favour of other musical groups, ultimately heading for Detroit – the home of the newly emerging Tamla/Motown record labels. By now Gay, good looking and stylishly dressed, exuded a confidence that was sometimes interpreted as arrogance. Motown boss Berry Gordy spotted his potential immediately. A growing bond between the pair was further reinforced when Gay married Gordy's sister Anna, who at eighteen years his senior was only seven years younger than Gaye's mother Alberta. Before the release of his first single in 1961, he added an 'e' to his surname as singer Sam Cooke had done before him, partly because connotations of the word were changing and also to distance himself from his father.

Although the Tamla record label brought opportunity, he was also subject to its strict formula. Gaye was pushed towards R&B, although he saw himself more as a crooner with a jazz backing track. Staff shaped the sound of the record while Gaye, a talented drummer and musical arranger, had sought to produce his own records. In fact, he initially had more chart success as a drummer on other people's records than as a solo artist. It wasn't until the mid 1960s that he began selling significant numbers of singles, and album sales still evaded him.

In 1967, he teamed up with Tammi Terrell and together they produced some powerful duets. A succession of hits came to an abrupt end, however, when Terrell collapsed mid-performance into Gaye's arms, suffering from the effects of the brain tumour that would kill her three years later. Much later, Gaye confessed he never really recovered from the trauma of losing Terrell, who was like a sister to him.

While Terrell was still ill, Gaye enjoyed extraordinary success with 'Heard it Through the Grapevine', his first number one and at that point the biggest hit in Motown's history. After her death, though, there was a period of introspection while he worked on *What's Going On*. His brother Frankie had returned from active service in Vietnam and told him troubling tales. The White House was in the clutches of the corrupt, and a new black consciousness was rampant. With lyrical dexterity, Gaye poured his concerns into the record which was diametrically opposed to the romantic songs with which he was normally associated and even contains evidence of early rap. Nervous of its political implications, Gordy branded it the worst record he had ever heard. But by now Gaye had sufficient influence to have the album released and its multi-layered sound with backing singers won critical and popular acclaim. One reviewer summed it up like this:

> *What's Going On* is not only Marvin Gaye's masterpiece, it's the
> most important and passionate record to come out of soul music,
> delivered by one of its finest voices, a man finally free to speak his

mind and so move from R&B sex symbol to true recording artist. … Besides cementing Marvin Gaye as one of the most important artists in pop music, *What's Going On* was far and away the best full-length to issue from the singles-dominated Motown factory, and arguably the best soul album of all time.

Already his drug-taking was an open secret, with Gaye insisting it improved his creativity. He moved from psychedelic to sensual soul with songs like 'Let's Get it On', released in 1973. It came out around the time he began dating teenager Janis Hunter. Inevitably, his marriage then collapsed and the divorce proceedings were acrimonious. Both the divorce and his love affair with Hunter played significant roles in his musical output.

The early 1980s saw Gaye with an unpaid tax bill, a second divorce and a driving drug addiction that threatened his recording career. Against all odds, however, he returned to the charts in 1982 with 'Sexual Healing'. There followed a tour which raised his profile but a short-lived reduction in drug consumption came to an end and he finally returned to his parents' home in Los Angeles, paranoid and plagued by thoughts of suicide.

It was Gaye himself who armed his father, fearful that drugs barons would threaten his family. His father warned him several times: 'If you ever lay a finger on me, I will kill you.' On the eve of Gaye's 45th birthday, a violent row broke out between father and son, with Gaye pushing the older man several times. As he'd promised he would, Gay fetched the gun and levelled it at his son, pulling the trigger twice. Gay was sentenced to five years probation after pleading guilty to voluntary manslaughter. He convinced the authorities he had been beaten by his son before producing the weapon. Fans have since been left to wonder whether Gaye's death was tantamount to suicide.

Martha Gellhorn

(1908–1998)

She is as good a journalist as has ever been. She was right at the major stories of the twentieth century, from the Spanish Civil War, the Second World War, Vietnam and pretty well everything in between. Some of her writing can be breathtaking. There's no ego in it. It is just a passion for what she felt she had to show people and tiny pieces of information that maybe other people wouldn't have thought to say. It really kind of brings home to you what it is that's going on. Being a writer I think that is about as good as it gets.

Camilla Wright (Editor of popbitch.com)

Her real courage was facing up to being old and ill, with her sight going and having cancer. She had a bad back, she had falls. She was very brave about old age and death.

Caroline Moorehead (Biographer)

JOURNALIST MARTHA GELLHORN bore witness to the most tumultuous events of the twentieth century. A war correspondent's career that began with the Spanish Civil War and ended with accounts of the street children of Brazil fighting for survival brought her to some of the most talked-about events of the century. Fearless at the front line she offered remarkable insight into the everyday lives of people caught up in conflicts. With a passion for observation that never wavered, she was described by one critic as having 'a cold eye and a warm heart'. When her powerful reports highlighted the suffering of innocents and risked alienating the American public, she was even banned from trouble zones by an anxious US government.

The daughter of a leading suffragette in St Louis who was a profound influence, Martha had three brothers. She was, she insisted, brought up in exactly the same way as the boys, believing she could achieve anything she wanted. When she was 16, her father took her to Germany, where he'd come from, and Gellhorn was infected with the desire to travel. Aged 21, she arrived in Paris in 1930 with a typewriter, a suitcase and $50. Her first relationship was in Paris with a married man. Together they went to America, and Gellhorn wrote about the effects of the Depression in what would now be described as faction.

Her first foray into war reporting was done somewhat reluctantly. She walked into Spain from France through the Pyrenees, attracted by the people gathering there to fight Fascism rather than the opportunities to work. She wrote to a friend of her mother's, saying, 'I'm going to Spain with the boys. I don't know who the boys are but I'm going with them.' It was writer Ernest Hemmingway who challenged her there, asking, 'Why don't you write something.' When she protested she knew nothing about war, he told her to write about what she did know, which was life in Madrid. She sent the piece to *Collier's* magazine in America, and it was published. Her name duly appeared on the masthead of the newspaper as 'war correspondent'.

She ended up married to Hemmingway, and they honeymooned in China which, like Spain, was riven with unrest. The marriage didn't last, probably thanks to professional rivalries between them. However, letters between the pair early in their relationship are evidence of genuine affection.

During the Second World War, Gellhorn went to Monte Cassino when it was under siege, to Omaha beach during the D-day landings and also reported on the Battle of the Bulge. She denied she was unduly brave: 'It's something that I have never thought about, and you can't take credit for a state of mind that just seems perfectly natural.' She relished the opportunities her job offered, though: 'The journalism was a wonderful chance to see everywhere what was going on in the world. If you are a journalist, you can go up to anybody and say please tell me. You can knock at any door. If you did that as a private individual they would say buzz off. ... I myself am consistently, forever and to this minute deeply and passionately interested in everything that is happening in the world, [journalism] gave me a ringside seat.'

Partly Jewish, her abiding support of Israel came mostly from seeing the carnage at a concentration camp. Gellhorn was one of the first people into Dachau and the scenes of abject misery there marked her outlook for the rest of her life. Her writing, about Israel and other emotive issues, was unashamedly partisan. 'This objective stuff seems to me to be both rubbish and boring,' she explained. 'If you are seeing something happening, the idea that you are so brain-dead and stony-hearted that you have no reaction to it strikes me as absolute nonsense. You are describing what you see and what you see is awful.'

As a young woman, she was tall, fair and shapely. Throughout her life and especially since her death, her love life has been pored over in a way that would never happen with a male equivalent. There's even been speculation that she slept with men to advance her career. It remains a curious charge as she once confessed, 'I only love the world of men and not the world of men and women.' The implication is that she was not a fan of sex.

After the war, she decided to adopt a child and visited fifty-two Italian orphanages before she found Sandy, her son. However, her career remained paramount. While she visited international trouble spots, he was sent to boarding school and grew plump and disconsolate. Much later, Sandy mooted that he would have been better off if his mother had been in the kitchen with an apron. Her reply to this charge was 'Stuff it, kid.' Later, she told Jenni Murray on Radio 4's *Woman's Hour*: 'We are very good friends now he has grown up. Amongst other things, I supported him. I couldn't very well have done that in an apron.'

In her later life, Gellhorn lived in London. English weather was, she said, 'a national catastrophe borne bravely by the inhabitants.' When she could no longer go on missions abroad, she made friends with newsreaders and foreign correspondents.

Before her death she revealed an admirable lack of self aggrandisement when she sent a message to a fan through a friend: 'Tell him that I never look back, which is true, or that I only look back on lost scenery ruined by the travel explosion. Tell him that I don't remember doing anything that calls for great pride. Tell him that one reason I cultivate my bad memory is that I remember well only what has caused me pain hence I prefer to live in the present. Just this very day will do me fine.'

Sir W. S. Gilbert

(1836–1911)

and

Sir Arthur Sullivan

(1842–1900)

*I cannot imagine why people don't love Gilbert and Sullivan. They are
part of my existence, part of the fibre of my life. I just have to think
those people are wildly mistaken. [Gilbert and Sullivan achieve] the
alchemy of sewing the music to the words so you can't think of one
without the other.*

Dillie Keane (Singer, composer and comedian)

*Lots of people are unable to embrace Gilbert and Sullivan pieces for
what they actually are; wonderful, enlightened, succulent, intelligent,
witty, moving lyrics and music. There is a very interesting and clever
chemistry of caricature and grossness, and real feelings and emotions.
It is a kind of puppet theatre that tells true-life stories.*

Mike Leigh (Film director)

CRITICS BELIEVE THEM to be jingoistic and anachronistic, blithely banging the drum for old British Empire days. But Sir William Gilbert and Sir Arthur Sullivan have legions of fans who take issue with that glib pronouncement, identifying warmth, wit and wisdom in their words and music. More than just relics of Victoriana, their most famous works are still often played and sung thanks to an appeal that crosses class and cultures. Today their names are synonymous. However, they were contrasting individuals from different backgrounds whose talents rather than characters were complementary.

Gilbert – known better to his family by his middle name of Schwenk – emerged from a stuffy upbringing which lacked affection. His father was a former naval surgeon who wrote stodgy novels. Aged 2 during his family's European travels, Gilbert was captured by Italian bandits and ransomed. His mother was so stand-offish that she lost touch with her son when he was an adult. She is thought to be the role model for some of the least attractive female characters he went on to create. A sometime clerk and barrister, Gilbert finally found his niche in the light verse tradition that flourished during the Victorian era. His poems and plays were smart and often satirical, and were published in magazines including *Punch*. He married but had no children.

Arthur Sullivan was the son of a bandmaster who had mastered most instruments by the age of 8. Obviously prodigiously talented, he studied music in Germany for several years before returning to London to work as an organist, teacher, composer and conductor. He won overnight fame in 1862 for his incidental music for a popular production of Shakespeare's *Tempest*. Conversely, he was famously fond of his mother and was the family patriarch after the premature death of his brother Fred, a father of eight. He was a popular bon viveur who enjoyed drinking, smoking, gambling and a Parisienne lifestyle but was nonetheless an accomplished musician with numerous credits to his name, including symphonies, opera and hymns, among them 'Onward Christian Soldiers'.

Impresario Richard D'Oyly Carte brought the two together in 1871 to collaborate on a production called *Thespis*, a Christmas pantomime barely remembered today but moderately popular at the time. Fortunately, the partnership endured and was ultimately so successful that D'Oyly Carte opened the Savoy Theatre in 1881 expressly to give their comic operettas a home. *Iolanthe*, *The Mikado*, *The Yeoman of the Guard* and *The Gondoliers* all premiered after the opening of the theatre, although *HMS Pinafore* and *The Pirates of Penzance* were already hits. In total there were fourteen Savoy operas, some of which have fared better through the years than others. Yet they all offer valuable insight into the way Victorians relished theatrical entertainment which mocked politicians and other celebrities of the day through words and music.

As librettist, Gilbert is deemed to have nurtured a topsy-turvy view of the world, the heart of which lies with the conviction that people are not what they seem. Score-writer Sullivan's genius was to challenge the status quo. Setting Gilbert's verse to music, he would invariably seek the contradictory rather than the easy option. Thus, audiences learned to expect the unexpected when the pair worked together.

Furthermore, Sullivan evolved his role into that of stage director. (Until then, Victorian theatres were notoriously chaotic.) Meanwhile, Gilbert noted down every detail he envisaged about the production, so actors worked inside a rigid framework. It was this kind of tight prescription that left Gilbert and Sullivan's operettas fossilised after the pair died, as the copyright for the words passed to the D'Oyly Carte Opera and the interpretation of the writer was never so much as tweaked.

During their partnership, Sullivan continued to work solo and produced some serious and monumental musical pieces. Although they worked together for years, the two men possessed radically different temperaments which would prove to be the undoing of the duo. In 1890, the pair quarrelled, ostensibly about the cost of carpet being laid in the Savoy Theatre. Underlying issues existed too, because both men felt their work was subjugated to the other. For three years, they were estranged and, although they worked together again later, the spark that ignited their most famous pieces was missing. Yet neither found the same level of success alone as they had done in the partnership. Nothing they wrote or composed won anything like the acclaim of the material they produced together.

If any hard feelings persisted after the quarrel, they apparently vanished with Sullivan's death from bronchial problems after prolonged ill-health. Gilbert described Sullivan's death as 'deplorable' and said: 'With Sullivan I never had to do that fatal thing, explain a joke. I remember all he has done for me in allowing his genius to shed some of its lustre on my humble name.' Although Sullivan hoped to be buried in the family plot, Queen Victoria decreed his final resting place was to be in St Paul's Cathedral.

Even before Sullivan's death, Gilbert had largely abandoned libretto and turned to writing plays. Most were lacklustre but one was distinguished by some success. *The Hooligan*, centred on a young thug in a condemned cell, was fully of gritty realism and social comment, a world away from his previous triumphs. He died after diving into a lake at his home to save a woman swimmer in danger of drowning, suffering a heart attack as he did so. A plaque dedicated to him on the Thames Embankment reads: 'His Foe was Folly, and his Weapon Wit'.

Such is their charm, Gilbert and Sullivan operettas have attracted armies of devotees since their inception and every year there are productions in England and across the world by the score. There's little doubt they bridged the cavernous gap between the more serious-minded operas that came before them and the American musicals that followed – including those by Rodgers and Hammerstein, Gershwin and Cole Porter – thus cementing their vital role in musical history.

W. G. Grace

(1848–1915)

Grace was the greatest. He had everything; he was physically imposing, he was in terms of statistics comfortably the best player of his generation – and of all time, I would argue. But he also was there when cricket became not just a village-green pastime but a proper international sport, and it took an iconic figure to make that transition work and to bring the English public with him. Grace did that, magnificently. He was the Henry VIII of the sporting world.

Piers Morgan (Chat show host)

He changed cricket singlehandedly in the 1860s and had more power, that he exercised quite ruthlessly, than anyone could imagine. When he was in his early twenties, when he was captain of Gloucestershire, he cancelled a county match between Gloucestershire and Nottinghamshire because he had given his word to a Yorkshire professional who wanted him to play in a benefit match. He cancelled what would have been the deciding match in the county championship. He had the beard of a man who was too busy with his net practice to shave.

Simon Ray (Biographer)

IF YOU SHUT your eyes on a summer's day and, above bird song and bees, hear the thwack of leather against willow, one image comes overwhelmingly to mind. Cricketer William Gilbert Grace was a man-mountain at the wicket whose monumental contribution to the game continues to loom large. Dead for almost a century, there are remarkably few who have come close to filling his ample blazer down the years.

Cricket commentator John Arlott recognised the debt cricket owes Grace: 'Look back through the swirl of two world wars to any one of a thousand English cricket fields and see there a tall man with a ringed red and yellow MCC cap perched on his head, a huge black beard falling down upon his barrel chest and a cricket bat looking like a toy in his hand and there's the Gloucestershire man of pure country strain who, without a moment of unfaithfulness to himself, became known to millions because he was not only the greatest cricketer of his age but one of the greatest men of his age.'

When it comes to Grace, the statistics speak for themselves. He scored over 54,000 first-class runs and took more than 2,800 wickets in a career that spanned forty-three years. Although his test career was comparatively brief, lasting only nineteen years, he played twenty-two tests, scored more than a thousand runs and was 'not out' seventeen times. Grace opened the batting for his country in a test against Australia when he was 50 years old.

He scored the first two triple-centuries in first-class cricket; he was the first player to score 2,000 in a season; he scored three back-to-back centuries on five occasions; he scored a century as well as taking ten wickets in fourteen matches. Aged 18 he scored 224 not out in a match against Surrey, which he left before its finish to win a quarter-mile hurdles race at nearby Crystal Palace.

All this in an era when pitches didn't have the smooth, lush surfaces they have today, so batsmen were hindered in their progress between the stumps. It's a mark of the man that he would regularly score at least double the amount of other batsmen in his team. 'When he was in, he made everybody else on the field look like a boy,' according to C. B. Fry, who was himself an outstanding cricketer.

There is, however, another darker side to Grace's legacy, as his gamesmanship was legendary. At the Oval in 1882, a young Australian batsman, Sammy Jones, got the nod from Grace to pat down a divot. Grace promptly orchestrated his run-out, to the fury of Australian bowler Fred Spofforth, aka the Demon Bowler. Spofforth was so fired up he skittled England out for just 77, causing an obituary for English cricket to appear in the *Sporting Times*. The cremation of the match stumps resulted in the Ashes, a minute urn that still inspires hard-fought contests between the English and the Australian cricket teams. Ashes statistics do not favour English cricket.

Grace was also a proponent of sledging, disrupting the concentration of opposing batsman by comments or insults, speaking with a distinctive Gloucestershire accent and a strangely falsetto voice. He was known to intimidate the umpires and other players with bulk and bat. Sometimes his on-field activities were branded as cheating, although he would hotly deny this was so.

That Grace was extremely competitive stems from his childhood experiences on the outskirts of Bristol. He was the eighth child of nine and played cricket perpetually with his father and four brothers with the avowed intention to win. (He played alongside two of his brothers in an England team in 1880.) Despite a life-threatening illness in his teenage years, he went on to top 6 foot 2 inches and become a brilliant technician of the game.

Although his promise was apparent, he pursued a medical career, according his father's wishes, alongside his sporting life. He was, however, late qualifying because he spent more time on the cricket pitch than studying.

He kept amateur status while liberating thousands of pounds from the game in what were loosely called expenses. As his reputation became firmly established – first playing for Gloucestershire, then London County and finally the MCC, as well as for England – the crowds flocked to see him perform and he was happy to cash in on his popularity. He was more recognisable to most people than William Gladstone when the latter was Prime Minister.

On a tour of Australia, Grace earned the enmity of people in the south east when he rudely extracted his team from the lavish hospitality that followed a game hosted at considerable cost in order to squeeze in another lucrative fixture before coming back to England. The local paper wrote, 'Instead of his brilliant and skilful play being remembered with profit and pleasure his name will become a synonym for mean cunning and systematic fraud.'

Off the pitch, he was shy and even modest. He worked as a doctor in some of Bristol's poorest areas, employing locums during the cricket season. In 1873, he married and subsequently fathered four children, but he was heartbroken when two died in their twenties, one of typhoid, the other of appendicitis.

It was with reluctance he finally gave up cricket in 1908, lamenting, 'I can still bat but I can't bend.' There's conjecture that the appearance of German Zeppelins over London during the First World War, at which he would angrily shake his fist, contributed to his early death.

An obituary in *The Guardian* said, 'Dr. William Gilbert Grace was by common consent the greatest and most attractive figure that ever appeared on the cricket field. In his all-round mastery of the game, in the length of years during which he stood far above all rivals, in the amazing sum total of his cricketing achievements, and by no means least of all in the popular interest he excited, no cricketer, living or dead, has ever approached him, and it is doubtful if any ever will.'

To cricket, Grace left at least two valuable nuggets of wisdom: 'When you win the toss, always bat' and 'There's no such thing as a crisis, only the next ball.'

Katharine Graham

(1917–2001)

She is a 360-degree person. By that I mean she had a lot of faults but she had many things to commend her. She showed a great lack of conceit. And that is very interesting in someone who had a lot of power. One might not admire all the angles she took, be they political or editorial, but she was a person who made a great journey. There was quite late in her life this coming from the chrysalis, her wings opening up and her capabilities being seen by everyone around.

Kirsty Young (Newsreader)

[On business trips] she would rip herself inside out to try and keep stuff in her head and not to make a mistake – and if she made a mistake she wouldn't be able to sleep that night. She could have had a life of ease, she could have had some public role, but she didn't have to let herself in for this terrible [punishment]. That is what I admire about her.

Carol Felsenthal (Unauthorised biographer)

S HE WAS SAID to be the most powerful woman in America, no mean feat in an era when women of her colour and class were generally confined to the home. Indeed, Katharine Graham emerged from domestic obscurity in her middle years to take the helm of one of America's most influential newspapers. Under her leadership, it would unleash the scandals of the Pentagon papers – a report about US conduct in the Vietnam war that the government badly wanted to cover up – and the Watergate bugging story, which ended with the resignation of President Richard Nixon. Her memoir, *Personal History*, won the Pulitzer prize in 1998.

Nothing in her background prepared her for the tumultuous media feats that defined her years as a newspaper publisher. She was born into immense wealth to industrialist Eugene Meyer and his wife Agnes Ernst Meyer. As a child, Katharine lived a cosseted life: the family's summer home at Mount Kisco, New York, had a dozen servants working inside and another twelve labouring outside in the gardens. But she had a remote relationship with her parents, particularly her mother. Artistic, self-confident and self-absorbed, Agnes judged her children by their achievements – and her standards were high. She found Katharine the least attractive, least creative and most gawky of her brood, and the pair did not see eye to eye. When Katharine went off to college she bought herself a range of clothes but later recalled how she wore one yellow sweater continually, never previously having been concerned with how clothes were laundered. She simply had no idea what to do.

On a whim, Katharine's father bought the *Washington Post* at a bankruptcy sale in 1933, determined to transform it into a vibrant, effective newspaper. To do so, he poured considerable amounts of his personal fortune into its coffers. Independently, Katharine sought a career as a journalist, working on the *San Francisco Chronicle* and proving herself with reports on labour unrest. (Her main aim was to stay away from Washington, where her mother generally lived.) Finally, she was tempted by her father to work on the *Post*, where she edited the letters page. There she fell in love with

Phil Graham, a Harvard law graduate, who became her husband and father of her four children. While Phil's star was rising at the *Post*, his wife was a stay-at-home mother. Only much later did she realise she was trapped in what today would be known as an abusive marriage:

> I thought he had done nothing but build me up and it was only looking back that I perceived that at the same time as building me up he was also in a way putting me down. This became more or less evident when I put on a fair amount of weight and he used to call me porky. He even gave me a French pig's head. I thought it was funny. It didn't occur to me afterwards that it wasn't funny. I became the butt of some family jokes.

With a shaky self-esteem buckling under a two-pronged barrage from mother and husband, Katharine remained in the shadows until Phil shot himself in 1963, having developed manic depression and begun an affair with a much younger woman. At the time, Phil had taken over the posts of publisher and chairman from his father-in-law, and his death left a power vacuum at the *Washington Post*. Aged 46, Katharine stepped into the breach, against advice, rather than sell the concern, primarily to safeguard her children's future.

She remained unsure of herself. Before staff parties, Graham found herself practising the phrase 'Merry Christmas'. When she met dignitaries, she was coached by several assistants using colour-coded briefing books. Initially, every day was a battle to remain buoyant. She described herself as 'an old brown wren in glittering company'. But she learned swiftly, almost instinctively, about journalism and the role of a newspaper proprietor.

The social contacts forged by her family, her husband and herself included political big-hitters like John F. Kennedy and Lyndon Johnson. Nonetheless Graham preferred to stay out of editorial policy so the newspaper could not be used as a tool by the elite. This robust position earned her the respect of newsroom staff, who began to treat her like one of the boys. Soon her conversation was peppered with colourful expletives, in typical newsroom fashion. She employed a tough editor, Ben Bradlee, and a talented businessman, Warren Buffett, to guide her.

In 1971, after the *New York Times* was gagged, the *Washington Post* published excerpts from the Pentagon papers, labelled 'sensitive' but construed as 'top secret' by Richard Nixon's government. Graham later described the decision to publish as 'anguishing', since she knew it would cause problems for close friends. Editor Bradlee believed her support for the story forged a new confidence at the paper. 'We had a great sense of someone who would be on the ramparts with us under any conditions,' he said.

It turned out to be the precursor for the Watergate scandal which dominated headlines for much of the 1970s. The unfolding story centred on a break-in at Democrat offices and the elaborate, high-level efforts to suppress it by high-level Republican figures. With Watergate came almost sinister threats. Attorney General John Mitchell told one reporter: 'Katie Graham is gonna get her tit caught in a big fat wringer if she publishes that.' Graham continued to publish, even when television licences owned by the *Post* were withdrawn.

It was something of a high point of her career in newspapers. Within the next decade she lost her appeal as far as reporters were concerned after she took on the pressmen and printers trying to protect old-style working practices in the onslaught of new technology. But even this was a personal victory for Graham, as she began her business career with only a scintilla of knowledge.

During her tenure, she worked to implement equality in the workplace for women. When she finally left the *Post*, she handed over the reins to her son Don. She died after a fall and in the report of her death on the ABC news channel she was called 'one of the twentieth century's most powerful and interesting women'.

Joyce Grenfell

(1910–1979)

She is the mother of female stand-ups. It is the things she doesn't say that make you laugh. That's such clever work. It is the timing. She is right up against it in terms of her patience but she is really trying. You can hear it all in the voice.

Arabella Weir (Comedian)

My mother first met Joyce when she was pregnant with me and went to interview her for the Girls Friendly Society magazine. Joyce took on our family of five children after our father died. She would invite us for Christmases and would send us trunks of her old clothes. She had the ability to watch a person, work out their entire life and describe it in a two-minute monologue. This often took two or three years, working away in her mind. She said she couldn't write a monologue about somebody until she knew exactly what their bedroom looked like.

Jamie Hampton (Biographer and friend)

MIMIC AND MONOLOGUER Joyce Grenfell modestly described herself as 'about eight feet tall with a face like a reflection in a spoon'. She may have felt gawky and flat-footed, but for the rest of the world it was her wit and charm that easily outshone any perceived physical shortcomings. Grenfell was one of the most gifted comedians of her generation. She appeared to popular acclaim on radio, television, in films and on the stage. During the Second World War she had a hectic schedule entertaining the troops. Using sharp observational skills and a spare, restrained way with words, she created a one-woman show that was characteristically a sketch of pent-up tension as she said one thing and meant another.

Quintessentially English in performance, Joyce was in fact born to an American mother and a half-American architect father. By the age of 5, she had crossed the Atlantic half a dozen times. She was the niece of Nancy Astor, the first woman to sit as an elected MP in the House of Commons. A great society beauty, Astor lived at Cliveden in Buckinghamshire, a grand house on the banks of the Thames, and it was here that Grenfell came to think of as home. Astor was also a convert to the Christian Science faith founded by Mary Baker Eddy on the premise that prayer could cure physical ills. She converted Joyce and her parents to Christian Science beliefs. Another relative thought to have had an effect on Joyce was Ruth Draper, her father's second cousin, who wrote and performed popular monologues in America. Grenfell admitted that as a child she loved to be the centre of attention. Her career betrayed a swift and agile mind, yet Grenfell left school at 15.

Despite her American heritage, she was firmly wedded to England and it was here she 'came out' as a debutante in her teenage years. Although she mixed with the higher echelons of society, she was not always impressed by wealth and aristocracy. Later in her career, after being invited by the Queen to perform at Windsor Castle during Ascot week, Grenfell wrote in her diary: 'Not my favourite audience; horsey, social upper crust and not all that bright.'

She married an accountant, Reggie, and might have spent her life as a housewife if not for a supper invitation from radio producer Stephen Potter in 1939. Everyone was expected to 'do a turn' afterwards and she performed a monologue based on a Women's Institute lecture she had recently seen. Another guest, a theatre director, insisted that she repeated the lines at his West End revue. She agreed only if she finished in time to catch the last train back to Taplow, near Cliveden. She was an immediate hit and her words did much to brighten wartime spirits. Her adult life was blighted by the separation of her parents, however, as she revealed in an interview given in 1971:

> The break-up of my mother and father's marriage I suppose was the time I was most unhappy in my life. It came as a terrible shock. We came in late at night and found my father standing in the drawing room and he said quite simply to me: 'Your mother's gone away.' I really can't talk about it, it was such a moment of horror. ... They did a most marvellous thing, they kept together and they made a happy family life for us to grow up in. We were unaware of this unhappiness and it was a very profound unhappiness. They denied themselves to give us this happy security and I shall never cease to be grateful for that.

That she never had children was another source of pain. But she committed herself to her work and her marriage, although she was wooed by international playboy Prince Ali Khan, who would go on to marry film star Rita Hayworth. They met in Cairo in 1945 as she completed an exhausting entertainment tour of Allied camps. No one knows precisely what occurred between them, but she returned to her husband in England.

In her autobiography, she revealed how she created characters: 'I always knew the character I was after. The way into it came through the voice and accent. It was the voice that brought the character into focus and with it instinctively came mannerisms and movements. I talked out loud to myself as I moved around our flat thinking in the manner of the creature I was trying to bring to life. The storyline was the last to be thought about.

Throughout the building up process, anything from two days to a month, I made notes to key words and phrases and so the piece took shape and only then did I write it out in full. A second character appeared one night when I was cleaning my teeth. I looked in the mirror and curled back my upper lip to make sure they were clean and gleaming. My teeth are as large as tomb stones and it is as well to keep them in good order as they are noticeable. It occurred to me that I had found a new face and I wondered how it would speak. It spoke in a clear, clipped educated manner and what it said was crisp and to the point. She is still my favourite character in my gallery of monstrous women, the wife of an Oxbridge vice chancellor.

Her life ended with cancer, which she tried to control with prayer, according to the tenets of her faith. After she was diagnosed she survived for seven years, taking painkillers only at the very end of her life.

Vasily Grossman

(1905–1964)

Here was a man who was not only very interested in the truth but also had the intellectual capacity and the skill as a writer to explore it. In that country where the truth could be so dangerous in those times, to dare to go into it in a full-hearted way and in a way doesn't go for simplicity, I think that is greatness.

Gillian Slovo (Novelist and daughter
of anti-apartheid activist Joe Slovo)

Truth is the first casualty not only of war but of ideology. Grossman talks about 'the ruthless truth of war'. It is truth and humanity that is the power in his books. He showed such an astonishing moral courage in being able to combine the two.

Anthony Beevor (Historian and author of
Stalingrad and Berlin: The Downfall 1945)

A T FIRST GLANCE, Vasily Grossman – bespectacled and portly, wearing an ill-fitting uniform and wielding a walking stick – promised little to his comrades-in-arms during the Second World War. But a curious blend of courage and conviction elevated him above the rank-and-file war correspondent in Soviet Russia. With words he produced images that seared into the national consciousness. And his words were those the ordinary Ivan looked to first, to discover what was happening on the fast-moving front line. But prose that could make readers shiver in a sketch of a Moscow winter or weep with a narrative on concentration camp conditions put him on a collision course with Soviet authorities, who preferred disinformation above observation. He was effectively silenced and his best works weren't published until years after his death.

Grossman was born in Berdychiv, in today's Ukraine, which at the time lay in the shadow of recent pogroms and famine. Although he was born into a Jewish family, his upbringing wasn't typically religious. His distinctive Jewish first name of Iosif was superseded with a pet name given to him by a Russian nanny. His father was a social democrat, while he himself supported the Russian Revolution in 1917.

After studying at Moscow State University during the 1920s, Grossman became an engineer and worked in the coalfields of eastern Ukraine. But all the while he was penning novels and short stories and finally he gave up working in industry to concentrate on writing. Russian writers Anton Chekhov and Leo Tolstoy were his inspirations. His first marriage was short-lived but produced a daughter.

Although he was left-leaning, his politics might have been construed as Trotskyism which, at the time, could have meant a death sentence. He was arrested and interrogated in 1933, before the purges – waves of killings ordered by Stalin – got under way. Even so, Grossman stepped in when a dissident writer Boris Guber was later arrested and murdered. Grossman had already married Guber's former wife Olga Mikhailovna, and he quickly adopted her two sons so they could not be guilty by implication of crimes against the state. When Olga was detained, Grossman revealed steely courage: he wrote to the head of Soviet home security, misquoting Stalin to claim she was being illegally held.

Despite some private misgivings about the Soviet Union, his stories tended to be patriotic. Accordingly, he was admitted into the Union of Soviet Writers in 1937 and was twice recommended for a Stalin prize.

Internal politics were forgotten when Hitler's forces attacked the Soviet Union in June 1941, despite the existence of a non-aggression pact between the two. The invasion had two immediate and life-changing consequences for Grossman. Unsuitable for active service, he was employed as a war correspondent by *Red Star*, the army's newspaper. And his mother was killed as German forces swept through the Ukraine. Although her death wasn't confirmed for years, Grossman knew Jewish people like her would be murdered by Germans and he felt guilty for not doing more before the war to save her.

As a journalist he went to the sites of all the major battles with the Soviet army, from Stalingrad to Berlin. He was also the first person to chronicle the events at the Treblinka death camp, after interviewing local people and about forty escapees.

His war correspondent's career began with a stroke of luck, narrowly avoiding capture as Kiev was swiftly surrounded by encroaching German forces. His experiences were featured in a novel, *The People Immortal*, which came out the following year. His next stop was Stalingrad, already ruined by warfare.

An arch-sceptic about Soviet propaganda of the era, he sneered at other stories dominating front pages: 'They are complete rubbish, with stories such as "Ivan Pupkin has killed five Germans with a spoon."' Instead, he listened quietly to the powerful recollections of officers and men of the Red Army, still exhausted from the fight. He didn't use a notebook, concerned that it would intimidate them. Instead he remembered their words and typed them later. His admiration for soldiers was palpable, and he understood not only their fears but the nature of their triumphs too. He got the following account from a successful sniper at Stalingrad:

> When I first got the rifle I couldn't bring myself to kill a living being. One German was standing there for about four minutes talking and I let him go. Then I killed my first one. He fell at once. Another one ran out and stooped over the killed one. I knocked him down too. When I first killed I was shaking all over. The man was only walking to get some water. I felt scared; I have killed a person. Then I remembered our people and I started killing them without mercy.

In July 1944, Grossman was with the unit that entered Treblinka, already flattened by retreating German forces. His account reveals he was among the first to understand the psychology of the Holocaust, highlighting the mechanics of the Nazi approach:

'The key to the second phase of handling the newcomers was the suppression of their will by constantly giving them short and rapid orders. These commands were given in that tone of voice of which the German army is so proud, the tone which proved that Germans belonged to the race of lords. The "r" at the same time guttural and hard sounded like a whip. *Achtung* carried over the crowd ...'

After the war, he worked on a book noting all the outrages against Jews carried out in Soviet Russia. Grossman was also a member of the Jewish Anti-Fascist Committee, which forged links with America. Stalin, however, was not only anti-Semitic but also paranoid about foreign influence. If Stalin had not died in 1953, Grossman would surely have been sent to a Siberian gulag.

He spent much of the 1950s working on his defining work, *Life and Fate*. Completed in 1960, it includes numerous suggestions that would rattle a totalitarian state. Although the Red Army soldier is still lionised, Grossman highlights how some Soviet people helped the Germans to kill

Jewish neighbours and that Stalin's Communism was a mirror image of Hitler's Nazism. It was the first time the spookily accurate comparison had been made behind the Iron Curtain.

While the backlash against Stalin among Soviet top brass was radical, it wasn't ready for this political heresy. Grossman's office was raided by the secret police who took copies of the book and even the typewriter ribbon used for the manuscript. Persistent pleas for his book to be released for publication were turned down by Soviet authorities. Grossman was told it wouldn't be published in Russia for at least 200 years, so dangerous were its ideas.

When he died from stomach cancer, Grossman assumed his greatest work would never be seen. Fortunately, one copy did remain in existence and it was ultimately photographed by dissidents and successfully dispatched to the West, where it was published in 1980. Eight years later, it appeared in Russian where it perplexed many who mistakenly thought he was critical of Soviet soldiers.

John Hammond

(1910–1987)

*He was one of the greatest producers and A[rtists] & R[epertoire]
men that the music business ever saw. He changed the face of popular
music, particularly in America but also around the world. Unique is
a terrible word to use, but you have to use it here. He was able to be
artistically true to the music he loved and also, very cleverly, make sure
it was heard. He is my role model.*

Joe Boyd (Record producer)

*At age 22 or 23 he was [organising] Bessie Smith's last recording and
Billie Holiday's first recording. At the time, nobody knew the connection
but he did. We can look back now and see these were two icons.*

Dunstan Prial (Biographer)

BRUCE SPRINGSTEEN, BOB Dylan, Aretha Franklin, George Benson, Count Basie, Benny Goodman, Leonard Cohen and Billie Holiday were among many musicians catapulted to stardom by one man. Without the insight and perception of music producer John Hammond, the soundtrack of the twentieth century might have been very different indeed. Hammond has been dubbed 'the most influential talent scout and music producer in history'.

More than that, he was a civil rights campaigner who was convinced that music in general and jazz in particular could dismantle the divide that kept blacks and whites apart in America. Although he couldn't immediately integrate society, he was able to bring together bands with talented musicians, both black and white, to achieve a winning sound. He also brought major black stars to white audiences, not least because he had a considerable personal fortune to finance such ventures.

Hammond was the great grandson of shipping magnate Cornelius Vanderbilt, born in Manhattan into US 'aristocracy'. Christened John Henry Hammond, he shared the same name with his father and grandfather. At first his love of music came from hearing his grandmother playing classical pieces on the piano. Soon afterwards, though, he was down in the basement among the family's servants listening to early blues and gospel recordings.

As a teenager he explored East Harlem, traditionally the haunt of black musicians, and heard jazz great Bessie Smith perform. He was also an accomplished violin and viola player. There were many wealthy young white men who experimented with jazz but soon conformed to family expectation. When Hammond dropped out of Yale in 1932, he was determined to choose his own path, one that would make a difference in an unjust world. Ultimately it became a lifelong quest.

To make his dream of a colour-blind society a reality, he funded recording sessions, venues and travel costs on behalf of talented but hard-up musicians. His crew-cut hair and toothy grin were soon welcome fixtures on musical circuits where he saw to it that the best musicians worked together.

Benny Goodman, for example, was sure his all-white band was as good as it could be. However, by 1936 Hammond was convinced that with black pianist Teddy Wilson the musical result would be sensational. Hammond was proved right. (Hammond's sister Alice went on to marry Goodman although the two men fell out soon afterwards.)

Three years earlier, Hammond went to a club in Harlem to hear Monette Moore, one of his favourite singers. Moore was called away and Billie Holiday, an 18-year-old with a troubled past and no musical training, took her place. On hearing her voice, Hammond immediately organised a recording session for Holiday with Benny Goodman and, within a few years, she was performing in her own right as a major recording star. In 1938 he brought together some of the most important recording stars of the era at the Carnegie Hall in New York for a groundbreaking concert called 'From Spirituals to Swing'. During the 1930s, Hammond not only made his living as a talent scout – helping to assure the future of the Columbia record label – he also wrote for Britain's *Melody Maker* magazine and some American titles.

During the Second World War, Hammond was called up to serve in the military, something he did not relish. He returned to the USA to find swing had given way to be-bop in modern musical preferences. It wasn't a style he enjoyed, and he spent most of the 1950s working as an executive for Vanguard Records, observing the rise of rock and roll with some mystification. In 1960, he spotted and signed preacher's daughter Aretha Franklin to Columbia, although her most soulful hits were made some time later.

His knack for picking winners returned in February 1961, however, when he persuaded Columbia records to sign an unknown folk singer, guitarist and harmonica player called Robert Zimmerman. For a while, other Columbia executives called Zimmerman 'Hammond's Folly', but the following year the artist changed his name to Bob Dylan – and the rest is history.

During the 1960s Hammond resigned his long-held position on the board of the National Association for the Advancement of Coloured People, the most enduring civil rights group in America, when he felt it did not oppose US involvement in Vietnam robustly enough.

His last major triumph on the music scene was to spot the promise of Bruce Springsteen, who he signed in 1972. Although already nicknamed 'the Boss', Springsteen was not yet a household name. Even when sales of his first two albums with Columbia were slow, however, Hammond kept the faith. Finally, with the release of *Born to Run* in 1975, Springsteen was on the road to mega-stardom.

When criticisms were made of Hammond it was usually that he got too involved with records and artists, leaving the creative team feeling stifled.

Hammond married twice and had three sons. One, who shared his name, went on to be a blues singer and guitarist. (John Paul Hammond was also named for Paul Robeson, a close friend of Hammond's.) His second wife Esme died after contracting HIV from a blood transfusion a year after Hammond's own death.

In childhood he learned that families such as his, imbued with wealth and opportunity, had an obligation to 'give back' to the community. Yet his pursuit of talent was more than simply weighing off his conscience. He believed music really could make a difference in an unjust world, helping to free the shackles that pinned poor but gifted musicians.

In 1971 he was given a Grammy Trustees Award for his work on the reissue of a Bessie Smith record. Fifteen years later he was inducted into the Rock and Roll Hall of Fame.

Tony Hancock

(1924–1968)

My mother had six children, and she didn't laugh very much. She was harassed, busy, hard up. The effect that the Hancock programmes had on her was extraordinary. My mother was doubled up [with laughter], she couldn't get her breath. It was joyful for me to see my mother's reaction. That was when my love and admiration for Tony Hancock started.

Pam Ayres (Poet and television personality)

The work rate was phenomenal. Once he hit his stride in 1954, over the next seven years he recorded something like 160 Half Hours either for radio or television. Performing comedy is the hardest job in the theatrical world. Dennis Norden summed up Hancock's legacy by coining the phrase 'the echo of remembered laughter'.

John Fisher (TV producer and Hancock biographer)

FOR A GENERATION, he was the king of comedy. First on radio and then through the new media of television, Tony Hancock depicted a flawed hero who nonetheless held an audience in his hand. So popular was he that the BBC received complaints from shops and pubs, which emptied when his show was scheduled. But in true 'tears of a clown' tradition Hancock was racked with self-doubt, his private life was a mess, and he took his own life in Australia in 1968 by consuming a deadly cocktail of amphetamines and alcohol.

Anthony John Hancock was born in Birmingham but moved to the seaside resort of Bournemouth when he was just 3 years old. His father Jack ran a laundry, then a hotel, but throughout he also worked as a semi-professional entertainer, specialising in droll monologues. Through his father, the young Hancock met some of the stage stars of the era when they came to stay at the family's hotel, and he was encouraged to wait in the wings during performances.

After a few false starts in show business, he was called up into the Royal Air Force as ground crew. Consequently, he joined Ralph Reader's Gang Show, a style of variety performance borrowed from the Scouting movement that spread throughout the armed services during the war.

In 1947, Hancock toured Britain with a gang show. Although he was dogged with insecurities throughout his life, he showed some grit and vigour in the early stages of his career, making an appearance on BBC TV as early as 1948. By the 1950s, he was a regular on BBC radio and soon became a household name. Through a show called *Calling All Forces*, which began in 1951, he met comedy writers Ray Galton and Alan Simpson. When they reunited in 1954 for *Hancock's Half Hour*, their combined skills propelled situation comedy to new heights.

The character they created was Tony Aloysius St John Hancock, of 23 Railway Cuttings, East Cheam, a pompous, petty and vain man aspiring to better himself. Inevitably, he always fell foul of events. If his own frailties didn't bring about his downfall, then the sharp-minded antics of co-star Sid

James certainly would. There was also a small cast of other characters on hand to burst his bubble. While this type of character-led comedy is old hat today, *Hancock's Half Hour* broke the mould when it was first broadcast. He was a radical change of diet for people used to the music-hall mentality and its typically knockabout comedy routines.

Galton and Simpson were skilful writers in any event. But in colluding with Hancock they got direct access to his personal foibles and incorporated them into scripts making him a caricature of his real self. For example, one episode focused on Hancock unbandaging his new nose following cosmetic surgery. Only later did his mother reveal that the Hancock family all had big noses and were often teased about it.

Hancock's Half Hour transferred to television in 1956 amid some scepticism about whether it would still work. It remained hugely successful and brought about a phenomenal fan base for Hancock. But fame began to cloud his judgement. Unwilling to be part of a double act and concerned about the soaring popularity of Sid James, he engineered a solo series in the 1960s. While it featured some vintage comedy, it lacked the staying power of his previous series. He also got rid of his agent and then dispensed with the services of Galton and Simpson. He sought fame in America and switched sides to work for ITV in Britain. The shows followed loosely the same format as his earlier series, but lacked the verve of previous years.

There's a theory that a high-profile interview in 1960 catastrophically altered Hancock's perception of himself. He was the first popular entertainer to be invited on *Face to Face*, hosted by John Freeman, who generally picked politicians, philosophers and intellectuals as his guests. Obviously nervous, he answered questions about the nature of comedy honestly, reflecting on how funny and sad were basic ingredients of a good sketch. 'I always wanted to be a comic,' Hancock told Freeman. 'Looking like this it was perhaps the only thing I could do.' Afterwards, Hancock's self-analysis seemed to lead to self-destruction, and he appeared to regard his own talents too highly. For although he was a smart man, he was some distance short of genius.

Unable to achieve the audience ratings he once commanded, Hancock became increasingly drink dependent. He was also involved in a car crash that impaired his capacity to learn lines. When he realised that autocues could bridge the gap, his professionalism took a dip while his drinking went on the rise.

As his alcohol intake increased, so did his mood swings. People had often mistaken the mournful expression staring out from beneath his trademark homburg hat as bad humour. 'I give the impression of being morose because I am concentrating on my work,' he insisted early in his career. But there's no doubt that ultimately his humour was compromised by drink dependency, fuelled by insecurity, and brooding introspection washed over him frequently. In addition, he had personal problems, with two marriages ending in divorce.

Hancock appeared on British television for the last time on 14 January 1968, as a guest on *The Eamonn Andrews Show*. Afterwards, he headed for Australia, hopeful that a new opportunity would revive his flagging career. In fact, his face was lined and ill, his comic timing awry and it proved difficult to launch the show.

He had been on the wagon for a few months, believing it was his last chance to revive his career. But he was overwhelmed by melancholy, perhaps because he realised a hoped-for reunion with his first wife was unlikely to take place. He took a deadly combination of pills and vodka and wrote a note saying 'Things just seemed to go wrong too many times.' He didn't live long enough to see himself proclaimed the father of modern comedy.

Mata Hari

(1876–1917)

To me she is a great feminist hero; she is a great survivor, she is an extraordinary chameleon, she reinvents herself at every turn. The men in her life are useless. They let her down, they beat her up, they are unfaithful, they betray her, they drink themselves into a stupor. Despite all that, she makes something incredible of herself. She made her living as a fabulous exotic dancer at a time when that really wasn't acceptable. Otherwise she would have been on the streets. She symbolises to me the treatment of women in an era when women were very much subjugated.

Fiona Bruce (Newsreader)

She was someone who stood out from a very young age. Early on she realised she had sexual cachet and she was going to use that. When she was executed in October 1917, she really did blow kisses. She didn't want a blindfold. That was her final performance. To the end, she understood it was all performance. She wasn't going to be victimised, she wasn't going to be beaten down, she was going to rise above it all – and that is damn hard to do.

Julie Wheelwright (Biographer)

THE MENTION OF her name brings forth images of exotica, seduction and sensual pleasures. But the archetypal femme fatale became a fatality when Mata Hari was shot at dawn for being a spy during the First World War.

There's no question that she was a bold, lone woman who relished her extravagant, exhibitionist lifestyle in an era when modesty and strict economy were the norm. However, there is considerable doubt about whether she knowingly spied to the detriment of a country she loved. Today no one is sure whether there was nailed-on evidence about espionage claims, and the court martial papers will be kept secret until 2017. The question is, did scapegoating prosecutors – determined she was a woman who deserved sound punishment for her lifestyle choices – get two issues mixed up in their minds before sentencing her to death?

Born Margaretha Zelle in Holland, she was described by her school friends as an orchid among the buttercups. Her father was a hatter who had made money speculating in oil shares and he spoiled his lovely daughter in her childhood. But soon her idyllic life was in ruins. Her father went bankrupt, her parents divorced, and then her mother died. At the age of 12, she was effectively orphaned and sent to relatives in Leiden. She seemed destined for life as a nursery nurse but she left college under a cloud after allegations of improper sexual relations with the headmaster. No one knows exactly what went on, but it would be typical, given the era, for a young woman to be dispatched by way of punishment rather than a man.

Still a teenager, she went to Amsterdam and advertised in a lonely hearts column. When she met Rudolph MacLeod, an army man twelve years her senior based in the Dutch East Indies, they fell instantly in love and were married within months. Even now, though, she didn't find the happiness she perhaps felt life promised her. After they moved to the Dutch East Indies, her husband began drinking excessively and visiting prostitutes. Worse still, their son Norman died and daughter Nonnie only just survived following a poisoning incident. After returning to the Netherlands, MacLeod took their daughter out to post a letter one day and they never returned. Margaretha's efforts to win custody of the little girl were frustrated when a private investigator discovered she was entertaining men at her home.

As a divorcee, she travelled to Paris with no more than a few coins in her pocket in 1904, initially working with horses in a circus. Within a year, though, she had changed track and was working as a dancer. Newspaper reports claimed that when she performed the audiences were 'absolutely out of their minds'. The secret of her success lay in a daring plan to exploit human nature. She called herself Mata Hari – meaning 'eye of the day' in Javanese – and developed what at first glance seemed a pseudo-religious/cultural dance. Although she had only a passing knowledge of authentic dance moves from her time in the Dutch East Indies, she had a certain grasp of how to draw in crowds, performing scantily clad and suggestively. (Nonetheless, she wore a body stocking to protect her modesty.) Her dancing earned enough money to fund her opulent lifestyle for some years. It is likely she supplemented her income by taking a number of lovers, treating none of them exclusively. She did, however, fall in love with a younger man who she hoped would share her future, but he failed to stand by her when she was later accused of spying.

As the First World War began, it seemed her luck had run out again. She found herself in Berlin, ready with a new show in a city where the theatres had been shut down. There followed a series of liaisons with both German and French military figures, both of whom apparently employed her as an agent. Unsure of the protocol, she failed to tell the French that she was working as a double agent. Probably her compulsion to spend money encouraged her to take everything offered. The intelligence services were in their infancy, although she did apparently head to Cologne for some training and was given a supply of secret ink by the Germans to impart secrets. Those who knew her believed it unlikely she would ever betray her adopted country, France.

She was finally arrested in Paris in January 1917 and interrogated seventeen times before facing a court martial. Years later, one of her prosecutors said, 'Mata Hari was a common spy; an intelligent woman who danced in a few musicals in Paris and who in some circles unknown to me may have had a certain reputation. She might have been able to make the best of her looks, although I have never been able to understand this attractiveness. I say again she was a plain, common spy.'

His opinion won the day. On 15 October 1917, British journalist Henry Wales watched her execution:

> She did not move a muscle.
>
> The underofficer in charge had moved to a position where from the corners of their eyes [the firing squad] could see him. His sword was extended in the air.
>
> It dropped. The sun – by this time up – flashed on the burnished blade as it described an arc in falling. Simultaneously the sound of the volley rang out. Flame and a tiny puff of greyish smoke issued from the muzzle of each rifle. Automatically the men dropped their arms.
>
> At the report Mata Hari fell. She did not die as actors and moving picture stars would have us believe that people die when they are shot. She did not throw up her hands nor did she plunge straight forward or straight back.
>
> Instead she seemed to collapse. Slowly, inertly, she settled to her knees, her head up always, and without the slightest change of expression on her face. For the fraction of a second it seemed she tottered there, on her knees, gazing directly at those who had taken her life. Then she fell backward, bending at the waist, with her legs doubled up beneath her. She lay prone, motionless, with her face turned towards the sky.

Henry V

(1386–1422)

He was the best possible soldier; wonderful military abilities combined with no stuffiness. [He was] right in there with the lowest soldier sharing their sufferings – pretty unique among big generals, even today.

Sir Ranulph Fiennes (Explorer)

He was an entirely focused person. There were so many warring people in his own kingdom, he got two of these gentry who had been fighting each other for years and said, 'If you haven't made up by the time I finish my tea, I'm going to hang you both.' They were so terrified of him, they did.

Dr Juliet Barker (Biographer)

W ITH PROPAGANDA PROVIDED by luminaries including Shakespeare, Henry V is securely lodged in the collective English consciousness as one of the nation's finest kings. His glowing reputation is at least in part deserved. A major player in the Hundred Years War and a man who led from the front, Henry V was deft – if harsh – both as a military campaigner and a politician. Thanks to him, warring factions in medieval England were united at least for a while. Abroad, he reclaimed Normandy for the English and was poised to claim the French throne before his untimely death from dysentery.

The eloquence bestowed on him by Shakespeare, however, was merely literary licence. Fluent in French and English, he studied Latin and history and owned a well-stocked library, but he was nonetheless known to be a man of few words. When he launched the battle of Agincourt in 1415, he simply said, 'Fellas, let's go.'

As Prince of Wales, Henry became a seasoned soldier at an early age, fighting against Owain Glyndŵr's Welsh forces and cutting his teeth as a commander from his young teens. From this he learned about logistics in battle which later ensured his success.

By the time Henry became king, English society teetered on the brink of civil war and was burdened by issues of faith and favour. Henry had to pull the strands of society together and fast if his monarchy was to survive. His relationship with his father was difficult. Henry was keenly aware that he was born to be the Duke of Lancaster and that he had access to the throne only because his father Henry IV had usurped the rightful king, Richard II.

Perhaps it was guilt about this early injustice that drove Henry to focus on bringing fair dealing to the English people. This made him popular, as did the extraordinary empathy he showed for the fighting men of his armies. Here's one view about him from an enemy, the French ambassador:

Although at first sight he gave the impression of being a proud prince, being of distinguished bearing and good height, he showed the greatest affability which he valued above all other virtues, to all people whatever their rank or status. He always avoided wordy replies and commonplace oaths, going straight to the point and contenting himself by saying 'it is impossible' or 'it is how it should be'.

He thought such simple statements should be considered just as effective as if he had sworn upon Christ and all the saints. He knew how to serve the cause of justice, sparing the lowly and humbling the powerful. He was as amazingly calm in adversity as in prosperity and if anything bad happened to his soldiers he would often repeat to them: 'As you know the fortunes of war vary but if you desire a good outcome you must keep your courage intact.'

As a soldier, Henry prepared meticulously for the battle ahead. He was known to adopt disguises in order to inspect the city he had in his sights or the field designated for army combat. At Agincourt, he knew the land where the French and English were to meet was sodden. With the English outnumbered – perhaps by as many as five to one – he lured the French into the marshy land between the armies through a funnel provided by dense woodland. French noblemen, eager to avenge earlier English victories, spewed forth. As the French advanced under a sky blackened with arrows, the front line – including heavily-armoured barons – buckled and many were drowned in the bog.

It was at Agincourt that one of the major stains against his character was recorded after he ordered that French prisoners should be killed. Although it was contrary to the etiquette of warfare, his men reluctantly complied with his orders. There was, however, cool rationality behind this stark brutality. Having believed the battle was won, Henry became aware not only of a potential resurgence of the French forces ahead of him but also of a possible attack from the rear. If the prisoners among his own forces had seized discarded weapons and created a third diversion then Agincourt might have been lost.

Afterwards, Henry returned in triumph to London. Confident that God was now smiling on the Lancastrian line, he chose to rule with integrity rather than a heavy hand, in a way that no other monarch of the era had done before. He also sensed there were more spoils to be had in France and embarked on another campaign there from 1417. During the siege of Rouen, he once again showed a steely side when he watched French women, children, the elderly and the infirm die in ditches rather than let them pass through his lines.

Nonetheless his success in France was sweeping, topped by his marriage to the Dauphin's daughter, Catherine de Valois. Although it was more a marriage of convenience than one inspired by true love, the couple had a son, also called Henry. He was nine months old when his father died. Henry had not laid eyes on him.

Despite his long absences, Henry remained popular at home. Unusually, his campaigns had the support of the people, although they brought little to the table for ordinary folk. Nobles had one eye on the profits that awaited them across the Channel, where the divided French were poorly led. Nonetheless, England was still only emerging from the longstanding soporific effects of the Dark Ages and was culturally behind its neighbour and rival France at the time. Henry's rule was only one step towards an enlightened age.

Henry V surrounded himself with men he could trust who worked, even after his death, to secure his legacy. His brother John, Duke of Bedford, succeeded him as military commander in France and continued to pile pressure on the Norman frontiers, winning further significant victories in 1423 and 1424.

But there was little anyone could do to preserve the gains made in the face of the ineptitude that his son eventually displayed. Henry VI of England was also Henry II of France, but he did not have the capacity to maintain a dual monarchy. The French finally found a hero to muster the forces in the shape of Joan of Arc. After thirty years, the English kingdom contracted and his legacy was virtually eradicated. Yet somehow the chivalry of Henry V shines through the ages, untarnished.

Henry VII

(1457–1509)

In 1485, Henry Tudor, who is an outsider, picks up the crown from the proverbial thorn bush and puts it on his head, having killed Richard III. No one would have given him any chance of surviving as a king after a long period of civil war. And yet at the end of his reign he becomes the first English king for almost 100 years to pass the monarchy on to his son Henry VIII, and the foundations of the early English modern state are laid by this man who probably knows less about England than any other monarch since William I.

George Osborne (Chancellor of the Exchequer)

He's an outsider in all sorts of senses. His father died before he was born, his family were on the losing side in civil wars during the 1450s so that he grew up as the ward of the opposite side. His teenage years are spent as an exile in the court of the Duke of Brittany who at any point could have decided to sell him back to Edward IV and Yorkists. [Yet] in many ways Henry's reign is the end of something old and the beginning of something new.

Dr Stephen Gunn (Tudor expert)

ENGLISH KINGS OF the second millennia tend to emerge as romantic figures after their images are blown and buffeted down subsequent centuries. Not so King Henry VII, who largely lacked looks, chivalry and charisma. There's just one area in which he shines above others. Henry was probably the best businessman ever to grace the throne and from this there was some feel-good spin-off that improved the lives of his subjects.

Henry was born a Tudor at Pembroke Castle with a distant claim to the English crown. With English politics mired in the War of the Roses between Yorkists and Lancastrians, it was not the most direct descendant of kings who would win the throne but the most powerful.

At first glance, it seemed like incumbent Richard III would be victorious at the Battle of Bosworth in 1485 against the forces rallied by Henry. After all, Henry was coming from France where he had spent many years in exile as something of a political pawn, his family having been beaten by rivals when he was a boy. But (Lancastrian) Henry had found a way to woo his traditional enemies, by promising marriage to Elizabeth of York, thus uniting two warring factions. It was enough bait to bring defectors onside at Bosworth, while others hesitated before belatedly pitching in for King Richard. Finally, Henry won the battle and plucked the crown from the bloody battlefield, as if the outcome reflected the will of God.

At the time, confidence in the monarchy was at a low ebb after a series of poor candidates and public unrest. Henry shared with his people a desire for peace and new opportunities for trade. However, the person who benefited most from this was Henry himself. He doctored the date of his accession to the day before the Battle of Bosworth, thus making everyone who fought for Richard a traitor who was compelled to give up their lands. Through a series of taxes, the king's purse continued to bulge. As England and Europe slowly recovered from the ravages of the Black Death, there were more people at work, creating greater wealth on his behalf. He also sold high offices to bring in cash and hard-line support. Although he began to loosen crown control of the Welsh, Henry kept the English aristocracy to heel.

But it is perhaps for the personal attention that he paid to the accounts that he is best remembered. His supporters call him prudent, his detractors downright mean. From the evidence of his household accounts, it is hard not to see Henry as rapacious, and he certainly used fiscal measures to exert political control. Crown revenue at the beginning of his reign amounted to £30,000 a year. At the end the figure was £100,000, and he died a millionaire.

Nor was there uniform contentment during his reign. Although Richard III left no direct heir, numerous plots against Henry surfaced, relating back to previous royal claims, specifically the child princes Edward and Richard, earlier locked in the Tower of London, who were missing, presumed murdered. Henry survived the challenges of two pretenders who posed as the princes in adulthood: Lambert Simnel, who was ultimately employed in the Royal kitchens, and Perkin Warbeck, who presented a far more serious threat and was finally hanged. Other figures who could have been rallying points for dissenters were executed, including Edward, Earl of Warwick, the nephew of Richard III, who was convicted on flimsy charges. It is believed that guilt about this death caused Henry to beat his breast and lunge for the crucifix as he lay dying.

Henry appears to have been a loyal husband and loving father. Certainly, the death of his eldest son Arthur – who, if he had lived, would have been king rather than second son Henry VIII – caused a tide of grief to engulf the royal household. This great mourning was repeated a few years later upon the death of Henry's wife, Elizabeth.

It is difficult to define just where Henry stands in our history, other than at the cusp of one of its greatest eras and the founder of a notable dynasty. Three opinions are to hand, although all the writers may have their own agenda.

In 1506, papal representative Polydore Vergil was commissioned by Henry to write a history of England. In it, Vergil described Henry like this: 'His body was slender but well built and strong. His eyes were small and blue, his teeth, few, poor and blackish, his hair thin and white, his complexion sallow, his spirit was distinguished, wise and prudent. His mind was brave and resolute and never even at the moment of greatest danger deserted him.'

At Henry's funeral, Bishop John Fisher eulogised: 'His politick wisdom in governance, it was singular; his wit, always quick and ready; his reason pithy and substantial; his mighty power was dread everywhere not only within his realm but without also. His people were to him in as humble subjection as ever they were to king.'

More critical but much later comes the view of Francis Bacon, who in his history of Henry VII, said: 'He was of a high mind, and loved his own will and his own way; as one that revered himself, and would reign indeed. Had he been a private man he would have been termed proud: But in a wise Prince, it was but keeping of distance; which indeed he did towards all; not admitting any near or full approach either to his power or to his secrets. For he was governed by none.'

Perhaps the best way to appreciate him today is to visit Westminster Abbey where a chapel named for him contains the grand marble tombs of him and his wife. It is a masterpiece of a mausoleum that has been termed 'the most beautiful chapel in all Christendom'.

Octavia Hill

(1838–1912)

There is a lot to cherish about Octavia Hill. She was ahead of her time. She was someone who facilitated things to happen and was not necessarily the one at the front of the band. This tiny lady, such an insignificant-looking woman, had the most exquisite pink rose named after her in 1995, the centenary of the National Trust that she founded. I think she'd rather like that.

Baroness Brenda Dean (Life peer and first woman
to lead a manufacturing trade union)

She was a tough little cookie. She was a persistent woman, not afeared of the great and the good of the day. She was always prepared to face up to people and speak out. I don't know if this was because she was the eighth of eleven children or because she was a little person, but she wasn't intimidated even if she did feel strongly some people were heroes of the hour.

Lord Richard Best (Director,
Joseph Rowntree Housing Foundation)

S LIGHT IN STATURE she may have been, but Octavia Hill, doughty Victorian reformer and workaholic, packed quite a punch. She was a teacher, conservationist, social worker, writer, artist, healthcare professional and general mover and shaker. Her legacy includes the National Trust, the concept of social housing and social casework and the army cadet force. She achieved all of this in spite of prolonged bouts of ill health, including mental breakdowns.

Hill was the granddaughter of Dr Thomas Southwood Smith, a prominent campaigner for improved sanitary conditions in British cities. Her parents James and Caroline were also radicals during notoriously conservative times. Hill and her siblings enjoyed a carefree childhood in rural Wisbech, Cambridge, until her father's bankruptcy forced a move first to the outskirts of London and later to the inner city.

As a young woman Hill began charitable works under the umbrella of the Christian Socialists (before the term had an overtly political meaning). With her grandfather, she heard author Charles Kingsley claim at a public meeting that four out of five children's lives could be saved if 'lady visitors' went to their homes to explain how disease and infection were caused and spread. It was the seed that germinated into public health education and Hill was inspired by it. She embraced the work so fully that Florence Nightingale, the founder of modern nursing, sent candidates to Hill for tuition.

Another major influence was John Ruskin, art critic and social thinker, who in 1864 helped finance her first housing project with money left to him by his father. Slums in Marylebone, London, were renovated and rented cheaply to poor families. Initially, she worked for him as an artist making creditable copies of old masters. He, however, correctly predicted that her artistic talents would give way to her charitable inclinations.

Through Ruskin and others she began networking to find sufficient funds for her numerous projects. It was the dawning of the philanthropic age and, without enormous means at her disposal, Hill was determined to make the most of other people's benevolence. There followed numerous housing projects aiming to eradicate diabolical housing throughout London, often allowing for small parks next to new homes. She dispatched middle-class women tutored in basic social care to collect rents and give advice to ill-educated residents, like early social workers. Hill was also among the first to realise that a 'green belt' was needed to stop all the capital's land being turned over to industry and housing.

She recognised the value of exercise and fresh air, and regularly led children from London tenements on lengthy walks into the countryside, on outings she considered vital for their bodies and souls. She also worked as a teacher in a London school founded by her sisters and herself in their twenties. However, from the evidence of a former pupil, it is by no means certain that Hill excelled in this area:

> Miss Octavia took us in drawing and accounts. During term time we had sixpence a week pocket money. We had to keep account of it and Miss Octavia scrutinised it. She was strict over it. And I believe I was a bit afraid of her. She was inclined to be stern and a bit uncompromising and sometimes a bit sarcastic. Miss Miranda, her sister, was so gentle and understanding and always ready to help.

A seventeenth-century garden in Deptford, London, was offered to Hill to maintain on behalf of the nation in 1884. What if she had the opportunity to preserve garden, coast, countryside and even homes 'for ever, for everyone'? With such a scheme, people would enjoy outside 'sitting rooms' and the 'healthy gift of air and the joy of plants and flowers'. Her vision was unshakeable, but she had considerable cajoling and bullying to carry out before it became a reality.

As early as 1902, an appeal to purchase Brandelhow overlooking Derwentwater in the Lake District got under way, winning support across the board, from the Royal family at one end of the scale and a steel worker from Sheffield who contributed sixpence at the other. He wrote: 'All my life I have longed to see the Lakes. I shall never see them now, but I should like to help keep them for others.' Brandelhow was finally purchased in 1904, and Hill described it to a meeting in Oxford: 'It comprises about a mile of the lakeshore. It commands views of Skiddaw in one direction and Borrowdale in the other. From its slope you can see the whole space of the lake, set with its islands. It has a crag and a meadow and a wood. On it the sun shines, over it the wind blows. It will be preserved in its present loveliness and it belongs to you all, to every landless man, woman and child in England.'

The eventual result of all this activity was the launch of the National Trust in 1907, the tangible result of Hill working in collaboration with Sir Robert Hunter and Canon Hardwicke Rawnsley. If this wasn't enough, she was still working on other projects. In 1889, Hill established the first Cadet Battalion in London, confident military discipline would give some disconsolate youth a new direction.

Although she did much to enhance women's lives, she was more activist than feminist. Her dearly held and desperately uncompromising views were a source of frustration for some. She sought to strengthen communities and supported voluntary work, yet she was vehemently opposed to women getting the vote or to government welfare, including the idea of pensions for older people. Although she now seems like an anachronism, her views were commonly held at the time. Throughout her life, she stressed the importance of encouraging self-reliance rather than a culture of dependency. Said one biographer:

> Octavia Hill's perspective on the role of women is a confusing one. She fought hard for women's rights in education and property ownership and encouraged women she knew to take on public office where they could. Her own public achievements

were hardly negligible yet she was adamantly opposed to suffrage for women and envisaged the working class woman staying at home and forming the stable world from which children would take their standards. Because of the contradictions in Octavia's character she's been consistently misunderstood.

William Hogarth

(1697–1764)

Hogarth has always been a hero of mine. He was fantastically funny and a brilliant artist. He is extraordinarily talented but also has a life that is moral and committed in ways that make him better than the average. His life always makes me feel rather inadequate, but maybe that's what great lives should do. Not only did he do the satire better than anybody for the next 250 years, but I think he had a very commendable life. The combination is very impressive.

Ian Hislop (Satirist)

He is above all the artist of London, and London is the capital city of what's about to become the most powerful empire the world has ever seen. It is a city alive with activity; there's huge immigration so the population is going up, there's the rise of the mercantile classes, there's new money, and this is a city that's undergoing a media revolution. Everybody's reading, looking, thinking, talking, and Hogarth is the artist who has plugged in to that.

Andrew Graham-Dixon (Art Critic)

THROUGH ARTIST WILLIAM Hogarth's eyes, we see the best of times and the worst of times in England during the first half of the eighteenth century. He was at the same time kindly and cleverly cruel, radical and downright rude. As a businessman, he was canny; as an observer, he was frequently callous. But students of his work are left under no illusions: life in London, across the spectrum of society, could be tough.

If Hogarth had special empathy for the capital's poor and destitute, it was perhaps because his father Richard spent five years in debtors' prison following a failed business venture. There are no records of Hogarth speaking about the hardships this put his family under. But his work frequently laments the lack of a safety net in society that would save people from the perils of destitution.

His father's imprisonment made Hogarth the head of his household at the age of about 12. Apparently in response, he became an apprentice to a silver engraver, William Gamble, for a six-year span and was determined to complete the course. His early talent was refined during this time. It also instilled in him a respect for industriousness.

Before he was 20, he was proficient at etching, painting and drawing. Unlike other artists of the era, he didn't stick to portrait painting, although he completed some notable examples. Instead, he chose to comment on society through action-packed pictures or sequences that told a contemporary tale.

While he was still young, his work became popular and his engravings were quickly pirated by fast-thinking businessmen of the day. In response, Hogarth pioneered the first copyright legislation, ultimately brought through Parliament in 1735. The Hogarth Act, as it was known, helped to protect his income. His work remained widely seen, however, as it not only appeared in newspapers but was also posted up in coffee houses and inns.

The recurrent themes of his moralising art would not be out of place in today's art world – the city, sexuality, social integration, crime, corruption, charity and patriotism. Yet his work often bears hallmarks that link it to the times in which he lived.

At the time, stern punishment was meted out thanks to the 'Bloody Code', with more than 200 offences punishable by the death penalty. Convicted villains who were hanged risked having their corpses sliced up by the anatomists, a matter for considerable shame at the time. Meanwhile, there loomed the horrors of debtor's prison or Bedlam – the Bethlem Royal Hospital for psychiatric cases in London, where tourists could pay a small sum to witness the 'lunatic' inmates. There is also evidence in his pictures of a long-running antipathy towards the French, in a century where conflicts between France and England were commonplace. But it is British people – specifically Londoners – who are Hogarth's favourite subjects.

In *A Rake's Progress*, first seen in 1733, Hogarth devotes eight canvases to the decline and fall of Tom Rakewell, who is entrapped by the vices of gambling and prostitution after visiting the capital. Tom ends up in Bedlam. *A Harlot's Progress* comprises six scenes charting the degeneration of Moll Hackabout from fresh-faced country girl to mistress, prostitute, jailbird and finally corpse. All the pictures are rich with detail.

Among the most famous of his works is *Gin Lane*, inspired by the story of a French immigrant who strangled her 2-year-old daughter in order to sell the toddler's clothes so she could buy her next drink. In Hogarth's picture, a drunken mother who drops her baby down a stairwell is the central figure, but there's much more to it than a single depiction. A carpenter is hawking his saw for a glass of gin. The pawnbroker is doing a roaring trade. It is dark rather than funny, a dire warning about alcoholism, aimed at working people. It was akin to propaganda and helped to persuade Parliament about the merits of the Gin Act 1751, restricting spirit consumption through licensing.

But his barbs are not reserved for the lower classes alone. In a series of sketches called *Marriage à-la-mode*, completed in 1745, Hogarth mocks the aristocrat father fallen on hard times who marries off his foppish son to the daughter of a rich merchant. Ultimately, she falls for the lawyer involved in drawing up the marriage agreement, the lawyer kills the son and is duly hanged for murder. The messages are clear: marry for love not money, and that you can't put a price on honour.

Hogarth did marry for love, eloping with Jane Thornhill, the daughter of an eminent painter. The pair did not have children and, perhaps because of it, became closely associated with London's Foundling Hospital, which opened in Bloomsbury in 1745. As prosperity grew, so did the opportunities for early philanthropists like Hogarth and his colleague, retired sea captain Thomas Coram. A founding governor of the hospital, Hogarth fostered some of the unwanted babies and children deposited there. He also painted a portrait of Coram, the driving force behind the project, to adorn the hospital wall. Coram was painted without a wig in a pastiche of the Baroque style which was popular at the time.

While he was swift to lampoon pretension, Hogarth was himself somewhat thin-skinned about criticism and became embroiled in some heated but rather futile disputes later in life.

He lived for years in Chiswick, at the time a village on the outskirts of London, and he was buried there in St Nicholas' Churchyard. Actor and friend David Garrick wrote his epitaph:

Farewell great painter of mankind
Who reached the noblest point of art.
Whose pictured morals charmed the mind
And through the eye correct the heart
If genius fire thee reader stay
If nature moved thee drop a tear
If neither touched thee turn away
For Hogarth's honoured dust lies here.

Harry Houdini

(1874–1926)

This is a man who comes from nowhere. He suddenly realises that to escape from stuff has more appeal than card flinging and builds that into a career that has never been equalled.

Paul Daniels (Magician and presenter)

[Houdini] felt he had to become expert at all facets of his field to be respected. That was what he was really searching for, great respect.

William Kalush (Magician and co-author of
The Secret Life of Houdini)

MAGICIAN, ESCAPOLOGIST AND the scourge of spiritualists who claimed contact with the dead, Houdini was a small man with a mighty reputation. Even today there is no one who is remembered so well for his dumbfounding stage skills. He was a winning blend of charisma, technical skills, endurance, physical strength and prowess at workaday magic. He perpetually challenged audiences to defeat him, imploring them to secure his bindings with their own padlocks. This inevitably drew in crowds who were awed and soon embraced him as 'the king of handcuffs'.

Houdini was born Erik Weisz in Budapest in 1874. Four years later, he and his family moved to America where his name was changed at immigration to Ehrich Weiss and his father became the rabbi of Appleton, Wisconsin. Although the young Ehrich – also known as Harry – lacked a formal education, he was bright enough to capitalise on the expanding demand for entertainment at the time. Having spent hours in rehearsal, he became a magician using card tricks and sleight of hand to thrill carnival audiences before he graduated to escapology. He was still an unknown when he met and married Beatrice Rahner, known as Bess, who became his lifelong assistant. To make a success of his career, he knew he needed publicity in every town and city he visited. So he normally performed at least one stunt in each venue involving escape from the town jail and its obliging sheriff, police officers or wardens.

Houdini's unusual career choice took a great toll on his body. This was one of the reasons he tried to break into film from 1906 when it was still cutting-edge technology. On film, he knew, he could perform an escape just once and it would still be seen by thousands of people. In fact his time in the film industry was not the blistering success he had hoped for, but a collection of footage illustrating some of his vintage tricks still exists.

There were low points in his career, including when he rubbished the reputation of the pioneering French magician Jean Eugène Robert-Houdin in print. Paradoxically, this was a man he had once respected so much that he took his name and added an 'i'. Unattractively, Houdini later wanted to prove himself the master of Houdin, rather than the acolyte.

And there were high points, including the success of several seemingly impossible feats like the Milk Can escape, when he was locked into a water-filled churn which was itself padlocked into a crate, before he made his escape. When this was widely copied, he replaced it in his repertoire with the Chinese Water Torture Cell. This time he was suspended by the ankles and lowered into a box filled with water, his method of escape screened from the audience by a curtain. In addition he regularly escaped from being bound in chains and put into a box that was weighted with lead and cast overboard in a river. Escaping from a straitjacket at a time when they were regularly used in hospitals, while suspended from a crane, was another speciality. Although the trick seemed impossible, he never implied a supernatural element to it. After triumphing at home and then abroad he is alleged to have worked as a spy although, if true, it was on a relatively small scale.

But perhaps Houdini's greatest legacy was the unmasking of unscrupulous spiritualists who faked contact with the dead. He did so at a time when ordinary people were investing money and immense emotion into the belief that the dead would communicate, not least because of the escalating number of casualties in the First World War. He didn't hate the concept of life after death or the comfort it could bring to the living. In a quest to discover the truth about life's eternal mystery, he made several pacts with family members, urging them to contact him from beyond the grave if they could. But he loathed the fraudulence that accompanied mediums of the era.

His personal life was distinguished by a closeness to his mother Cecilia. As his father lay dying, Houdini promised to take care of the family as a whole and his mother specifically. It was after her death, when a medium allegedly relayed a message that Houdini knew his devoutly Jewish mother would never have uttered, that his enmity to spiritualism intensified.

It is possible that his campaign ultimately cost him his life. Houdini died of peritonitis on 31 October 1926. The story usually associated with his death is that students in Canada who saw him after a show seized upon a challenge he regularly issued, that he could withstand a blow anywhere on his upper body. The students threw punches before he had tensed the muscles to provide protection. He was already complaining of stomach pains, probably associated with untreated appendicitis. Recent research, albeit ambiguous, has pointed to evidence that the spiritualists' lobby claimed a measure of credit for his death. There's also speculation that he had discovered a sinister secret of one of his chief targets, Margery 'the Medium' Crandon, involving the disappearance of adopted boys.

There seemed synchronicity in the fact that Houdini died on Halloween. To exploit this unearthly link, his widow Bess held a séance every year for a decade after his death, hoping that he might resolve the issues that so perplexed him in life. When there was no sign sent from beyond the grave by the husband she adored, she abandoned the project, adroitly observing that ten years was long enough to wait for any man.

Alfred Edward Housman

(1859–1936)

A. E. Housman has been my hero ever since I was 17, when the headmaster came into the school room and read to us A Shropshire Lad *poem 62. For some reason I was caught. I had always loved the idea of the scholar poet. I understood what he was talking about, a certain clarity and succinctness. At that age life sometimes seems full of disappointments. From that point onwards the old boy never let me down. He's not the greatest poet in the English language, I hasten to say, but for me he has brought me more delight than all the others.*

Colin Dexter (Novelist)

His work is so allusive, there are so many other voices clamouring to get out of his poems. Sometimes it is as if the only kind of friendship he could have was with the dead. He is like a shy man at a party. He surrounds himself with so many other people and hopes he is going to blend in with the background. His poems work like those blue remembered hills [he writes about]. They seem terribly simple, they seem almost graspable, but they keep slipping out of your reach. The closer you think you are getting to them, the simpler they seem, the more they seem to have these lurking depths, these depths of despair.

Dr Robert Douglas Fairhurst (Professor of Literature)

'*A* ND I WILL *friend you if I may, in the dark and cloudy day.*'

A few spare words that speak of loyalty and longing, hope and despair, of soul mate and soul searching. It was the pain of unrequited love that inspired poetry like this from A. E. Housman. Not for the first time in the lyrically inclined down the ages, the creative juices flowed in abundance with every fracture line of the heart.

For Housman, though, the outlook was particularly bleak. The object of his passion was a fellow student at Oxford who wanted nothing more than platonic friendship. Moreover, as if to sharpen the exquisite pain, Housman shared rooms with him not only at Oxford but also later when they both landed jobs in the same place in London. While Moses Jackson, the man of his dreams, was a scientist and an athlete, Housman was bookish and somewhat prissy. Ultimately, Jackson went on to live thousands of miles away with a wife and children, and Housman retired to the dusty upper shelves of academia, nursing his wounded feelings. But in this five-year friendship Housman invested a lifetime of love, and the anguish of sorrow and loss became the fuel that fired his writing.

Housman's mother died when he was 12, although his solicitor father married again. The early loss of his mother made Housman sceptical about faith, but he retained an interest in the rituals of religion. He became what he termed 'a high church atheist'. A talented scholar, he took what's now known as Classics at Oxford University. Having gained distinctions in his first year, he ultimately flunked the degree for reasons that have never been fully illuminated. He then secured a job in the patent office in London, alongside Moses Jackson, and they both shared lodgings with Jackson's brother. It is known that they quarrelled at one stage, but they seem to have been reconciled before Jackson's departure for a job in India in 1887. Housman was not, however, invited – or even told about – Jackson's wedding two years later.

Determined to vindicate himself following his lack of degree, Housman devoted his free time to studying classical texts. After a decade he showed himself sufficiently accomplished to win the post of Professor of Latin at University College, London, in an extraordinary vault into university life.

In 1895, the year that public attitudes towards homosexuality hardened in the wake of the Oscar Wilde trials and also that Jackson left England, Housman wrote his first and perhaps his best-received poetry cycle, *A Shropshire Lad*. Its tone is at best disappointed, at worst desolate. Some of it is inaccurate, Housman having been born in Worcestershire. The 'blue remembered hills' of Shropshire that he knew in childhood were always viewed at a distance and became a fantasy landscape for him. With ample resources at his disposal he drew upon numerous scholarly references. Beyond the nod to English nature there's a sense of foreboding that strikes deep into the psyche.

Initially Housman published *A Shropshire Lad* at his own expense after it was turned down by publishers. However, it soon won long-term popularity with the public and it was put to music by composers who seized on the words as lyrics. Later many men took it into the trenches with them.

In 1911, Housman moved to Cambridge to become the Kennedy Professor of Latin at Trinity College, Cambridge where he kept fixed habits and unexciting routines. He immersed himself in ancient texts, setting rigorously high standards in translation and lambasting those who in his view failed to observe the same. For a considerable period, poetry was his second priority behind this academic challenge. He was not warmly remembered, being curt with students and abrasive with fellow scholars. Yet he was known to have possessed a sense of humour which occasionally revealed itself.

It was the more dramatic and relevant poetry of the First World War that ultimately put Housman's verse in the shade. Criticism that it now seemed stale and mannered must have stung the hard-working Housman. Only when he heard Jackson was dying with stomach cancer did he gather together a collection of work, which he called *Last Poems*, especially for his friend. Jackson wrote back in pencil with a shaky hand. Meticulously, Housman went over the outlines in ink in order that the words would endure for longer. After Jackson's death, Housman wrote to a mutual friend: 'Jackson died peacefully on Sunday night in hospital at Vancouver, where he had gone to be treated for anaemia, with which he had been ailing for some years. I had a letter from him on New Year's Day, which he ended by saying "goodbye". Now I can die myself: I could not have borne to leave him behind me in a world where anything might happen to him.'

While it must have been obvious to Jackson, Housman kept his homosexuality veiled, although he is known to have paid for rent boys and pornography in Paris. By contrast he felt life was fleeting and it was important to live for the moment and consequently indulged in aircraft travel as often as possible.

After his death, Housman's brother Laurence collected together more poems and a revealing essay that he'd written that frankly outlines the enduring love for Jackson that he knew would never be reciprocated.

M. R. James

(1862–1936)

He is one of my all-time heroes, one of the greatest writers of the supernatural that's ever lived. He's affected a whole generation of horror and supernatural writers. Every horror writer is trying to capture the essence that M. R. James invented of creeping, psychological, unseen horrible things that are unspoken, unknowable and they enter the psyche, rather than giving somebody a fright. Now if one can even do a fraction of that in the way that James did it you would be a genius.

Muriel Grey (Writer and broadcaster)

He was an astonishing scholar. He catalogued every single collection of medieval manuscripts in Cambridge, which is an astonishing feat but he had a cataloguer's mind. He was great at lists and physically describing things. He is the best writer of ghost stories in the language and that's quite a claim because there's an awful lot of rivals.

Sir Christopher Frayling (Professor)

A S CHRISTMAS DAY beckoned, students and staff at a Cambridge college clustered in the spare light of a single, flickering candle to hear an accomplished academic spinning his latest ghost story. Yelps of nervous laughter only added to the tension as shadows in the common room lengthened. The collection of Edwardian spine-chillers spawned by this tradition is now regarded as the foremost of the genre. Storyteller Montague Rhodes James is thought a master of the ghost story craft.

It wasn't his day job. James was a professor and later a provost who specialised in divinity, particularly the apocrypha, early Christian writings that fall outside the confines of the Protestant Bible. As a Christian fundamentalist who kept his emotions very much in check, he was perhaps one of the most unlikely candidates for delving into the unknown. But from childhood his fertile mind tuned into the dark possibilities of the paranormal. By giving life to his inner dread he became an icon for generations of ghost and horror stories. According to writer H. P. Lovecraft, James was 'gifted with an almost diabolic power of calling horror by gentle steps from the midst of prosaic daily life'.

As a child in a Suffolk rectory, James was a prodigious reader who also suffered from nightmares. Perhaps surprisingly, he showed an interest in grisly martyrdoms of ancient times. In 1931, he clearly recalled to the *Evening Standard* how he first became interested in ghosts: 'In my childhood I chanced to see a toy Punch and Judy set, with figures cut out in cardboard. One of these was The Ghost. It was a tall figure habited in white with an unnaturally long and narrow head, also surrounded in white, and a dismal visage. Upon this my conceptions of a ghost were based, and for years it permeated my dreams.'

As a schoolboy at Eton, he was remembered as 'the learned boy'. Although he found life less compelling at Cambridge he was nonetheless well suited to the bookish existence of a don: 'It is a constant puzzle – if not puzzle, surprise – to me that I have never shared the ambitions or speculations about a career which ordinary people have and ought to have; choice of profession, home of one's own and all such. I believe there never was a time when I have had more of a programme than to find out all I could about various matters and to make friends. Positions and objectives have been the same. It has not been the case of amiable modesty but something more like indolence or, if a long word is better, opportunism.'

Through his studies, he picked up remarkable details about folklore, legend, rituals and traditions which he incorporated into his stories, lending to them the atmosphere of a non-fiction essay rather than a made-up tale. Although characterisation is generally recognised as his weak spot, the main protagonist was generally an antiquarian or academic seemingly in a similar mould to himself. He was clear about the necessary ingredients for a successful ghost story: 'The ghosts should be malevolent or odious. Amiable and helpful apparitions are all very well in fairy tales or in local legends but I have no use for them in a fictitious ghost story.' He also specialised in bringing horror forth from the mundane at a measured pace: 'Let us then be introduced to the actors in a placid way. Let us see them going about their ordinary business undisturbed by forebodings, pleased with their surroundings and into this calm environment let the ominous thing put out its head, unobtrusively at first and then more insistently until it holds the stage.'

He did not embrace the explicitness of sex and violence that came to the fore after *Dracula* was published in 1897. His brand of spectre, ranging from the ominous to the grotesque, came in from the peripheral vision in stories that were filled with suspense until the unspeakable being manifested itself, with dire consequences ensuing. 'If any of [the stories] succeeded in causing their readers to feel pleasantly uncomfortable when walking along a solitary road at nightfall, or sitting over a dying fire in the small hours, my purpose in writing them will have been attained.'

It was all the more curious that James was so successful on paper, given that he was notoriously poor at expressing emotions face to face. A hard worker and a conservative, he was in many ways a remnant from Victorian times, who disliked intellectual debate and the scientific enquiry which was at the time threatening the foundations of Christianity. He betrayed no feeling for the working classes, was opposed to women studying for degrees and inhabited an entirely male world, save for his attachment to the widow and daughter of a close friend. There's no evidence he was a homosexual, but he was almost certainly celibate.

In 1930, he received the Order of Merit, six years before his death, while he was provost at Eton. He bequeathed to the literary world some cult classics, bearing a similar style to the following excerpt from 'Oh, Whistle and I'll Come to You, My Lad':

> One last look behind, to measure the distance he had made since leaving the ruined Templar's church, showed him a prospect of company on his walk, in the shape of a rather indistinct personage, who seemed to be making great efforts to catch up with him, but made little, if any, progress. I mean that there was an appearance of running about his movements, but that the distance between him and Parkins did not seem to materially lessen. So, at least, Parkins thought, and decided that he almost certainly did not know him, and that it would be absurd to wait until he came up. For all that, company, he began to think, would really be welcome on that lonely shore, if only you could choose your companion.
>
> In his unenlightened days he'd read of meetings in such places that even now would hardly bear thinking of.

Roy Jenkins

(1920–2003)

He was clever, funny, wise. He is often thought of as being stiff and rather pompous, but he wasn't at all. In some ways he was curiously insecure. Politics was his destiny and in his blood. He was the man who created the 1960s revolution, he really changed the culture and the climate of the times.

Polly Toynbee (Journalist)

When I first met him, he was rather slim and dashing. He broadened out when time went on, and certainly by the time he got back from Brussels he was the corpulent Roy that one saw later. He was a man of great charm and warmth and everybody felt this. He was unique in having this combination of talents, of being someone who had a major impact on events.

Lord Taverne (Former junior minister)

The great advantage of our partnership was that he was much older, he had all that experience under his belt which I didn't have. Therefore I felt we were a good partnership. He was a great leader of the SDP [but] in the House of Commons he somehow faltered. He lost his nerve, he didn't like it. It was a very uncomfortable place for him to be after having so many successes at the dispatch box.

Lord Steel (Former leader, Liberal Party)

A LTHOUGH ROY JENKINS was never Prime Minister, he was the instigator of radical policies that changed the face of British society in the 1960s. As Home Secretary, Jenkins created a shopping list that included reforms to the laws governing abortion and homosexuality, a scrapping of censorship in theatre, the introduction of suspended sentences and a ban on the use of the birch in jail.

Right-wing politicians lambasted him for being the architect of the permissive society, while the left felt he was a snob who betrayed his working-class roots. Stranded in the wilderness of the political centre ground, he eventually helped form a new party, although his lofty ambitions to be the country's leader were thwarted by in-fighting.

Jenkins was born in the mining valleys of South Wales. His father Arthur was a mining agent who went to Oxford University and became a Labour MP. Enmeshed in politics from childhood, he saw his father jailed for rabblerousing during the 1926 General Strike. Jenkins later insisted his father had been trying to quieten the mob rather than incite it, and the incident was a cause of shame for his magistrate mother Hattie.

Although the Second World War beckoned, Jenkins completed three years at Oxford himself before joining the army. He was a captain in the Royal Artillery and then a code-breaker at Bletchley Park, among many credited with cracking the German ciphers.

In peacetime, his aims to enter Parliament were frustrated, first in 1945 when he failed to be elected in the Solihull constituency, and again the following year when he wasn't selected for the Pontypool seat vacant following the death of his father. But in 1950, when Labour was elected with a five-seat majority, Jenkins won the newly created seat of Birmingham Stechford. He remained the area's MP for twenty-six years. He was a close ally of Labour leader Hugh Gaitskell, although the pair had political differences, chiefly over Europe. Jenkins was a firm believer in the wisdom of a European collective, while Gaitskell, among many in the Labour movement at the time, was firmly against it.

When Harold Wilson became Prime Minister in 1964, Jenkins began to flex his political muscle. He first accepted a role linked to aviation and then turned down a job in education to wait for the big prize, the post of Home Secretary, which was his by Christmas 1965. With firm ideas about the liberal reforms needed in Britain, he set about changing the nation's social agenda. Thanks to him, Britain got its first race relations board. For the first time, homosexual acts between consenting adults in private became lawful, and women who wanted abortions for medical reasons were given legal rights. If he didn't draw up the necessary bills himself, Jenkins supported other like-minded politicians in doing so. After two years as Home Secretary, he was Chancellor of the Exchequer, inheriting a fragile economy and gaining few friends with his attempts to shore up the pound.

His devotion to a united Europe left him at odds with many prominent Labour politicians. As the official party line swung away from Europe in 1972, Jenkins resigned from his party post as deputy leader and so diminished his chances of ever leading the party. A successful cross-party campaign ahead of a national referendum in 1975 kept Britain in the Common Market, as it was then known. Jenkins orchestrated the 'yes' to Europe contingent, alongside former Conservative leader Edward Heath and Liberal chief whip David Steel. Consequently, Jenkins was offered the job as President of the European Commission.

His growing taste for a new politics was finally revealed in 1979 when he was offered the chance to deliver the annual Dimbleby Lecture on the BBC. He used the prestigious platform to call for a new party that would cover the centre ground in a political landscape which had Margaret Thatcher leading the country on the right and Labour lunging to the left. From the ensuing flurry of political activity there emerged a 'gang of four' – Roy Jenkins, David Owen, Shirley Williams and Bill Rodgers – who created the new Social Democratic Party in 1981. Its name was chosen to reflect a successful brand of European politics.

Moderates from all sides were drawn to the cause, and Roy Jenkins resumed his Parliamentary career in 1982 when he was elected MP for Hillhead in Glasgow. The outcome of the by-election had been far from certain. With only days to go before the poll, Jenkins set about a personal initiative to reach the voters. He kept an automatic counter in his pocket and clicked it every time he shook someone's hand. At the end of the campaign, he discovered he had met over half of the adult population of Hillhead.

Despite enormous early promise, however, the party began to founder. Personally, Jenkins found life at the dispatch box more trying than previously after being subject to poisonous barracking from former allies. There was also rivalry between himself and David Owen for control of the party. During the 1983 election there was uncertainty among members of the new party, although a belated alliance with the Liberal Party put them within two per cent of Labour's share of the vote. But the vote did not translate into Parliamentary seats, and enough of the country was besotted with Margaret Thatcher following her strong leadership during the Falklands crisis the previous year to re-elect her with an increased majority.

A relatively poor showing in the 1987 election – in which Jenkins lost his Hillhead seat – led to calls for a merger between the Liberals and the Social Democrat Party. Supported by Jenkins and David Steel, this became a reality, but the move fractured the middle ground which the creation of the SDP had been supposed to unite.

Jenkins was now dogged by ill health, but that did not stop him becoming Chancellor of Oxford University, and he continued a flourishing sideline as a respected author. Nor was his contribution to politics finished. He was for a while a valued adviser to Tony Blair when the latter was reorganising Labour and running the country, although there were policy areas on which neither could agree. It remains impossible to say whether his defection from Labour ultimately caused the party to unite.

Samuel Johnson

(1709–1784)

[Johnson is] a mixture of transparent genius and this extraordinary emotional fragility and originality. He gets to the heart of human nature and he mobilises language in a very special and powerful way. He tried to defeat people in conversation. He is remembered for the way he puts his finger on human emotions.

Boris Johnson (Journalist and politician)

He took the part of poor people, of mad people, of people on the edges of society. He gave lots of money to the poor. He had a deeply humane and humanitarian spirit. He hated people who loosely talked flim-flam, people who were hypocrites.

Peter Martin (Biographer)

'*D*ICTIONARIES ARE LIKE *watches. The worst is better than none,
and the best cannot be expected to go quite true.*'

Samuel Johnson knew he was up against it when he was asked to write a
dictionary of the English language. Quill in hand, he diligently wrote 42,773
entries in a monumental enterprise that took nine years to complete. Often
definitions were accompanied by quotations from poets and playwrights.
It is the work for which he is best remembered but perhaps not the one he
most enjoyed. During the writing of it, he was beset by depression, made
worse by anxiety about finances.

Johnson was already established as a writer, poet, essayist and ready wit
when he was commissioned to write a dictionary by a collection of publishers
in 1746. His was not the first English dictionary, but it was certainly the
best by a considerable margin. (The esteemed *Oxford English Dictionary*
did not appear until 1928.) It was a belated addition to British shelves in
many ways as the Italians and the French had been enjoying the advantages
of a national dictionary for many decades. And theirs took much longer to
compile as Johnson worked fast and furious to complete his tome.

Although he often cursed himself for being idle rather than industrious,
the endeavour reveals extraordinary application, drawn as it was from
copious reference books and written up by himself and six clerks.
Johnson was one of the few men in London who were intellectually able
to undertake such a task at the time. It didn't earn him much money, but
there was a prize at the end which interested him far more, a Master's
Degree from Oxford University in recognition of this mighty act of
scholarship.

The mind of a genius was masked with unprepossessing looks, as one
contemporary pen portrait by his friend Fanny Burney reveals: 'He is indeed
very ill favoured. He is tall and stout but stoops terribly. He is almost bent
double. His mouth is almost continually opening and shutting as if he was
chewing. He has a strange method of frequently twirling his fingers and

twisting his hands. His body is in continual agitation, see-sawing up and down. His feet are never a moment quiet. And in short his whole person is in perpetual motion.'

From the description of his compulsive twitching it seems Johnson suffered from Tourette's Syndrome, then unknown in medical circles. He was also scarred by scrofula, which he suffered as an infant after being wet-nursed by a nanny with tuberculosis. He was blind in one eye and partially deaf, a sickly child who grew into a colossally sized man.

He was born in Lichfield, Staffordshire, where his father owned a bookshop. Having proved himself a good scholar at a local school, he went to Oxford University after his mother inherited a legacy of £40. But when his father's business went to the wall, he was compelled to give up university life, to his rage and frustration. When a fellow undergraduate left a pair of shoes to replace Johnson's very worn pair, he launched them in fury at the unfortunate student. It is why the degree given for the dictionary meant so much.

For a while he worked as a teacher in Lichfield, although he was not very successful. He managed to secure some short-term writing jobs and was married, aged 25, to widow Elizabeth Porter, a woman twenty-five years his senior.

Then he decided to make his way to London with former pupil David Garrick – destined to become one of the leading actors of the era – where Johnson made a living as a hack working in Grub Street, a poor thoroughfare in the city where would-be writers mustered. Johnson eventually defined Grub Street like this: 'originally the name of a street ... much inhabited by writers of small histories, dictionaries, and temporary poems, whence any mean production is called grubstreet.'

Soon he was joined by his wife, but guilt about living off her money led him to haunt the streets of London, often in the company of poet Richard Savage. His wife sickened in London and died in 1752 while he was still part way through writing the dictionary. He was torn apart with grief, fearing he had mistreated Elizabeth, who he called Tetty, while she was alive. Her death further slowed the progress of the masterpiece.

Johnson is considered a Tory by inclination, but the term doesn't have the same connotations as it does today. He was certainly conspicuously kind-hearted, as the profile of his household reveals. Among the destitute who found a home with Johnson was Mrs Anna Williams, a blind poet who became his housekeeper. A cataract operation that he paid for failed to restore her sight. She lived constantly at odds with Mrs Desmoulins, the widowed daughter of Johnson's godfather. And neither were partial to Robert Levet, a quack doctor who Johnson nonetheless rated highly as a house guest. The most enduring addition to the household was Francis Barber, a Jamaican lad who became Johnson's manservant. Eventually Barber's wife and children lived in the Johnson household too. Johnson loathed slavery and railed against it publicly at any opportunity. Despite this army of household helpers, when his cat Hodges was hungry Johnson would often take to the streets to buy the fortunate feline oysters.

In 1765 he moved out of his house and into the home of Henry and Hester Thrale, who cared for him during a fit of mental illness. He would return to his London house at weekends to ensure everyone was well. The 'black dog' of what was then called 'constitutional melancholy' was caused at least in part by guilt for imagined slights or failings. One day in his late middle years, he remembered that many years before he had failed to do an errand for his father in Uttoxeter. Although it was years after the death of his father, he set off to the market town to stand bareheaded in the rain by way of atonement.

He was a friend to many eminent London residents including artists and writers, most significantly perhaps bon viveur James Boswell. It was Boswell who wrote Johnson's biography, committing conversations the pair had enjoyed to print. It is through Boswell's eyes that Johnson is often best remembered.

Three weeks before he died, Johnson began destroying his papers, feeding a fire all day every day for a week. Still his conscience could not be calmed with recollections of his kindnesses. When it came, his death was violent with misgivings – as a lifelong Anglican, he greatly feared going to Hell.

It is, though, for his contribution to the English language that Johnson is remembered, which far outweighs any perceived misdemeanours during his colourful life.

Robert Kennedy

(1925–1968)

After the tragedy of his brother's death, he completely took himself apart and rebuilt himself and you saw someone coming to understand the grinding nature of poverty and destitution. Had he become President, he might have changed that. There was huge potential and it was cut down that day [of his assassination] in California. I don't think any of us believed we were going to see so many decades of the uninspiring leadership that followed.

Ken Livingstone (Politician)

His father called him the runt of the family, and that was a lucky thing to be in the Kennedy family. Older ones were expected to be great from the word go. They had to be superstars right away and it was a terrible burden on them, whereas Bobby was allowed to be a child. That allowed him to feel a sense of empathy for the less well off, he could sympathise with those who had been left behind. For many years that quality was buried in him. After his brother was killed, he was able to get in touch with those feelings of vulnerability and compassion.

Evan Thomas (Biographer)

F ROM RUTHLESS RIGHT-WINGER to outspoken civil rights activist, Bobby Kennedy went on a political journey that seemed destined to end at the White House. After shedding youthful prejudices, Kennedy offered hope of a brighter future to the poor, to a downtrodden black population and to soldiers being dispatched to the killing fields of Vietnam.

The collective dreams of a significant proportion of the people of America – and the world – ended abruptly when three bullets ripped into him after he secured California's Democratic presidential nomination, in an almost eerie echo of what happened to his older brother, President John F. Kennedy, who had been shot dead five years previously.

Bobby Kennedy did not start life as an archetypal people's champion. He was born into the ambitious and wealthy Kennedy clan, the American equivalent of aristocracy. Although he was reputedly his mother Rose's favourite, he struggled to gain the attention of his father Joe. 'I was the seventh of nine children,' he once explained. 'When you come from that far down you have to struggle to survive.'

Scholarly studies were a strain, and his Harvard education had a welcome interruption when he joined the US Navy Reserve during the Second World War. Eventually, he qualified as an attorney, although it was as an aide to his brother John's election campaign, first as a senator then as President, that he came to prominence. He also sat on a series of investigative committees during the 1950s, where his reputation was as a hard taskmaster rather than a bleeding heart, professing a particular fondness for 'witch-hunter' Senator Joe McCarthy, who persecuted people for perceived left-wing tendencies.

When John F. Kennedy was elected President in 1960, he made his loyal brother Bobby Attorney General. (The appointment was made at father Joe's instigation to protect John from FBI probes.) Two years later, they were at the heart of crucial decision-making as the world was poised on the brink of nuclear war during the Cuban missile crisis. The brothers favoured tact and discretion rather than military might to secure a withdrawal of Russian weapons from the island and they averted an apocalypse. Already,

Bobby had a civil rights agenda, although he did approve phone taps for activist Dr Martin Luther King following unfounded accusations that King was consorting with communists.

Following the assassination of his brother in 1963, Kennedy experienced grief, loss and finally a sense of renewal, when he read widely and thought deeply. Through literature he discovered a fresh passion for society's disaffected, and he dedicated his life to the less fortunate, branding the existence of poverty in a world of plenty 'an evil'.

In 1964, he successfully ran for the Senate and embarked on a programme to assist New York's poor. He also pioneered civil rights legislation that would bring about the end of the prejudicial Jim Crow laws, segregating America's black population.

Two years later, he visited South Africa under white supremacists' apartheid rule. In a speech in Cape Town he backed the black population with the words: 'Each time a man stands up for an ideal, or acts to improve the lot of others, or strikes out against injustice, he sends forth a tiny ripple of hope.' It was a quote that later appeared on his memorial stone.

In a surprise move, Kennedy decided to run for president in 1968 on a platform of racial and economic justice:

> I run to seek new policies; policies to end the bloodshed in Vietnam and in our cities, policies to close the gaps that now exist between black and white, between rich and poor, between young and old in this country and around the rest of the world. I run for the presidency because I want the Democratic party and the United States of America to stand for hope instead of despair, for reconciliation of men instead of the growing risk of world war.

In April that year after the assassination of civil rights campaigner Martin Luther King, he went into a black area of Indianapolis without a police escort to speak from the back of a flatbed truck:

For those of you who are black and are tempted to be filled with hatred and mistrust at the injustice of such an act against all white people, I would only say that I can also feel in my own heart the same kind of feeling. I had a member of my family killed. He was killed by a white man. We have to make an effort to understand, to get beyond these difficult times. My favourite poet was Aeschylus. He once wrote: 'Even in our sleep pain which cannot forget falls drop by drop upon the heart until in our own despite, against our will, comes wisdom.'

Mystery still surrounds the precise chronology of Bobby Kennedy's assassination, which occurred just a few months after that speech. At the time it was thought Sirhan Bishara Sirhan, captured at the scene, was a lone gunman. The Palestinian was eventually sentenced to life for murder. However, a post-mortem revealed that the bullets inside Kennedy were fired from behind at close range, while Sirhan had been at the front of the politician before he fell. Sirhan is believed to have fired eight shots in total before he was wrestled to the ground while there was evidence of fourteen bullets being unleashed. Rumours of CIA involvement have since abounded. What is certain is that an adept and farsighted statesman, a husband, father and son, a man of integrity who might have shaped history, lay dead. Union leader Paul Schrade, who was alongside Kennedy that fateful day and suffered gunshot wounds, recently said: 'I think we were in a position of really changing this country. What we lost was a real hope and possibility of having a better country and having better relations around the world.'

Genghis Khan

(c.1162–1227)

His story is amazing. But the history of the West was written by Western historians and this becomes just a historical blip. There is an element of real racism here. We don't know enough about Genghis Khan because Genghis Khan was a Mongolian who lived on the other side of the world. It is almost as if there has been some attempt to write him out of history. He is one of the most important historical figures of all time.

Joe Queenan (Commentator, author and broadcaster)

Genghis himself was remarkably flexible. He saw that he could not possibly run an empire without bureaucrats and was very happy to employ talent wherever he found it. He had a lot of Muslims as officials and a lot of Chinese as advisers, and he could not have invaded without them. What he lacks is a legacy of an increase in human happiness which I think we would have to add to anybody's life to call them truly great. But looking back in history very few people have actually done this, so it makes him an extraordinary leader.

John Man (Biographer)

FEW MEN HAVE thrived on a reputation for genocide in the same way as Genghis Khan. He lived up to the epithets associated with his name: 'the mighty man slayer', 'the scourge of God' and 'master of thrones and crowns'. Indeed, for many Genghis Khan is a byword for ethnic annihilation. That he accrued a mighty empire unrivalled in size and variety by essentially barbarous means is well known. He is less famous for a range of other achievements, among them the construction of a skilful bureaucracy, the advocacy of religious tolerance and a series of laws that made life safer, especially for women.

Historian John Keegan offered a commonly held view about Genghis Khan and his Mongol hordes at the 1998 Reith Lecture:

> Mongol conquest had a single purpose, to extract by violent extortion the revenue that would allow them to enjoy in luxury rather than poverty their nomadic and warrior way of life. So determined were they to remain horse warriors that in China large areas of agricultural land were turned back into pasture for the grazing herds and the disposed peasants massacred. Genghis himself said that the greatest pleasure in life was 'to chase and defeat the enemy, seize his possessions, ride his horse, leave his married women weeping and use his body as a nightshirt'. It is not surprising in view of Genghis Khan's world outlook that no political, cultural or intellectual achievement can be associated with their rule whatever. Their society found no place for any man who was not a warrior and they ended as they began, an army on horseback.

But to accept that the Mongol army achieved known world domination through carnage and chaos would be superficial. One of his most extraordinary feats was to unite a series of warring tribes with himself at their head by 1206, something he carried out in his forties rather than in his youth. The charismatic and dynamic Genghis Khan was a military genius who took the art of warfare to new heights. This was especially crucial as the Mongol army was almost always outnumbered in its battles.

With no shortage of ambition, Genghis Khan plotted routes through the highest mountains and across previously impenetrable deserts to reach his targets, cashing in on the element of stealth and surprise this created. The men were inevitably tired when they arrived at an area of conquest thus they had to ensure that victory was swift and all-embracing. Indeed, the Mongol army only stalled when it went out of its comfort zone to fight in cities, where different techniques to the usual slash and burn approach were needed. The Mongols depended on their horses to maintain a lightning pace across Asia's hostile interior, with five animals to each warrior. Accordingly, they needed access to acres of pasture. But they were also notoriously unsentimental, drinking horse blood and eating horse flesh in times of desperation.

Without doubt, Genghis Khan's army was brutal. Prisoners were used as human shields in battle, women were raped in front of their husbands before both were slaughtered, while noblemen were slowly suffocated in the centre of a table with Genghis Khan and his men feasting alongside. (Perversely, Genghis Khan would have insisted this was tantamount to a noble death.) But Genghis Khan was not without scruples. Those who surrendered without raising arms to the Mongols were sometimes spared. Fighters who switched sides during battle were massacred, as he had no tolerance for betrayal. His most bloodthirsty campaigns were mounted after his own or his kinsmen's peaceful traders or diplomats were killed. Of course, the levels of violence on display in equivalent campaigns elsewhere in the world, including the Crusades, was comparable.

Men followed him because they were loyal, they received rich rewards and they subscribed to his own belief that he was a divine ruler heaven-sent to bring the territories to heel. While he was alive, his empire extended to four times the size of that secured by Alexander the Great. After his death, his heirs doubled it again until it spanned between the Pacific Ocean and the Adriatic Sea. To help counter the problems of communication he established a pony express that was not rivalled for speed until the age of the train. While his motives for conquest are not certain, the ostentatious wealth that travelled along the Silk Road, the region's primary trade, was surely an incentive. Genghis Khan's first foray into today's China was in 1207 when his triumphant Mongol forces were outnumbered many times over. He was at least 50 years old before the region was finally subjugated.

Given the time frame, his life is obviously shrouded with mystery. *The Secret History of the Mongols* has, however, survived to at least offer a theory about his early life. While undoubtedly sprayed with folklore, it is the earliest literary work associated with the Mongols, who were largely illiterate and relied on captured Muslims or Chinese or cooperating Uighurs to harness writing skills.

The history says Genghis Khan was born Temüjin, a name rooted in 'blacksmith'. After murdering a half-brother for the theft of a sparrow and a fish, Temüjin received a vividly worded rebuke from his mother. Life changed following the murder of his father and history portrays a hand-to-mouth existence for Genghis Khan's family before his ascendancy.

Fittingly, his death came after a fall from a horse in which he sustained fatal internal injuries. His body was taken back to his homeland and buried in a secret place according to Mongol tradition. Although there's no shrine for him, he did leave something behind that's evident to this day. His genes are thought to be present in 16 million people today. Scientists have drawn this conclusion after studying the populations in what was once the Mongol empire and considering the Mongol way of life – vanquishing local people, living with numerous concubines and establishing a certain lineage.

While he is still seen as a devil in some countries, Genghis Khan remains a hero to Mongolians and a symbol of the country.

R. D. Laing

(1927–1989)

My brother suffered from paranoid schizophrenia, and I grew up feeling that R. D. Laing had told the world that it was families, particularly mothers, that were responsible for their children having schizophrenia. I was devoted to my mother and I felt she already had a sufficient burden, seeing her son go mad in front of her eyes. [Laing] did a disservice to families and mothers but he was a brilliant writer, and the more I have read about him, the more I have learned about him, the more I wish I had met him.

Carole Stone (Networker)

The end contribution of his life in my mind is really the unquantifiable degree of humanity that he infused into the psychiatric profession. The point at which my father qualified was really the dark ages of psychiatric treatment. We are talking about insulin coma treatment, electro-convulsive therapy, padded cells, lobotomies, even trepanning. It was into this climate that my father came in the early 1950s, and to him the way people who had been diagnosed as schizophrenic were being treated was no less than totally barbaric behaviour.

Adrian Laing (Son and biographer)

TO PSYCHIATRIST AND guru R. D. Laing, it seemed family life was tough. For evidence, he looked at 1950s Britain where families were idealised in the media at a time when more children suffered mental illness than went to university. He scrutinised his own family, having been brought up by a mother who burned his toy horse because he seemed to love it more than her. 'We are effectively destroying ourselves by violence masquerading as love,' he declared.

His onslaught on family life brought him notoriety – which he relished – as well as loathing and adulation in equal measure. Combined with his wild drinking and drug-taking and the extraordinary rages that marked his later life, it leaves a somewhat skewed view of a psychiatrist who became a household name. For his contribution to the world really lay in the treatment of the mentally ill, who for the first time were dealt with like human beings under his care.

Ronald David Laing was born in Glasgow and named for silver-screen star Ronald Coleman. As an adult he was known as R. D. or Ronnie. His mother was, he felt, cold-hearted while the rest of the austere lower-middle-class family were regularly rocked by rows. Although he didn't always understand the arguments, he could feel the destructive emotions wash over him in childhood. From an early age he strove to better understand interpersonal relationships.

His family were straight-laced, repressed Presbyterians and, although his accounts cannot be verified, he told lurid tales of his mother's unnatural attitudes. Speaking on the BBC in 1985, he said, 'My second eldest daughter, when she was 15, told me that my mother had told her that she had made herself or acquired a little figurine called Ronald that she was sticking pins in, into its heart, to give me a heart attack.'

In spite of a chilly domestic atmosphere, Laing excelled in Greek, Latin and English at school then studied medicine at Glasgow University despite a more abiding interest in philosophy. He was then posted to the British Army Psychiatric Unit at Netley in Hampshire, peopled largely by men emotionally damaged in the Second World War. He was appalled by the free use of drugs and invasive techniques, while he felt he achieved better results by simply talking to patients, one to one.

When he returned to Scotland, he eventually qualified in psychiatry and joined the staff of Gartnavel Royal Hospital, where he established a rumpus room. The aim was to have a clean, safe, drug-free and friendly environment for the mentally ill that would withstand behavioural episodes. Laing discovered he had a natural gift for communicating with disordered minds. In an experiment reported in *The Lancet*, he treated a dozen women patients in the rumpus room, where they were allowed to dress in their own clothes and socialise, and were treated normally. All the women were eventually discharged. However, they were also later readmitted for treatment as their newfound stability came to an end.

In the early 1960s, Laing moved to London to begin a radical practice in Wimpole Street which soon attracted the attention of film and literary stars, including Sean Connery and Sylvia Plath. He believed that breakdowns were really breakthroughs, and that insanity was 'a perfectly rational adjustment to an insane world'. With others, he founded the Philadelphia Association, to provide an alternative to the era's mental hospitals. He opened a community house in East London, where doctors and patients could live and work together.

His books, beginning with *The Divided Self*, sold thousands. Laing was recognised as the figurehead of a counterculture that surged across Britain, Europe and America in the 1960s and found himself facing of an army of followers. Condemnation from the British medical establishment only reinforced popular support for him, although he perpetually rejected claims that he was anti-psychiatry.

In fact, his own life was by now already spiralling out of control. His first marriage broke up acrimoniously, and his drinking and drug-taking were escalating. After a spell overseas seeking further enlightenment among Eastern faiths, he returned to Britain to discover he was no longer the focus of publicity. To the consternation of many, he began practising re-birthing techniques, claiming to cure various afflictions as patients re-enacted their own births amid a circle of onlookers. He later became a poet of dubious verse but failed to recapture the media interest that had once surrounded everything he did. He left a series of failed relationships behind him. He had ten children, but was a notoriously flaky father – ironically repeating many of the parenting blunders that he railed against in his earliest books.

He ultimately died on a tennis court mid-match, in the process of beating a younger man in forty-degree midday heat. Anthony Clare, writing in *The Guardian*, said of him: 'His major achievement was that he dragged the isolated and neglected inner world of the severely psychotic individual out of the back ward of the large gloomy mental hospital and on to the front pages of influential newspapers, journals and literary magazines ... Everyone in contemporary psychiatry owes something to R.D. Laing.'

Burt Lancaster

(1913–1994)

I have a particular affinity to Burt. I don't know what it is that attracted me to him but I always liked his quiet desperation. You always felt there was a serious brain going on in there, that he was doing the best he could. Lots of his movies were sleepers. People didn't realise the quality of them until time had passed and didn't realise how talented he really was, how ahead of his time he was. He was always very underrated as an actor. It was his vitality that shone through at the beginning.

Gerry Anderson (Broadcaster)

His energy, his physical presence on the screen is what drew me to him. He was a performer, he wanted to connect with his audience. In the 1950s, megastars didn't take on character roles until they were over the hill and they had to. He deliberately took them on to stretch his range. One of the most interesting things about him is that he seemed impervious to critical ridicule. He knew what he was doing.

Kate Buford (Biographer)

267

THE ILLICIT SHORELINE embrace of an army sergeant and an officer's wife as they are washed over by the warm waters of a Hawaiian tide is one of the most suggestive scenes in Hollywood history. It's both passionate and poignant, as the pair rolling in the waves have no idea their futures are about to be shattered by the surprise Japanese invasion of Pearl Harbour.

In 1953, when *From Here to Eternity* was released, filmmakers were still working within the confines of the Hay's Code, a so-called good-taste guide issued in 1930 which decreed: 'No picture shall be produced that will lower the moral standards of those who see it. Hence the sympathy of the audience should never be thrown to the side of crime, wrongdoing, evil or sin.' Although the vice-like grip of the code had been loosened, it still overarched the activities of writers and actors. Burt Lancaster, who played Sergeant Milton Warden to Deborah Kerr's Karen Holmes, revelled in his role as it flew in the face of prudish censorship.

Lancaster was a lifelong liberal who worked hard to break down traditional barriers in the film industry by launching an independent production company to challenge the major studios. Although he fitted the bill as a Hollywood heartthrob, he also accepted roles that would challenge his acting abilities rather than merely bank massive pay cheques. 'Most people seem to think I'm the kind of guy who shaves with a blowtorch. Actually I'm bookish and worrisome,' he once said.

Burton Stephen Lancaster was born in East Harlem in 1913, the son of a post office clerk from a family descended from Northern Irish protestants. A restless youth, he eventually ran away to the circus and honed his legendary body strength as a working acrobat during the Depression. His tough itinerant life came to an end as bookings for his act declined, and he became a lingerie salesman in Chicago, impressing customers by doing handsprings on the counter. With the onset of the Second World War, he joined the army and was attached to the forces' entertainment division.

When he returned to visit his family in New York he won a part in a play that ran for just three weeks. Yet his performance was so electrifying he was spotted by a Hollywood talent scout and, with undue speed and simplicity, his future was assured.

His first film role was in *The Killers* in 1947, which catapulted him to fame. Later Lancaster admitted: 'I woke up one day a star. It was terrifying. Then I worked hard toward becoming a good actor.' On the set he learned a lot about the business of being a film star, as he later recalled with disarming honesty: 'The first picture I ever did was called *The Killers* and in it I had a scene with a girl called Ava Gardner, at that time 19 years old and easily one of the most beautiful women who ever lived. When I had to kiss her I found myself very deeply stirred and it took the form of some embarrassment and the director threw everybody off the set except ourselves. After that I never had any difficulty making a love scene.'

Soon he was known as a 'brawny Apollo', a 'brute with the eyes of an angel' or, more enduringly, 'Mr Muscles-and-teeth'. He went on to star in seventy motion pictures, not all of them sure-fire hits. Unlike fellow stars, he refused to restrict himself to roles of a particular genre. So when audiences settled in expecting a formula performance they were often disappointed with Lancaster. Some films were instantly branded disasters. Indeed, many of his movies have only become cult classics years after they were made. His choices were led by a personal integrity that also inspired him to carry out all his own stunts, a move which he believed embellished action films with authenticity.

It was this same spark that led him to form a film company, to give himself more creative control and a broader brief. In an era governed by a proscribed Hollywood diet, this was a pioneering leap forward for independent filmmaking. Most high-profile stars were relatively unconcerned about taking responsibility for what appeared on the screen or improving a film's intellectual edge. It didn't signal the end of his blockbuster days, though. He was Marshal Wyatt Earp in *Gunfight at the OK Corral*, made in 1957, and Robert Stroud, *The Birdman of Alcatraz*, in 1962. He won an Oscar for his title role in *Elmer Gantry*, a 1960 film about an evangelical salesman. However, his career was pit-stopped with less commercial films including *The Leopard* and *The Swimmer*.

Off screen he backed liberal causes both financially and personally. He was part of the vanguard that stood up to McCarthyism, the witch hunt carried out in Hollywood to persecute presumed communists and socialists. In command of his own film company, he hired people who were blacklisted elsewhere for their political beliefs. He marched alongside Martin Luther King in the latter's quest for civil rights and was vociferous in his opposition to the Vietnam War. His cash went into the campaigns of politicians who were demonstrably liberally minded. Later, Lancaster was an outspoken supporter of AIDS charities, fuelling rumours that persisted in his career about bi-sexuality.

Lancaster was married three times, was a father of five and conducted numerous affairs. As he grew older, he was plagued by poor health, surviving a gall bladder operation and open heart surgery only to be disabled by the effects of a massive stroke from which he did not recover.

Bob Marley

(1945–1981)

People hear his music and associate him with a little illegal plant and his many girlfriends, and they don't really know the man. When I was very small I sent him some poems and he wrote back to me. I was so chuffed. I don't think that since Bob Marley there has been another person with his songwriting ability.

Benjamin Zephaniah (Poet)

[At the time he died] his myth took a quantum leap, because he was frozen in time, because he never got old, because he still looked fantastic when he went. That is really the reason why he is the colossal worldwide artist that he is.

Chris Salewicz (Biographer)

OUT OF A Jamaica held at bay by gangs and gun culture came Bob Marley, man of music and faith who took reggae music and the Rastafarian message around the world.

He was the son of a black mother and a white, British army father and his lighter-than-average skin made him the object of some derision in his community. After his father left the family, he and his mother moved to Trench Town in Jamaica's capital, Kingston, so named because it was built over an open sewer. Amid the deprivation arose the culture of Rude Boys, a gang modelled on those that roamed the streets of some American cities. In Jamaica they were sharply dressed, armed themselves with ratchet knives and were a matter for concern in many parts of the community.

Marley may have aligned himself with the Rude Boys for a while but he was mostly concerned with making music. In the early 1960s, he met other musicians including Peter Tosh and Bunny Livingstone, with whom he ultimately formed the Wailing Wailers. The sound they pioneered, a fusion of rock, rock steady and ska, began to find a following. At the time, music in Jamaica was generally played in public through enormous sound systems that were transported by truck to venues across the island. In 1963, his hit 'Simmer Down' was directed at fellow Rude Boys, urging them to curb their rebellious behaviour to sidestep the worst attentions of the law.

In 1966, working as a voice coach, Marley met Alfarita Constantia Anderson – better known as Rita – a single mother in a singing group. 'Did I have any idea that in a few short months this Robbie Marley, the shy guitarist, would become the love of my life?' she wrote in her autobiography. 'Did I suspect that he'd become a major force, world renowned, an icon of musical history? No! What was on my mind was Aunty's warning: "Don't you dare stay too long because you have to give the baby titty when she wakes up."'

They were soon married. But for now both his musical career and his family life were disjointed. Marley went to America, where his mother now lived, to earn some cash in a factory immediately after his marriage.

There followed a few hits but initially it seemed Marley's success might be confined to the Caribbean. Although the West Indian population in Britain was enjoying roots music and its Jamaican offshoots, it was a marginal market which got no radio airtime. Only in the 1970s did the renamed Bob Marley and the new-look Wailers become international recording stars.

Record producer Chris Blackwell had already established his Island Records label. In Marley and his colleagues he saw musical potential wrapped up in social aggravation but decided to take a chance: 'They were like real sort of rebels so I made a deal with them which in a sense was risky, to give them some money and go off and make a record. Everyone said, "You will never get a record and you will never see the money again and that will be that" because they had a bad reputation. The amount was £4,000. A few months later I went to Jamaica. I know enough about recording to know every penny of that £4,000 was in the record.'

Marley's first album recorded in London was *Catch A Fire*, which propelled the group to stardom. After 'I Shot The Sheriff', a track from the second album, was recorded by superstar Eric Clapton, Marley's reputation was copper-bottomed.

In tandem with his musical career there came a religious journey inspired by the Rastafari faith, which emerged in Jamaica out of Christian worship in the 1930s. Its adherents worshipped Haile Selassie, one-time ruler of Ethiopia, as an incarnation of God or Jah. Marley often sported the Rastafari colours of green, gold and red. He certainly abided by its principles of charity and preached peace whenever he could. 'Me only have one ambition, y'know. I only have one thing I really like to see happen. I like to see mankind live together – black, white, Chinese, everyone – that is all.'

However, dreadlocks and Rastafari followers' free use of cannabis for spiritual purposes bred the perception that it was a rebel cult. For his part, Marley defended his use of marijuana with the words: 'Herb is the healing of a nation. Alcohol is the destruction.' His was a message of enlightenment rather than revolt and he became a political icon in Jamaica even though it remained illegal to smoke marijuana there. Elsewhere he was considered a prophet for his Biblical interpretations.

When he was criticised for living in a better part of town after finding some success he told people: 'I'm just bringing the ghetto uptown.' Although largely apolitical, he reluctantly agreed to perform in a free concert on behalf of the People's National Party led by Michael Manley during the 1976 election campaign, which is remembered for being marked by violence. Shortly before it was due to begin, his house was stormed by gunmen and Marley was shot and injured. By way of response he appeared in the concert as scheduled regardless of the wounds, even poking fun at his would-be assassins from the stage. But he left his homeland soon after to recuperate and tour, recording the album *Exodus* in the process.

Although there's doubt about the exact incident that caused it, Marley suffered an injury to his toe during a football match in the 1970s that refused to heal. It is thought to be this that led to cancer spreading through his body, leading to his untimely death in 1981. Afterwards there were a flood of paternity claims. Rita recalls: 'There were people much older than Bob who claimed he was their father.' He had at least ten children, maybe more. Many ended up following a musical career.

Marley's following has continued to expand despite his demise. Eppie Edwards, deputy director of the National Library of Jamaica, put it like this: 'Marley is more popular in death than in life because a lot of his work is still being discovered and recognised. The message of his songs was peace, looking out for the underdog, love. Simple as that.'

Groucho Marx

(1890–1977)

Looking at his FBI files recently, his name was misspelled as Graucho. Almost everybody in the world knew him as Groucho. He was inimitable. He was an iconic figure in the 1930s, the 1940s and to some extent the 1950s in a way that few people were. He seemed to get involved in some quite left-wing causes. He had a social conscience, he minded about things and he was willing to take risks and put his name on them.

Roger Graef (Filmmaker and criminologist)

Groucho's claim to greatness lies in the fact that he succeeded in life several times over. For the most part, his brothers succeeded once, maybe twice. But Groucho kept going at either end of the Marx Brothers' story.

Glenn Mitchell (Author of *The Marx Brothers Encyclopaedia*)

'*L*AST NIGHT *I shot an elephant in my pyjamas – and how he got in my pyjamas I'll never know.*'

It's one of many one-liners delivered deadpan by Groucho Marx, the low-sloping, cigar-smoking, quick-thinking, woman-chasing wit who brought an original brand of zany comedy to the silver screen. With two of his four brothers he made it big on both sides of the Atlantic. They appeared first on Broadway, then in Hollywood, and later Groucho became a popular television game show host.

The Marx Brothers were born in New York to a tailor and his wife, Minnie, who harboured high-flying ambitions for her boys. Her uncle was already a Vaudeville star, and she was determined that those were the footsteps her family should follow. Initially a singing act, with one brother on the piano and another on the harp, the boys discovered how to improvise in order to win round a hostile audience. Almost from the start of his career, Groucho wore a thick greasepaint moustache with matching eyebrows and steel-rimmed glasses, which meant he was almost unrecognisable when he was off-stage. At first he delivered lines in a mock German accent but, after the U-boat sinking of the *Lusitania* in 1915 with numerous American passengers aboard, that was unceremoniously dropped.

No one – even Groucho himself – was sure about how he got his name. At birth he was Julius Henry, while his brother Chico was Leonard and Harpo was Adolph, later known as Arthur. Two other brothers, Zeppo and Gummo, who sometimes appeared with the trio, were named Herbert and Milton. (A sixth brother died in infancy.) The word Groucho might have been taken from a cartoon, to reflect his disposition or because he was in charge of the purse, also known as a grouch.

The Marx Brothers were finally elevated from Vaudeville to Broadway in 1924 with the musical comedy *I'll Say She Is*. Five years later, Hollywood beckoned and they made a film version of *The Cocoanuts*, one of their popular plays. They filmed at Long Island City during the daytime and rushed back to Broadway in the evenings to perform in *Animal Crackers*. Although the film production had shortcomings, the absurd slapstick style honed through the years by the brothers now reached much bigger and highly appreciative audiences. Two of their biggest films, *Duck Soup* and *A Night At The Opera*, were made during the 1930s. But without sharp direction their uncontrolled antics and wide-ranging anarchy drifted. By 1941, the brothers had decided to retire although there remained a strong fraternal bond between them.

For Groucho, this was an opportunity to explore the more serious side of his nature. A lover of Gilbert and Sullivan operettas, he also had an immense appetite for literature. Having dropped out of school at an early age, his appreciation of books was largely self-taught. He began corresponding with the poet T. S. Eliot among others, and collections of his letters were published in his lifetime and after his death. Sometimes the letters were hilarious, like the one he wrote to Warner Brothers when legal proceedings were threatened after Groucho planned a spoof on *Casablanca*:

> Dear Brothers, Since I last wrote to you I regret to say there have been some changes in the plot of our new picture, *A Night in Casablanca*. In the new version I play Bordello, the sweetheart of Humphrey Bogart. Harpo and Chico are itinerant rug pedlars who are weary of laying rugs and enter a monastery just for a lark. This is a good joke on them as there hasn't been a lark in the place in 15 years.' (*A Night In Casablanca* was finally made in 1946, largely to help Chico pay off gambling debts.)

Usually the topics covered in the letters were more weighty, but he would characteristically include a PS that took the form of a joke. Before his death, a book of letters first published in 1967 was archived for posterity in Washington, a fact which made the comic proud, following his paucity of education. In 1972, he told interviewer Frank Muir: 'The award that I like is that I wrote one book that is in the Congressional Library in Washington. That I'm proud of. I've settled for that.' Today three autobiographies and as many as possible of the salvaged scripts he wrote are alongside it.

Away from the relentless puns and pistol-shot comedy, he once attempted a role in a serious play. The critics were fierce in their response, and Groucho found himself trapped in a caricature. He was always generous with praise for the straight actors – including Margaret Dumont in Marx Brothers films and George Fenneman on the radio and TV show *You Bet Your Life* – who were his faithful foils. During the show, which aired on various stations between 1947 and 1961, Groucho improvised hilariously with contestants with sensational results.

Always the joker on screen, there was less to laugh about in his private life where his relationships with women were largely unsuccessful. He married three times, had three children and was with a partner when he died of pneumonia. His death came three days after Elvis's and was overshadowed by it. The longest-lived of all the brothers, he had insisted: 'I intend to live forever, or die trying.'

Ultimately there was no epitaph on his gravestone, just a Star of David, his stage name and life dates. Here is a selection of some of the one-liners by which he is best remembered:

> Politics is the art of looking for trouble, finding it, misdiagnosing it and then misapplying the wrong remedies.

> I never forget a face, but in your case I'll be glad to make an exception.

> I find television very educating. Every time somebody turns on the set, I go into the other room and read a book.

Military intelligence is a contradiction in terms.

She got her good looks from her father. He's a plastic surgeon.

Those are my principles. If you don't like them I have others.

Henri Matisse

(1869–1954)

He seems to say in his work and by the way he has lived his life that in the ordinary there can be the extraordinary. This was an ordinary man from an ordinary background, according to conventional perception. And yet from this man bursts the most amazing imagination. Why is the colour green that he chooses always exactly the right colour green for that moment in that canvas?

Frank Delaney (Writer and broadcaster)

He is one of those artists whose art is one with his life. They are not separable. Matisse was a radical and a revolutionary from the start, one of the [most] reckless and rashest human beings who has ever existed, with a passionate heart which led him from the beginning.

Hilary Spurling (Biographer)

HENRI MATISSE WAS a rare commodity: an artist who found fame and some fortune in his lifetime. He became a master of vivid colours, fundamental forms and fluid ideas. For him, art filled every aspect of his life. 'The work is the emanation, the projection of self,' he said. 'My drawings and my canvases are part of me. They add up to Henri Matisse. I could also say my drawings and canvases are my real children.' Before his death Matisse received the Légion d'Honneur, a distinguished medal in his native France. He had, however, served a long apprenticeship before he reached these lofty heights.

He was born in northern France into what he considered to be a repressed family where all forms of self-expression were discouraged. Initially, he wanted to become a lawyer. But during an illness he was given some paints by his mother and he began a lifelong love affair with colour. Without any particular encouragement from his family, he left for Paris to study art. He later explained:

> When I started painting you didn't argue with your superiors and only ventured your opinions discreetly and cautiously. I spent my time in the Louvre, copying under the influence of acknowledged masters like Raphael, Poussin, Chardin and the Flemish. I felt the Impressionist methods were not for me. I wanted to see beyond their subtle gradations of tone and their continuous experiments. ... Coming out of the Louvre, crossing the Pont des Arts, I saw other subjects for my art.

He married in 1898, and his wife Amélie's income from a hat shop kept them in food. She was also his chief model for some time, a mother to his daughter from a previous relationship and a rousing cheerleader: 'I didn't know what he was doing but I knew that what he was doing was good.'

Matisse and a number of fellow painters became known as Fauvists, meaning wild beasts, a name derived for their free use of primary colours straight from the paint pot, rather than mixed on the palette. Matisse later recalled the difficult years before his talent was embraced: 'We didn't have the money to buy a beer. Hunger was a problem. So we watched what others were doing and decided to try and do the same as them, to please the public. We couldn't, so much the better for us. Collectors started to notice us and eventually risked 100 francs for one of our paintings.'

His life was further shaped by a turn-of-the-century scandal that rocked French society. It centred on a woman called Thérèse Humbert, who borrowed a fortune, claiming she owned a safe that contained a legacy from an American millionaire that would provide collateral. Ultimately, the safe was found to be empty. Matisse's in-laws worked for Humbert and were made scapegoats by a furious French public. He did much to save their reputation and secure their freedom. It is believed that Amélie and Henri received a bag of jewels as a wedding gift from Humbert before her scam was discovered. Amélie sold the gems in order to buy a picture by Paul Cézanne, one of her husband's favourite artists. Thereafter Matisse and his family sought life out of the spotlight, frantically avoiding public attention at any cost.

It is with this in mind that Matisse made the following comments:

I'm an ordinary man, a devoted husband and father. I've got three lovely children. I go to the theatre, ride, have a comfortable home, a fine garden that I love, flowers, etc., just like any man.

What I dream of is an art of balance, of purity and serenity avoiding disturbing or depressing subjects, an art for businessmen as well as for authors, a soothing calming influence on the mind something like a good armchair which helps one to relax when exhausted.

In fact, Matisse never lost the radical edge that characterised his work. Influential collector Gertrude Stein alighted on Matisse, much as she did his friend Picasso. As she invested in Matisse canvases – and encouraged family and friends to do the same – so he was propelled into the art-loving public's eye.

He travelled the world and finally settled in the south of France, where he felt the warmth was a contributory factor to the success of his work: 'In order to paint my pictures I need to be in the same state of mind for several days. And I can only do this on the Côte d'Azure. The north, especially Paris, develops the mind with its rich culture and its wealth of museums. But it is too unstable an atmosphere for work as I see it. And the richness and silver clarity of the light in Nice seems to me indispensable for a painter.'

Still, ties that bound him to his childhood in the darker realms of northern France were evident, particularly his soft spot for the pigeons kept by his northerly neighbours. Although the couple had two sons, Matisse and Amélie split. He was later diagnosed with cancer, which nearly killed him. He saw the post-illness, bedridden phase, which lasted more than a dozen years, as a 'second life'.

Much later in his life, Matisse switched from secular to religious subjects, most notably the iconic Chapelle du Rosaire in Vence, which he completed as a tribute to a nun who once nursed him. Speaking in 1941 he said:

> As far as I am concerned, anything is capable of inspiring an artist and making him work. Sometimes you paint grand subjects and others you paint everyday things that seem banal. I have the same respect for nature, the same religious feelings about a wide range of subjects: fruit, flowers, landscapes, faces. Above all, it is the feeling I have when I see those things that keeps me working.

He continued to work with paper, collages and drawings while France was occupied by Nazi Germany, although his days of sculpting, printing and draughtsmanship were largely over. Initial plans to skip the country were abandoned when he realised he would be deserting a nation already in a terrible mess. 'If everyone of any value leaves France, what's left of France,' he asked himself. And these were anxious days with his former wife and daughter arrested by the Gestapo while son Jean was a saboteur working for the French resistance. (His other son Pierre was by this time an art dealer in New York.)

Matisse remained close to his family and stayed friends with Picasso. Before he died he donated 100 paintings to a museum dedicated to his work in his birthplace.

Lise Meitner

(1878–1968)

It is an extraordinary life. She made her way through a particular time when women weren't accepted into university. Education was made difficult for her. She surmounted these problems. I've been brought up in an age where I have taken for granted the fact that as a woman I can vote, I have had an education, I've been allowed to do all those things. [Meitner] did not have those easy opportunities. She was thrown into a world she couldn't come out of with glowing colours and all the awards.

Jenny Agutter (Actress)

Physics was to be more of a calling than a career and it was seen as a battle for ultimate truth. Lise Meitner has been written out of much of the history of twentieth-century physics despite the fact she made significant contributions to radioactivity and nuclear physics. She was one of the co-discoverers of nuclear fission which led to nuclear weapons and nuclear energy.

Dr Jeff Hughes (Senior lecturer in the history of science, Manchester University)

A T A REMOTE border crossing under cover of darkness, a 60-year-old woman stole out of Germany to escape certain death at the hands of the SS. Her hands were empty, except for a diamond ring that didn't signify love but insurance, in case she had to bribe border guards. But her head was bursting with the science that would usher in the nuclear age.

Lise Meitner was born in Vienna into a secular Jewish family, although she converted to Protestantism in her twenties. This meant little to the Nazis who came to power in 1933 with a fundamental agenda of anti-Semitism. As an Austrian citizen, Meitner worked in Berlin for five years under the radar of the ruling Nazis. Only after Austria was absorbed into Hitler's Third Reich in 1938 did she become vulnerable to anti-Jewish legislation. Ultimately, she was denounced by a fellow scientist in Berlin and, as she fled Germany, her case came up before Heinrich Himmler, head of the feared SS.

Later she recalled her final hours in Germany: 'So as not to arouse suspicion I spent the last day of my life in Germany in the Institute until eight at night, correcting a paper to be published by a young associate. Then I had exactly one and a half hours to pack a few necessary things into two small suitcases.'

She walked away from a research project on the brink of success at the Kaiser Wilhelm Institute to which she had devoted her adult life. It was not the first time bigotry had stood in the way of her career.

After formal education which ended in Austria at the age of 14, she was privately tutored at the expense of her parents because there were few opportunities for women to extend their studies, especially in scientific fields. She had been drawn to the value of scientific endeavour after her grandmother warned her, 'If you sew on a Sunday the heavens will come tumbling down on you.' Meitner duly took out needle and thread that day to discover first hand that the heavens stayed firmly in place.

She was finally admitted into the University of Vienna in 1901 and was inspired to major in physics by teacher Ludwig Boltzmann. She was only the second woman to gain a PhD from the university and she then worked as Boltzmann's assistant. His suicide less than a year later left her with an uncertain future at a time when women were not employed on university faculties. With the help of physicist Max Planck, she finally moved to the Institute of Experimental Physics in Berlin. Soon afterwards, she teamed up with Otto Hahn and they began working together at the city's Chemical Institute – although Meitner was initially barred from entering the all-male building. Together they worked in a woodshed on the Institute perimeter.

When she was finally admitted, it is fair to imagine there was still a bitter taste of discrimination in the air. Meitner was by nature shy. Nonetheless, she had to confront this issue on a daily basis and constantly felt the need to prove herself. When she authored papers she signed them 'L Meitner', leading many people to assume she was a man. Indeed, one invitation to contribute to a scientific encyclopaedia was withdrawn when the publisher discovered her true gender.

During the First World War, Meitner interrupted her research to work as a radiologist in the Austrian army. She reunited with Hahn after the conflict in a continuing effort to sort out the tangle that surrounded uranium's mystifying characteristics. Indeed, she was so absorbed in her work that she failed to read the political writing on the wall that meant her exit from Germany was inevitable, even after she was asked to stop lecturing in the mid 1930s.

After her eventual departure Hahn stayed in touch with Meitner and kept her up to date with his work by letter and even during a covert meeting in Copenhagen. It was a letter about the perplexing response of uranium under test conditions that led Meitner, in collaboration with her nephew Otto Frisch, also a physicist, to identify the process of nuclear fission. She realised that the atom was splitting and producing immense energy in doing so.

It was a significant moment that engendered huge excitement, not least with Hahn who made use of Meitner's findings on the way to winning the

1944 Nobel Prize for Chemistry. Neither Meitner nor another colleague, Fritz Strassmann, was given any credit by Hahn. Although there is no doubt a deep and enduring friendship had developed between Meitner and Hahn, he even told some people that, had she still been in Berlin, she might have talked him out of the discovery. Meitner was admirably unrattled by these events, however. After nuclear fission led to nuclear weapons – which were used to devastating effect in Japan in 1945 – she was happy to disassociate herself from the controversial process she had helped pioneer.

While she helped Hahn in Germany along the road to fission, her nephew Frisch shared the information with the Allies. Meitner was invited to become part of the Manhattan Project, the Allied initiative to develop nuclear weapons that began in 1943. Her refusal was instant and absolute.

After the war a film was developed by Hollywood to tell the nuclear story, and once again she was invited to contribute. 'I would rather walk naked down Broadway than be involved in a film like that,' she told friends. Indeed, after years of experiencing discrimination on the grounds of her sex and faith she was by now happy to say just what she felt. With affection, Frisch described her as 'short, dark and bossy'.

She moved to England for the last eight years of her life. After she died, aged nearly 90, an epitaph composed by her nephew was carved on her gravestone: 'A physicist who never lost her humanity'.

Still, the scientific community did not forget the Nobel Prize 'mistake' that had been made. In 1982, physicists in Germany discovered through nuclear synthesis the world's heaviest element, which they named 'Meitnerian' in her honour.

André Michelin

(1853–1931)

and

Édouard Michelin

(1859–1940)

I admire them tremendously as the great entrepreneurial marketeers of the twentieth century. They saw first of all, as rubber ball manufacturers, that they could make bicycle tyres and then they had the foresight to see that motoring was going to be a big thing.

Sir Terence Conran (Designer,
retailer and restaurateur)

They were great myth makers. We are reliant on their public relations machine for knowledge of the Michelins themselves. Needless to say, they come out of it quite well. André ends up as the marketing man par excellence whereas Édouard is the hands-on factory patron.

Dr Andy Martin (Professor of French)

I T IS RARE to be on the leading edge of a new trend. The Michelin brothers managed it not once but twice, producing the first easy-change pneumatic tyres for bicycles and cars then launching an innovative tour guide. One spawned an internationally known cartoon figure in an early triumph of branding. Both continue to thrive today.

In fact, the Michelin brothers did not introduce the rubber industry to France. Their maternal grandfather, Aristide Barbier, was responsible for that in collaboration with his cousin Édouard Daubrée. From a base in Clermont-Ferrand in France's Auvergne region, they produced various goods including rubber balls. The company failed to prosper after the death of its founders and, by the time André Michelin took over the firm in 1886 it was teetering towards disaster. Although he was a gifted engineer, André knew little about rubber. Indeed, he was primarily interested in the metal framework firm he ran in Paris. Consequently he urged his younger brother Édouard to join him in the enterprise. At the time, Édouard was a painter with perhaps more ambition than artistry, as one critic's account of one of his religious scenes in 1885 indicates:

> The two disciples whose hearts were on fire with love and faith according to the gospel, have repulsive faces and the reborn Christ has the look of a criminal who has just escaped hanging. One wonders why the painter, inspired by the resurrection of the man-god, a miracle if ever there was one, suppressed the whole ideal and sublime aspect of this subject and turned it into a vulgar and commonplace scene.

It may have been with a measure of relief that Édouard changed direction to take up the role of managing director in Clermont-Ferrand where he was anxious to save the family firm from ruin and learn about the business from the grass roots.

The story about how the Michelin brothers became makers of bicycle tyres is an enduring one. Apparently, a cart drew up outside the Michelin factory one spring afternoon with a bicycle stowed in the back. The cycle had a puncture in its air-filled Dunlop tyres, design by Scottish vet John Dunlop and patented by him in 1888. (Prior to air-filled tyres, bicycles, which had developed throughout the nineteenth century, rolled along on solid wheels and were widely known as bone-shakers.) Dunlop's invention certainly added considerably to a rider's comfort. But a puncture was an unqualified disaster because the tyres were glued to the wheel and took time to lever off and even more time to replace.

The Michelin brothers finished the puncture overnight, but when Édouard took the cycle on a trial run the following day he experienced a second puncture. Together they set about inventing a detachable tyre that could be removed with a minimum number of tools. When cyclist Charles Terront won the Paris-Brest-Paris race in 1891, it was on Michelin tyres and he triumphed despite suffering a puncture.

It was the advent of the auto industry. Early cars also ran on solid tyres or wooden wheels with a metal rims. The Michelins saw the possibilities of air-filled tyres on cars – once again enhancing comfort – and set about persuading manufacturers. By now, the brothers had evolved as specialists in their fields. André was the company marketing man, while Édouard was head of research and production. In 1894, the pair attended a trade exhibition in Paris and, seeing Michelin tyres stacked up at the side of their stand, Édouard remarked the shape was similar to that of a man. This gave Andre an idea and, using a drawing by the illustrator O'Galup, the first Michelin man was conceived.

In France he is called Bibendum, taken from a Latin verse by Horace that in full reads 'Nunc et Bibendum'. The translation of 'it is time to drink' was transformed into the slogan 'Michelin tyres drink obstacles'. Bibendum was at the forefront of a new vogue for branding which grew in momentum throughout the twentieth century and is still thought vital to commercial success today. Although his shape and his actions have changed, the logo is instantly recognisable.

In 1899, Michelin tyres were on the electrically powered Jamais Contente, the first car to exceed 100 kph. But it was the pleasure principle rather than speed that took most people out onto the roads. With an able mind always open to a business opportunity, André realised people wanted to travel and use cars and bikes for their leisure. In doing so, they increased sales for bicycle and car tyres. Accordingly, he hit on the idea of a guide that would help to lure people to new areas, laying a foundation for domestic tourism. The Michelin guide, initially bearing a red cover, was at first issued free by agents.

> This book seeks to give any information that may be useful to a driver travelling through France, to supply his car, to repair it to permit him to find a room and a board, to communicate by post, telegram or telephone.

Its target audience was primarily chauffeurs who would need to know where they could charge car batteries or change tyres, with roads being in particularly poor repair. In 1900, when the guide first appeared, one estimate puts the number of cars throughout France at just 3,500. After the First World War, the number of cars increased while the number of chauffeurs decreased. After 1920, there was a charge for the guide. The Michelin brothers allegedly instituted the change after discovering a lop-sided garage bench propped up with a pile of their guides. If people paid for it, they reasoned, the guide would inspire more respect. André went on to open a travel information bureau in Paris to assist people with travel arrangements. The first regional Michelin guide appeared in 1926.

During the First World War, the Michelin factory produced aircraft at cost for the French government. Between the wars, the Michelin company took over car manufacturers' Citroën. Édouard's sons Pierre and Etienne were appointed to the company board but both died before the start of the Second World War, during which the extensive site at Clermont-Ferrand was bombed by the Royal Air Force after it was considered a vital cog in the Nazi war machine.

Wolfgang Amadeus Mozart

(1756–1791)

*He brings this terrific exaltation to his work, and I don't think there is
any man I know of who has brought more joy to the world. In fact we
probably know very little about this genius, despite the fact we have
wonderfully tender and funny and wicked and revealing letters. But
what do we know about his genius? Precious little.*

Michael Morpurgo (Author and former Children's Laureate)

*There is so much that is enigmatic about him. He is such an expressive
and human composer and has that ability to inhabit all the different
characters he uses in his operas. They are all alive. Each one has their
own life and dynamic, and I think that is particularly fascinating.
You want to know what kind of mind created this and what kind of
experience helped him produce this extraordinary understanding.*

Stephen Johnson (Music journalist)

MOST 5-YEAR-OLDS ARE content to run, skip, jump or play with wooden bricks. Not so musical genius Wolfgang Mozart, who was already performing his own material in front of adoring audiences, having mastered the keyboard at the age of 3.

Mozart possessed a remarkable talent that made him an honoured guest in royal courts and country houses across Europe. Capitalising on the talents of his 'wunderkind', father Leopold established a punishing schedule beginning in Mozart's early years. It was this tough work ethic instilled from infanthood and conducted in an era of primitive transport and rampant disease that brought Mozart's life to a premature end, so perhaps it is fortunate he made an early start.

Although he was only 35 when he died, he had already written a vast collection of work numbering more than 600 operas, symphonies, chamber music, arias and choral pieces. He worked to order, taking commissions from eminent religious figures or the nobility at a time when composers were uniformed and ranked as household servants. But he was also among the first to work as a freelancer, helping to establish a bold new future for the composers who followed in his wake.

Wolfgang Amadeus Mozart was one of seven children born to parents Leopold and Anna Maria. Only he and his sister Maria Anna – known affectionately as Nannerl – survived. Originally he was named for several saints linked to his birth date and there are several different versions of his name in circulation.

Although Leopold was an accomplished musician, he was quickly cast in the shadows by his children's prodigious abilities when they were both young. Both soon achieved complex piano pieces to note perfection, while young Wolfgang could learn the craft of any instrument within minutes, usually playing by ear. Realising their talents were both a gift and an asset, Leopold organised a strenuous tour of Europe that began when Wolfgang was about 6 and lasted for a decade. The Mozarts were a sensation, Leopold declared: 'We are already being talked of everywhere. Everyone is amazed, especially at the boy, and everyone whom I have heard has said his genius is incomprehensible.'

As a child with apparently casual mastery of music, Wolfgang was especially endearing, as one incident involving Emperor Francis and Empress Maria Theresa of Austria recalled by Leopold reveals: 'Their majesties received us with such extraordinary graciousness that when I shall tell of it people will declare that I have made it up. Suffice to say that [Mozart] jumped up on the Empress' lap, put his arms around her neck and kissed her heartily.'

Nannerl's musical abilities were equal to Wolfgang's, but she was compelled to stay at home with their mother once she was considered an appropriate age for marriage. Mozart's own appeal inevitably diminished as he grew older, despite his father's best efforts to manipulate his age for the purposes of public concerts. As a young adult, he began playing and composing in earnest, determined to make a decent living despite a lifestyle that entailed arduous travelling. He went to live in Salzburg under the dual strictures of his father and a dour archbishop for whom he worked. His days in Salzburg and later Italy were often mundane, as he revealed in a letter to his sister:

> My dear sister ... Now I will begin to describe my life here. I get up at nine, sometimes even at ten, and then we leave the house and eat lunch at an inn and after lunch we write. Then we go out and have supper. And what do we eat? On ordinary days, half a chicken or a roast meat. On fast days a little fish, then we go to bed.

Although he was successful, he was never complacent: 'It is a mistake to think that the practice of my art has become easy to me. No one has given so much care to the study of composition as I. There's scarcely a famous master in music whose works I have not frequently and diligently studied.' He did, however, clash with his father and with the Archbishop, who eventually sacked him. He was 'fired with a kick to the arse', Mozart told his father.

After the death of his mother in 1778 as they sought fresh prospects in Paris, Mozart's output matured with evidence of deeper emotions and greater sophistication. It was on that fateful tour that he met his future wife, Constanze Weber, although initially he had fallen in love with her sister Aloysia. After they married in 1782, only two children survived out of six born to Constanze. Perhaps because of this, the couple were hugely loving and supportive to one another.

Unable to compose during bumpy coach rides across Europe, Mozart tended to capture tunes in his head and note them down later. He was also famous for writing letters full of earthy humour, although he only did this to close confidantes.

Later he became a freemason, genuinely believing in the movement's concepts of brotherhood and social equality. Similar ideas were sweeping Europe as it shaped up for the French Revolution. Mozart was even appointed master of his lodge for a year. His freemason links enabled him to borrow money when times got tough – there's talk of Mozart and Constanze dancing blue-lipped around their home when there wasn't enough money to buy coal for the fire. Mozart certainly developed a taste for luxury which he couldn't always afford, and he remained relatively poorly paid despite his obvious talent.

When Mozart fell ill for the last time, it came at the end of a succession of serious ailments. This time, however, he failed to recover from a chronic kidney condition, and ensuing infection. Stories that rival Italian composer Antonio Salieri poisoned him seem far-fetched and lack credibility.

Although Mozart wasn't the only eminent composer of his age, he is considered one of the all-time greats among music lovers, scholars and composers themselves. Joseph Haydn, the Austrian composer some twenty years older than Mozart, wrote to Leopold saying, 'I say to you before God, as an honest man, your son is the greatest composer whom I know in person and by reputation. He has the taste and what is more he has the most thorough knowledge of composition.'

Napoleon

(1769–1821)

For a small chap who wasn't even French, he conquered the whole of Europe. [At the time] the French needed a hero. He was very clever with artillery, that was the secret of his success. The great flaw as far as I'm concerned is that he believed in luck.

Stuart Hall (Commentator)

In France, every child will study Napoleon in secondary school, some with despair, some with pleasure. He symbolises meritocracy. His great achievement was to take the positive heritage of the revolution but he was a man of order. He reorganised France on the principle of the revolution but made France orderly.

Isabelle Tombs (Historian)

Napoleon created a myth of himself. When Napoleon was exiled to St Helena after the Battle of Waterloo, he spent a lot of time writing and he wrote the history how he wanted it to be not how it actually was, creating a legend.

Peter Hicks (Napoleon Foundation)

A T FIRST GLANCE, Napoleon was a diminutive Frenchman with a world domination complex. However, closer investigation into the life of the one-time ruler of France reveals not everything is as it seems. A perception that Napoleon was short materialises from mocking English cartoons of the era. Napoleon was born in Corsica, which was indeed a French territory, but the island owed much more to long-term Italian influences than to France, a country hated by many nationalists there. Nor was it a desire to rule the world that motivated Napoleon so much as a thirst for a united Europe, albeit one that he himself led.

Although Napoleon liked to portray himself as a man with humble beginnings, he was in fact born into a relatively powerful family on Corsica. At the age of 15, he was admitted into the elite military school in Paris, having put aside early ambitions to join either the French or the British navy. With sunken eyes, a yellowy skin and a frequently haggard appearance, he didn't seem promising material for the military yet he made progress up the ranks.

He was sometimes resident in Paris during the turbulence of the French Revolution, which occurred from 1789 when King Louis XVI was overthrown. At other times, he was in Corsica, occasionally campaigning against the French in some complex realpolitik. At the time, he identified more closely with the republicans than the ruling classes. Indeed, at Toulon in 1793, he led French republicans against the British, who were occupying the port after it was yielded by royalists. And when he was given charge of a Royalist uprising in Paris in October 1795, he had no compunction about turning cannon on the rioters, killing 1,400.

Napoleon then turned to Italy to secure new areas of influence for the infant French Parliament. He distinguished himself with a rapid deployment of forces and skilful use of artillery borne on carriages. He rallied the starving and disenchanted men of his army, promising them health and wealth in Italy. Moreover, he rewarded them with medals, creating the Légion d'Honneur in 1802. The Austrians – in charge of large parts of Italy before it was united – were left reeling by the dynamism of his operations.

Then he hit on the idea of invading Egypt, controlled by the Ottoman Empire. With France in command in Egypt, the British shipping lanes to India would be easily disrupted. He returned home in 1799 without outright victory in Africa but with no notable defeat to blemish his reputation. On this occasion, he was mistakenly fêted as a hero. He had in fact deserted his post on hearing alarming news from home about the state of affairs in France.

Bloodletting revolutionaries had gone too far, and the public appetite for the revolution diminished. While the new rulers of France backed away from the reign of terror, they were ideologically divided, and enemies including Austria and Prussia were flirting with the idea of invasion. In pursuit of strong and orderly government, Napoleon and others staged a coup in 1799. The Consulate was established and, to the surprise of some of his colleagues, Napoleon declared himself First Consul.

Newfound power didn't stop his military ventures. He went across the Alps to regain land lost to the Austrians while he was in Egypt. Then he set up camp by the English Channel as he contemplated invasion of France's most enduring enemy, Great Britain. There was, however, a short-lived peace between the two countries while Napoleon was distracted with problems in distant Haiti, where rebellion among slaves had liberated the colony. It was only a matter of time before he was at war once more with Britain, and there were countless campaigns in Europe that generally went well.

He made landmark advances on the home front, too. The revolution had largely swept clean the legal framework of Royalist France. Successive governments in the interim had passed numerous laws. Napoleon saw the urgent need to codify the laws and set up a commission to do so. He attended its meetings when he could. Although Napoleon was becoming increasingly conservative, the heart of the legal system remained equality before the law, religious freedom and the abolition of feudalism. Although the paperwork was completed by 1801, the code wasn't published until 1804, the year Napoleon declared himself emperor. He garnered more power after popular votes in France appeared to back him.

On 2 December 1804, clad in white silk with a purple cape lined with Russian ermine, Napoleon arrived at Notre Dame Cathedral, to be crowned emperor by Pope Pius VII. Although the oath he took that day compelled him to uphold the principles of the revolution, he began to seem a more distant figure. No longer did he seek the counsel of others before making big decisions. He also had courtiers who resembled those beloved by royalty. From then on, his pursuit of power appeared more craven. His personal power reached its height in about 1810, by which time he had conquered twenty countries and married for a second time, to an Austrian princess who ultimately produced an heir.

Increasingly autocratic in his approach, Napoleon made a disastrous error in deciding to invade Russia. Usually his troops moved fast, living off the land, to make high-impact strikes against the enemy. There were few roads in Russia, which slowed the forces, and there was little to eat along the way. The Russian forces continually eluded him until both sides fought an inconclusive battle at Borodino. Finally, Napoleon's forces retreated from Russia in the worst winter weather, which felled thousands.

His empire was weakened by the failed exploit, and several European states formed an alliance to defeat him. On 18 March 1814, the Allies marched into Paris. Napoleon abdicated and was exiled to the island of Elba. As his funds dwindled, Napoleon decided on one last throw of the dice. He and some loyal soldiers left Elba to travel through France and return triumphantly to Paris for a rule of 100 days. But the resurgence ended at the Battle of Waterloo, after which Napoleon was dispatched to the South Atlantic island of St Helena.

It was a flat end to an extraordinary life, and Napoleon knew there was no going back. He wrote, with feeling, 'Glory is fleeting, but obscurity is for ever.'

Lord Horatio Nelson

(1758–1805)

I can see a man who is a risk taker, a brave man, a man of vision. The great negative is that he risked others. He is still a hero. He did what it took and he had to be ruthless to some extent. He is a man who did his duty to England and England expected him to do just that.

Benedict Allen (Explorer, writer and

TV documentary maker)

He is an archetypal icon. He was physically very conspicuous. If a man loses his right arm and has to fold an empty sleeve across him and has a blind eye over which he never wore a patch, he is conspicuous. He was a hero at a time when people needed heroes. Here was a genius, a superb sea officer, but he was not the sentimentally humane man which Victorian legend made him.

Terry Coleman (Journalist and author)

FROM THE TOP of a pillar in London's Trafalgar Square, a statue of Lord Horatio Nelson gazes into the middle distance, untroubled by the chaos unfolding below. It is a measure of the man that he was given top spot in the capital by a society in awe of his achievements. Although history has tempered the adulation in which he was once held, he is still regarded as an embodiment of duty and valour, as a man who laid down his life for his country.

Nelson was born in Burnham Thorpe, Norfolk, to a clergyman and his wife. His mother Catherine, who was a grandniece of Britain's first Prime Minister, Sir Robert Walpole, died when Nelson was a child. However, her brother Maurice Suckling became instrumental in his career. Suckling was in command of HMS *Raisonable*, when Nelson joined its crew as a midshipman at the age of 12. In 1773, Suckling saw to it that Nelson was on the ship dispatched to search for the elusive north-west passage in the Arctic Circle that would link Europe and North America. On this voyage, Nelson is said to have shot at and then clubbed a polar bear on an ice floe. It is difficult to discern whether this act of foolhardy bravery actually happened or is one of the legends that became attached to Nelson after his death.

Suckling – who himself became comptroller of the Royal Navy in 1775 – continued to speed Nelson's promotion through the ranks. By the age of 19, Nelson was a master and commander and, just a year later, he was post captain, which meant he could be in charge of a frigate or bigger. And it was as captain of HMS *Hitchingbroke* in 1779 that he captured a Spanish fort at San Juan in Spain. Nelson showed tremendous initiative and daring but was rewarded with a bout of fever that forced his return to England. In 1784, he served in the West Indies where he met and married Frances Nesbit, a widowed mother.

An outbreak of peace paused his career but in 1793, with the French revolutionary wars under way, he was given command of HMS *Agamemnon*, to serve with Lord Hood's fleet in the Mediterranean. Nelson helped wrest

Corsica from the French but was blinded in the right eye by enemy shot in 1794 at the siege of Calvi.

There was another bold display from Nelson in 1795 when he distinguished himself at the battle of Cape St Vincent against a large but unwieldy Spanish fleet. Six days later, he was promoted to Rear Admiral of the Blue and awarded Knight Commander of the Bath in recognition of his courage and skill. Two years on, it seemed his soaring career might be ended by a battle injury that resulted in his right arm being amputated. In fact, by cutting such a distinctive figure, he turned the disability into an advantage.

In 1798, he was back in action in Egypt at the Battle of the Nile when he redefined naval strategy by successfully attacking the French fleet at night. Three years later, at the Battle of Copenhagen, he pulled a victory out of the jaws of defeat by brazen tactics.

Yet even as one triumph followed the next, Nelson was apparently unpopular with his men. On one passage home from the West Indies he became infamous for flogging half his crew and the marines aboard. He spoke to officers only to give orders and refused to eat with them. In 1801, he wrote to the admiralty asking to be relieved of his command because the men in the ranks detested him.

His affair with Lady Emma Hamilton, conducted openly at a time when both were married, also scandalised society. Eventually Nelson left his wife to live with his mistress and her husband. Lord Minto, who was otherwise a fan of Nelson, had harsh words to say about his private conduct: 'Lady H goes on cramming Nelson with trowelfuls of flattery which he goes on taking as quietly as a child does pap. The love she makes to him is not only ridiculous but disgusting. Not only the rooms but the whole house, staircase and all, are covered with nothing but pictures of both him and her, of all pieces and sorts and representations of his naval actions, coats of arms, pieces of plate in his honour. An excess of vanity which counteracts its own purpose.' His reputation was also tainted by his role in the 1799 uprising in Naples. Although the dispute was largely resolved, Nelson – imbued with a sense of duty to the established order – penned the rebels in ships in the harbour rather than overseeing their agreed escape to Toulon. Later, more than 100 were executed in Naples. It has led to some commentators branding Nelson a war criminal.

But it was for his strategic mastery of sea battles that he is so fondly recalled by many. He pioneered new tactics of cutting through enemy lines to capitalise on the Royal Navy's superior, swift gunnery. Combined with a loyalty lately inspired in lower ranks, it was dubbed 'the Nelson touch'. In a letter to Lady Hamilton shortly before Trafalgar, he revealed how he outlined his battle plans to his men: 'I believe my arrival was most welcome not only to the commander of the fleet but almost to every individual in it and when I came to explain to them the Nelson touch it was like an electric shock. Some shed tears, all approved. It was new, it was singular and it was simple.'

Although he was only 46 at the time of Trafalgar, his hair was fully white and he was physically weary. Two stories that cling to Nelson are true. He did dispatch the famous signal 'England expects every man to do his duty'. And he did ask Captain Thomas Hardy to kiss him as he lay dying. A theory that he said 'Kismet, Hardy', meaning 'it is fate' falls because the word wasn't in use at the time.

England won the Battle of Trafalgar and Nelson possibly averted a planned invasion of England, although the victory didn't put an end to Napoleonic ambition. Perhaps Nelson's biggest error was wearing a coat emblazoned with substantial honours as he stood on the deck of HMS *Victory*. Despite the smoke and frenzy of battle, he stood out sufficiently that he could be picked off by a French sniper with relative ease.

Subsequent biographies made it difficult to distinguish between the myth and the man and helped elevate his national status.

Bernardo O'Higgins

(1778–1842)

I often question what makes a hero. Is it the man that makes the moment or is it some freak incident in history? I see in the persona of Bernardo a Greek tragedy in Latin American guise. I wonder what his recollections were about who he was and what he had done and how he was being perceived. Did the man die in penurious regret?

Brian Keenan (Beirut hostage)

He was a great-hearted man but he was really not good as a politician. He wanted to reform society, he wanted to give the poor their share of the cake, but he couldn't get on with the bigwigs. He pushed a liberal, progressive policy but he was hemmed in all sides by people who were on the make and on the take and he was pushed into exile in very quick time indeed.

Hugh O'Shaughnessy (Writer, South American Affairs)

'**O**'*HIGGINS MAY BE a comparatively rare name in County Roscommon or around the Ring of Kerry but it is a name you can't get away from here in Chile. His image is found on the currency and you can keep your share of that currency in the Bank O'Higgins. Or you can spend it on an O'Higgins ticket for a bus that will take you to the Parque O'Higgins, where you can stroll and feed the ducks. There are few O'Higgins in the telephone book but those who can claim him among their ancestors are not slow in telling you. Bernardo O'Higgins is revered here because at the beginning of the last century he led the successful bid to rid the country of centuries of rule by Spain and transform it into an independent republic.'*

These scene-setting words by Hugh O'Shaughnessy shed light on a little-celebrated class of hero: South American freedom fighters of Irish ancestry. O'Higgins the Liberator is among the most famous today, but he wasn't alone in battling to throw off Spanish colonial rule. He fought alongside another Chilean hero, Juan Mackenna, while across the Andes in Argentina Admiral William Brown from County Mayo fought the Brazilians and Spanish and developed the national navy to become a fêted figure there. At the same time, Simón Bolivar was surrounded by medics of Irish extraction during his independence campaign. William Lamport had earlier ignited calls for liberty in Mexico, while Argentinian-born Che Guevara, perhaps the most celebrated twentieth-century revolutionary, was of part-Irish extraction.

That O'Higgins would become such a pivotal figure was by no means certain at his birth. He was the son of an Irish-born engineer, Ambrosio, who'd found favour with the Spanish regime in Chile and been made a Marquis. Bernardo's father was 58 when he was born, while his mother was still a teenager. His father was so ashamed of the illegitimate child he had a tombstone carved for him, to make it seem like the child had died while in fact the infant was spirited away for nursing.

Initially, Bernardo was brought up with his mother's family until his absent father arranged for a formal education. The youngster went to Peru,

Spain and then England for schooling. During this time he came across the radical thinking that pervaded Europe at the time and philosophies of equality that became emblematic of the French revolution.

Although he never met his father, he was filled with dutiful affection as his letters home reveal: 'My misfortunes have quite doused my hopes of seeing my father, my mother and my country again. May God preserve your precious life. Farewell my precious father. Until heaven grant me my desire to embrace you, until then I shall not know any pleasure or happiness.'

In 1801, O'Higgins senior died, leaving extensive estates to his son. He might have continued life as a gentleman farmer had it not been for Napoleon's adventures in distant Europe seven years later, which took the French tyrant into Spain where he placed his brother on the throne. By 1810, O'Higgins had joined the revolt against French-led Spanish occupation in Chile, although widespread opposition was splintered into quarrelsome groups. In the battles against Spanish forces sent to quell the uprising, he rallied his men with the cry: 'Live with honour, or die with glory! He who is brave, follow me.'

Defeated in 1814, O'Higgins and his followers were exiled to Argentina for three years, where he worked with General José de San Martin on plans to liberate his homeland. He and his soldiers made their way home through the unforgiving Andes mountain range in a military exploit that compared with Hannibal's two thousand years previously. Although he wasn't a gifted strategist, he was a brave and passionate soldier, which helped him secure victory against the Spanish in 1818. Afterwards, San Martin declared: 'In the space of 24 days we have crossed the highest mountain range in the world, overthrown the tyrants and given liberty to Chile.'

O'Higgins took the reins of powers and instituted reforms in agriculture, the military, education and healthcare. Under Spanish rule, Chileans were divided into classes that determined people's place in society. O'Higgins was determined to scrap these ideas. Although he was benevolent he found it difficult to rule at the same time as being popular. When his programme for the poor was in jeopardy, O'Higgins said: 'If they will not be happy by their own efforts then they shall be made happy by force and by God they shall be happy.' Moreover, he offended the nobility with a plan to scrap hereditary titles and worried the powerful Catholic Church. For a while he teetered between democrat and dictator before being deposed by an erstwhile colleague.

In 1823, he left Chile with his mother, half-sister and illegitimate son. His revolutionary days were not over, however, as he joined forces with Simón Bolivar, who was fighting for independence in the middle of South America. With Bolivar's success and the ensuing unprecedented freedom on the continent, O'Higgins considered his mission complete.

A patriot to the end, though, he yearned to return to Chile. In 1842, he was given an honorary army appointment by the Chilean government which then voted to allow the exiled ruler back home. He made his way to a Peruvian port intending to sail home but was cut down by a heart attack. He died in Lima without ever seeing his homeland again. In 1869, his body was returned to Chile, where it had several different resting places until it was finally given a crypt. Gone but not forgotten, he is commemorated regularly in Chile and, to a lesser extent, in Ireland and London as well.

George Orwell

(1903–1950)

The power of great fiction is so much greater than that of dry political essays. George Orwell has been incredibly important, [his books] Animal Farm *and* 1984 *in particular, in creating my most important political drivers – the pursuit of protecting civil liberties and latterly promoting human rights. The writing is a great testament to his humanity.*

Shami Chakrabarti (Director of Liberty)

Every book and practically every bit of journalism that Orwell wrote is a projection of his own inner uncertainties and doubts. All Orwell's heroes and his single heroine are more or less the same, people oppressed by this extraordinary intolerant, all-seeing society that grinds them down ... the individual being confined by great oppressive forces targeted on this single puny individual consciousness.

D. J. Taylor (Biographer)

A S A PUPIL at Eton, a policeman in Burma, a tramp and an anti-fascist, George Orwell experienced life in every shade in the political prism. According to *Newsweek*, Orwell was 'the finest journalist of his day and the foremost architect of the English essay since Hazlitt'. His descriptions of life in the north of England, in Paris and at the front line in the Spanish Civil War were required reading for a news-hungry public.

Today his books are better remembered than the articles he left behind, with *Animal Farm* and *1984* lodging themselves at the top end of the popularity polls for literature in the twentieth century.

More subtly, however, it was his instinctive grasp of the power of language that perhaps should be at the forefront of everybody's mind when his name is mentioned. He was alert to the perils of propaganda and the threat it posed to people. 'Political language – and with variations this is true of all political parties, from Conservatives to Anarchists – is designed to make lies sound truthful and murder respectable, and to give an appearance of solidity to pure wind,' he commented. Ultimately he believed individual freedom was paramount, declaring himself a democratic socialist.

George Orwell was born Eric Arthur Blair in India, the only son of a civil servant. As a child, he returned to Britain with his mother and two sisters, winning a scholarship to a prestigious preparatory school, St Cyprian's in East Sussex. From there he went to Eton, where he undoubtedly did not fulfil his initial academic promise, although he did rub shoulders with some of the most prominent intellectuals of his generation.

Unable to go to university through lack of funds, Eric went to Burma to work as a policeman for the imperialist British authorities. The experience triggered in him an abhorrence of the colonial system, although he always had a military bearing which led most people to think he was in the services. During his time in Burma, he wrote an essay called 'The Hanging', which, although similar in feel to at least one other article on the same subject, marked out his skill as a wordsmith:

At each step his muscles slid neatly into place, a lock of hair on his scalp danced up and down, his feet printed themselves on the wet gravel and once in spite of the men who gripped him by each shoulder he stepped slightly to one side to avoid a puddle on the path. It is curious but until that moment I had never realised what it means to destroy a healthy conscious man. When I saw the prisoner step aside to avoid the puddle I saw the mystery the unspeakable wrongness of cutting a life short when it is in full tide.

After five years in Burma he came home on medical grounds in 1928. He adopted his penname – George for the patron saint of England and Orwell for a Suffolk river – in time for it to appear on his first novel, *Burmese Days*, published in 1934. This coincided with a period of abject poverty, its effects amplified in Orwell by his poor health. He worked in near slave conditions in Paris while it was still in the grip of an economic depression. After a teaching job, he worked in a second-hand book shop in London, the basis of his novel *Keep the Aspidistra Flying*.

In the mid 1930s, he lived in some of England's northern cities at the suggestion of socialist publisher Victor Gollancz, to report on a gritty reality that remained largely alien in the south:

> More than anyone else perhaps the miner can stand as the type of the manual worker, not only because his work is so exaggeratedly awful but also because it is vitally necessary and yet so remote from our experience, so invisible as it were that we are as capable of forgetting it as we forget the blood in our veins. In a way it is even humiliating to watch coal miners working. It raises in you a momentary doubt about your own status as an intellectual and a superior person generally for it is brought home to you at least while you are watching that it is only because miners sweat their guts out that superior persons can remain superior.

With the outbreak of civil war in Spain, where socialists rallied to fight for the republicans against General Franco, Orwell enlisted in one of the left-wing militias. Initially he felt the army was classless, united and took grave exception to the words of a newsman he met who said, 'This war is a racket, the same as any other.' But the callous intervention of Soviet commissars left him horrified. Shot through the neck by a fascist bullet, he found himself in comparable danger from a Soviet-orchestrated purge of socialists loyal to Trotskyite ideals. He relayed his experiences in *Homage to Catalonia*: 'Every war suffers a kind of progressive degradation with every month that it continues because such things as individual liberty and a truthful press are simply not compatible with military efficiency.'

By now his politics were coloured by his experiences and, at the outbreak of the Second World War, there was no question of him being a pacifist. Instead he enthusiastically joined the Home Guard. Later publisher Fred Warburg said: 'There was practically nothing about the Home Guard that didn't suit Orwell's temperament until it began to be efficient. The only snag with the Home Guard was that he was convinced three-quarters of the officers were fascists or potential fascists.'

Yet Orwell had matured sufficiently to believe that Oswald Mosley, leader of the British Union of Fascists, should not be silenced. 'Even a fascist should be allowed to express an opinion,' he said.

He worked for the BBC during the war, putting artful spin into his use of words. Eventually he left to write *Animal Farm*, published to immense acclaim and offering financial security for the first time. Later, *1984* was published, a chilling sci-fi style account of totalitarianism. Afterwards such scenarios became known as 'Orwellian'. Shortly before *1984* was published, he provided a list of thirty-seven active socialists and communists to a friend in the Foreign Office. Although it was a disloyal act, it better reflected his abhorrence of the Soviet Union than his lack of care for friends.

He married twice, with his first wife Eileen accompanying him to Spain. He died of tuberculosis soon after marrying for a second time and is buried in Oxfordshire.

Thomas Paine

(1737–1809)

*He was arguably the man who made the American Revolution possible.
He played a major role in the French Revolution. [But] in Britain we
have an incredible disregard of our own revolutionary tradition. I wish
I could write with the clarity he has. He stripped away so much of the
mystery of politics, and he allowed us to see things far more clearly
than before. He had an extremely important legacy, not just as a radical
but also as a writer.*

George Monbiot (Writer)

*Everybody has heard of Thomas Paine, but it is amazing how little
people know of his life. When people talk about the Norfolk hero, it is
Nelson they mean, not Thomas Paine.*

Chad Goodwin (Chairman, Thomas Paine Society)

HOME-GROWN REVOLUTIONARIES have been few and far between in Britain in the past three centuries. Radical Thomas Paine was hailed as a hero in America and France after he produced stirring, stark speeches and pioneering pamphlets. At home in England, he was hung in effigy with a copy of his controversial book in one hand and a corset in the other. The Brits, it seemed, were not as ready for the rebel cause as their neighbours and colonial brethren.

Born in Thetford, Norfolk, Paine – the son of a Quaker corset-maker – eventually abandoned his education in order to become an apprentice to his father. It was not the career he had dreamed of and, until the age of 37, he tried his hand at various trades including seaman, shopkeeper and excise officer. In his spare time, he joined a debating society and helped the poor. He also wrote a paper explaining why excise men like himself should be paid better wages.

Paine had two unhappy marriages and finally went bankrupt before heading for America, with letters of recommendation in hand from Benjamin Franklin, who he had met in London. It was here he got the opportunity to turn his hand to writing as a job and discovered it was where his natural talents lay. As well as working as a journalist, Paine is credited with a passionate tract on slavery:

> Christians are taught to account all men their neighbours; and love their neighbours as themselves; and do to all men as they would be done by; to do good to all men; and Man-stealing is ranked with enormous crimes. Is the barbarous enslaving our inoffensive neighbours, and treating them like wild beasts subdued by force, reconcilable with all these Divine precepts? Is this doing to them as we would desire they should do to us? If they could carry off and enslave some thousands of us, would we think it just? – One would almost wish they could for once; it might convince more than Reason, or the Bible.

British aggression at Lexington Green, where the opening salvoes of the American Revolution were fired, persuaded Paine about the merits of independence. His response was the publication in 1776 of 'Common Sense', a pamphlet which advocated self-rule of the colony on a strictly democratic basis and rejected piecemeal concessions offered by the British. Until it appeared, there was division among the colonists as to the best way forward. 'Common Sense', published anonymously, swung public opinion in favour of independence. If Paine did not invent the phrase 'United States of America' at this time, he certainly popularised it. Although he didn't sign the Declaration of Independence, he is nonetheless considered a Founding Father in American history.

Initially, Paine found work in the new American republic but a zealous desire to expose corruption earned him more enemies than friends. On hearing the Paris Commune was looking for a design for an iron bridge for the River Seine, he crossed the Atlantic and ended up commuting between Britain and France in his role as engineer. In France he witnessed some of the cruelties that preceded the French Revolution. In England, he saw influential Edmund Burke dismiss the growing discontent across the Channel with ill-informed statements. Once again, Paine chose to make his voice heard in printed form. The result was *Rights of Man*, a plea to overturn the traditional and especially the hereditary aspects of political power in favour of democracy driven by talent. Once again, it created a stir when it was published – and not entirely in the way Paine might have hoped.

While its notions of liberation for the poor and universal suffrage were used to underpin the Revolution in France, Paine was charged with seditious libel in England. Although the book was priced cheaply and sold well, a campaign conducted by the British government to tarnish Paine's reputation with the black art of propaganda did far more to publicise his work than the writer ever did. But when the *Rights of Man Part II* appeared in 1792, Paine finally fled Britain, chased to the shore by an angry mob.

He sought refuge in France where he and his radical ideas were warmly welcomed until the Revolution's sting in the tail – known as the Terror – got under way. Like numerous other observers of the Revolution, he failed to see what was coming and the unfettered bloodshed at the guillotine washed over radical politics like a tsunami. Among many, Paine was denounced as a royalist by the vengeful Maximilien Robespierre, self-styled leader of Revolutionary France, and only escaped the guillotine by a whisker. It seemed to the British this was proof, if any were needed, of the perils of radicalism.

It's tempting to conclude that facets of Paine's personality did him no favours at this time. One Frenchman called him 'drunk with vanity' following the success of his writings: 'He knew all his own writings by heart but he knew nothing else.' While Paine was languishing inside a French jail, however, he completed *The Age of Reason*, a contemplation of religion that was way ahead of its time – and it was this that sent his popularity ratings to an all-time low. He favoured Deism above organised religion, writing: 'All national institutions of churches, whether Jewish, Christian, or Turkish, appear to me no other than human inventions set up to terrify and enslave mankind, and monopolize power and profit.'

As a consequence, he became universally loathed in what was still a largely God-fearing European society. After gaining freedom once again, he remained in France for a while until Napoleon began his dictatorship, eventually flying in the face of everything Paine espoused. In 1802, Paine left France for America, where he spent his last years dogged by the ill-effects of disease and drink.

His funeral was sparsely attended and obituaries were generally unkind. One read: 'He had lived long, did some good and much harm.'

This wasn't the end of Paine's story, however. William Cobbett, another radical and pamphleteer, exhumed Paine's bones and brought them back to England with the intention of organising a public memorial. The grand plan never happened and, worse still, the skeleton vanished after Cobbett's death in 1835. Its whereabouts remain unknown. A memorial planned by Cobbett at the time was never built.

Frank Pakenham,
7th Earl of Longford

(1904–2001)

He lived a great life that intersected with the great events of the twentieth
century. He was the most extraordinary and fulfilling company. I really
did admire his principle and his morals stands. To me, he was kind of
an accessible father. He was terribly respectful towards me. He was a
wonderful friend.

Jon Snow (Newsreader and former Longford employee)

He liked the attention. His dress was eccentric. You could often see
what he had been eating for the last few days down the front of his
clothes. He would often turn up at the front door with someone odd
that he'd met in the street.

Peter Standford (Biographer)

I was number five in a family that became eight. He used to give
everybody who happened to be in the house pocket money. It was
a brilliant method of being sure his children got something even if
various others did too.

Rachel Billington (Daughter)

MOORS MURDERER MYRA Hindley was Britain's most hated women. After being convicted of two murders in 1966, her crimes with accomplice Ian Brady became the benchmark by which other acts of evil and depravity were judged. But while British people uniformly recoiled at the sight of the peroxide hair and pouting lips of her police mugshot, one man sacrificed his good reputation to become her ally and her friend. Lord Longford, who was convinced she had killed under Brady's malign influence, spent decades trying to win her release on the grounds that she had redeemed herself and was now a politically held prisoner. He continued to support her case for freedom, even after she admitted further murders and helped locate a body on Saddleworth Moor that she'd buried years earlier.

A prison visitor since the 1930s, Longford aspired to wholesale reform in jails. He devoted his time not only to high-profile prisoners like Hindley but also to sick and dying convicts who saw no one from one month to the next. Former Tory Cabinet minister Lord Hailsham opposed him politically but lauded Longford for his humanitarian work: 'His concern for the outcasts of society is perfectly genuine. Even when one is most exasperated at the impracticality of some of his demands or the apparent irresponsibility of some of his behaviour, one is glad from the bottom of one's heart that there exists in the world a man so single-hearted that he is prepared to espouse such hopeless causes.'

Born Frank Pakenham, he was a second son neglected by a mother who idolised her eldest at his expense. His father Thomas died in the First World War during the Gallipoli campaign. Frank went to Eton then Oxford, where he got a first in Philosophy, Politics and Economics. He also met his future wife, Elizabeth Harman. She was a socialist, as was his former roommate at Oxford, Hugh Gaitskell.

'I was Conservative,' he admitted later. 'I wasn't very sure when I went to Oxford what I wanted to do, but by the time I finished, particularly after I got this first and therefore seemed rather a promising figure and was one of the few Conservatives with even the feeblest claim to economics, I had quite a nice little career waiting for me. I began work in the Conservative research department. It lasted until just after I married. I can't imagine my wife would have tolerated it.'

Indeed, the couple had one of the happiest marriages in politics, lasting some seventy years. The pair were politically united after Pakenham joined the Labour Party, becoming a councillor in Oxford and skirmishing with British Union of Fascists founder Oswald Mosley. The marriage survived his surprise conversion to Catholicism in 1940. Although she was initially concerned about his change of faith, Elizabeth became a Catholic herself six years later.

Pakenham opposed appeasement policies and, following the outbreak of the Second World War, he enlisted as a private on the Ox and Bucks Light Infantry. A ceaseless target for officers who believed he should follow his class rather than his conscience, Pakenham suffered a breakdown before even making it to a battleground. He returned home to serve in the Home Guard, nursing a long-term wound to his family pride. More fruitfully, he spent much of the early war years helping William Beveridge to hammer out a report that laid the foundations for the welfare state.

At the end of the war, he hoped to become Labour MP for Oxford but was beaten by Quentin Hogg, who later became Lord Hailsham. Instead he became Baron Pakenham of Cowley, entering the House of Lords and joining Clement Attlee's government as a junior minister. His accomplishments in government look even better from a present-day perspective. Initially, he worked in occupied Germany, fighting the conquered nation's case. He was driven by the conviction that Germany needed to once again become an industrial power to secure future peace – although many of her erstwhile enemies wanted to keep the country in ruins. He also outraged many Britons by announcing that Germany had been forgiven for hostilities. Back at home, he oversaw civil aviation and did much to establish Heathrow Airport, one of the most successful British enterprises ever. Later he became First Lord of the Admiralty.

Attlee saw beyond Pakenham's shambolic bluster to his unquestioned intellect and ability. Later, Pakenham told how he tried to resign on numerous occasions on matters of principle. 'He would write me a letter in a very friendly way. "My dear Frank, I have noted the point you mentioned and I hope to see you later, yours ever, Clem", leaving one absolutely sunk. I tried it two or three times.' He was valued by Gaitskell too but Harold Wilson, when he became Labour leader and later Prime Minister, was pleased to be rid of Longford when he resigned in 1968 over Labour's failure to raise the school leaving age.

In 1961, he inherited the earldom from his brother and became known as Lord Longford. However, it wasn't the only name he was known by in Britain. His campaign for Hindley earned him the title 'Lord Wrongford' in the British press and a somewhat wrongheaded crusade against pornography that included a trip around Danish sex clubs left him known as 'Lord Porn'. He bore the constant, cascading criticism of British newspapers with remarkable equanimity, convinced that all publicity was good publicity. His opposition to homosexuality also made him a target. The notion that he was a soft touch for criminals wasn't entirely accurate, but he remained determined to help those who had transgressed. Unfortunately, his lively campaigning provided scant comfort for the victims of crime.

Longford was never afraid of incurring popular wrath for a cause he believed in and hoped his epitaph would be 'the outcast's outcast'. In 1990, journalist and broadcaster Bernard Levin summed up the political dilemma Longford posed: 'Everybody asks the wrong question about Lord Longford, viz. is he barmy? The question is not worth asking: of course he is barmy. What we should be discussing is something quite different: is he right?'

Pablo Picasso

(1881–1973)

Seeing his pictures changed my life. I realised suddenly there were no rules. Picasso showed me you can be outside the box the whole time. The wheel didn't have to be round. He didn't affect my photography, but he affected my way of thinking and looking at things.
David Bailey (Photographer)

There is enormous strength in Picasso from the very beginning to the very end. Even if you hate the stuff, it's powerful.
Brian Sewell (Art critic)

D ISCUSS THE NATURE of modern art, and the name Picasso soon falls from the lips. With an able hand and a fluid mind, he pushed back the perimeters of art in the twentieth century, and his name came to define a style as well as a clutch of masterpieces.

Although his work became radical, his upbringing was extremely conventional. His full name alone, Pablo Diego José Francisco de Paula Juan Nepomuceno María de los Remedios Cipriano de la Santísima Trinidad Clito Ruiz y Picasso, betrays middle-class roots. He soon chose to live by his mother's maiden name. The son of an art teacher, Picasso's irrepressible talent was spotted early. But attempts to school him were largely frustrated by his desire to go it alone.

At the turn of the twentieth century, he flipped between France and Spain, soaking up the works of great artists and getting a feel for street life. His work went in phases, beginning with realism followed by caricature. Then came the celebrated Blue period, where the lines were predominantly dark and the themes melancholic. The subjects were often those who dwelt at the margins of society. One of the most celebrated works was dedicated to a childhood friend and poet, Casagemas, who had committed suicide. The Blue period lasted for three years until 1904.

Thereafter Picasso's palette became brighter, with the advent of the Rose period, and his subject less sombre. Afterwards, he flirted with the classics then became entranced by the work of Henri Matisse, who was leading the Fauvists, which translates from French to mean wild animals and relates to the garish colours used by artists pursuing this style. Indeed, he became something of a concern for other artists who saw their own ideas freely incorporated into his work. He batted accusations away with the words 'Bad artists copy, great artists steal.'

His interest in Iberian sculpture led naturally to a taste for African art. Picasso began painting in simplified but striking style. In 1907, he painted a signature piece, *Les Demoiselles d'Avignon*, featuring five figures, two of which were comparatively natural and three strangely angular. He was finding his way into the entirely new arena of Cubism alongside close colleague Georges Braque, but wasn't sure what response it would have. Consequently, he kept *Les Demoiselles d'Avignon* under wraps until 1916.

According to Thomas Hoving, who wrote *Art for Dummies*: 'Cubism is essentially the fragmenting of three-dimensional forms into flat areas of pattern and colour, overlapping and intertwining so that shapes and parts of the human anatomy are seen from the front and back at the same time.' Picasso's paintings of women in Cubist form seem to betray an ambivalent feeling, although his love life was nothing if not colourful. He had four children and a number of significant relationships. One of his partners, Françoise Gilot, who in 1965 published a book about her life with Picasso, developed a theory about his approach to partners:

> His attitude towards women is one of an adolescent even now and I think also he is very frightened of death so if he will see the sign of death on another human being, like being older, that will frighten him. Maybe he has always been in search of youth. He says that even as a painter it takes a long time to become young.

By 1913, Cubism had caused a sensation in the art world, and Picasso led the Cubist movement from the front, perpetually tweaking his style and making the movement more fluid. If he was questioned about apparently random shapes on the canvas, he would characteristically reply: 'I don't paint what I see, I paint what I think.' While the art world was divided about its worth there was no doubt that he did what he did expertly and with feeling. It wasn't the end of his artistic journey, though. Before his death, he experimented with classical forms once again and with surrealism.

The great conflicts of the twentieth century had a marked effect on Picasso's output. In 1937, he painted a massive and disturbingly brutal canvas called *Guernica*, depicting the German bombing of a Spanish town during the country's bitter civil war. It's the work that perhaps most defines Picasso, even today. When the Second World War erupted, he was in Paris. He chose passive resistance to the Nazis rather than armed struggle. He refused to sanction their rule with acceptance of 'bribes' of extra food and coal rations commonly offered to eminent intellectuals at the time.

In October 1944, he joined the French Communist Party and remained a member until his death. Motivated more by the quest for peace, equality and social justice than by pure politics, his membership has been condemned as a stunt. Fellow artist Salvador Dalí said: 'Picasso is a Spaniard, so am I. Picasso is a communist, neither am I.' There's a belief he was manipulated by the communist media after the war. However, his work of the period reflects his continuing concerns about man's inhumanity to man.

He was working throughout the cold war, when the threat of nuclear holocaust loomed large. Perhaps the most iconic art he produced in that time was the dove of peace, adopted as a potent symbol by anti-war groups. With a few flourishes of a crayon, he created an enduring emblem. He was inspired by the hosts of pigeons that flocked to the ledges of his studio. They were also reminiscent of the pictures his father had painted when Picasso was a child. Picasso's daughter was born shortly before the Paris Peace Congress, and he named her Paloma, the Spanish word for dove. It wasn't just one Picasso peace dove but many. He produced numerous variations on posters, prints and badges for different peace initiatives.

For the rest of his life, he was lauded as an idol in the art world, although critics felt his best work was already a distant memory. He found a fresh interest in sculpture, pottery and making prints which, despite his great age, bore his hallmark of intensity and originality.

He finally died while hosting a dinner party. Memorably, his final words were: 'Drink to me, drink to my health, you know I can't drink any more.'

Pope John Paul II

(1920–2005)

This pope was quite remarkable. It isn't only the historical features, such as him being the first non-Italian pope since 1520 or the huge length of the pontifical reign, the second longest in papal history. It was the character, the charisma, the holiness of the man himself. I met him in 1996, when I had between fifteen and twenty minutes alone with him. He spoke fluent English. He ranged tremendously in the conversation he was having with me, but throughout it all I had a sense of being closer to God just by being with this man. There was an almost tangible link to the early Church. I have met churchmen galore, and I have only met with real holiness three times and that was certainly the most intense.

Ann Widdecombe (Former politician)

He was a pope that Catholics loved but disagreed with. They were saying to themselves, we'll make the rules. They had become relativists. Pope John Paul II was the prime absolutist who said moral relativism does not work, and he came to Ireland to say it at a time when Ireland was discovering relativism as freedom. John Paul's understanding of moral relativism as simply taking a popular vote on what is right and what is wrong is a failure to understand that people derive moral lessons from experience.

Malachi O'Doherty (Writer)

A S THE INSPIRATIONAL leader of more than a billion Catholics worldwide, Pope John Paul II became as familiar in his twenty-seven-year reign as any head of state or royal. Even those outside the Catholic faith were left in awe at the workload of a man who was ultimately in the winter of his life. He visited 129 countries, spoke fourteen different languages and survived illness and assassination attempts. The first non-Italian pope since 1522, he made immense efforts to impart God's message while at the same time building bridges with other religions. Perhaps he will be best remembered for his people-aware use of the Popemobile, a glassy cart he used to travel through the throngs who gathered to see him on visits.

Pope John Paul began life as Karol Józef Wojtyła in the Polish town of Wadowice. He was the youngest of three children, though one – Olga – died before he was born. As a child, Karol was close to his brother Edmund. However, his joy in family life was extinguished early; firstly with the death of his mother when he was 8 and then, four years later, when his doctor brother died of scarlet fever.

In his youth he was a keen athlete, regularly playing in soccer matches between the Catholic and Jewish populations of Wadowice. He was always the first to volunteer for the Jewish team if they were short of players. Alone with his father in a spartan apartment behind the church, the pair would often hone their football skills using a ball made of rags.

He moved with his father to Krakow in 1938, where he enrolled at university and pursued his interests in poetry and theatre. He was also a fine singer. But the storm that started the Second World War soon engulfed him. With Nazi invasion, he sidestepped deportation by getting a job as a stonecutter at a quarry. Life was tough for Poles under occupation, though, and in 1941 the privations claimed the life of Wojtyła's father, whose final wishes were that his son would train for the priesthood. Eighteen months later, Wojtyła fulfilled them by joining an underground seminary in Krakow – at a time when the Nazis began brutalising Catholics who opposed the regime. He continued working by day until 1944, when the Germans began rounding up able-bodied Polish men. At this point he took shelter in the Archbishop of Krakow's palace.

After the war, Catholics like Wojtyła faced a new and powerful enemy: Communism. It became increasingly difficult for him to complete his extensive studies in theology and philosophy while working as a pastor. The Catholic University in Lublin survived, however, and he won a chair in Ethics there in 1956. From that launch pad, he ascended the hierarchy of the Church, becoming Archbishop of Krakow aged 38, and a cardinal by the age of 47. On the face of it, he compromised with Communism so he wasn't suppressed by the state. In reality he had little time for its strictures and looked forward to its defeat.

His weighty intellect was in evidence with many papers on Church practice authored by him, all well received. Yet he wasn't the automatic choice for Pope upon the death of John Paul I in 1978, who held tenure for just thirty-three days. Support was split between the two other candidates, both Italian, one conservative and one liberal. Wojtyła finally secured sufficient support in the eighth ballot and chose to go forward with the name of his predecessor.

In post, Pope John Paul II was broadly a moderate reformer. He did much to support young people and linked up with other world faiths. Perhaps drawing on the love of theatre he knew as a young man, he relished the chance to travel when other popes had previously lived a somewhat withdrawn existence behind the Vatican walls. In 1979, he went to Ireland to celebrate mass in Phoenix Square with more than a quarter of the country's population. When he visited Cuba in 1998, Communist leader Fidel Castro was uncharacteristically deferential.

And it was in Communist countries that he wrought the greatest changes. He tacitly supported Solidarity, the Polish freedom movement, from its inception in 1980 as the first non-Communist trade union. Union leader Lech Walesa later said that the Pope, in secret messages, had told him:

'Don't be afraid.' Behind the scenes, the Pope warned Soviet authorities he would travel to Poland and man the barricades if they invaded. Within a decade, the Communist leadership in Poland fell along with the rest of the Eastern-bloc countries, domino-style. In 1994, *Time* magazine named him Man of the Year, saying he generated electricity 'like no one else on Earth'.

There was criticism, too. He reiterated Catholic opposition to the use of birth control when the rampant spread of AIDS among African Catholics could have been hindered or even halted with official sanction for condoms. His conservative resistance to condoms, women priests and homosexuality was intended to reinforce the core strength of the church.

In 1981, in St Peter's Square in Rome, the Pope was felled by two bullets fired by Turk Mehmet Ali Ağca and only survived after five hours of surgery. Two years later, he forgave Ağca during a private meeting. This and a subsequent, less serious assassination attempt were linked to the prophecies made by children who saw a vision of the Virgin Mary at Fatima in Portugal in 1917. There's still doubt whether the incidents are a jigsaw fit, though, as the vague and loose terms of the prophecy are open to interpretation. Even after sustaining these injuries, he continued a busy schedule. In Britain, Cardinal Basil Hume said, 'I can't see him changing, and he's not the kind of person who would want to be sealed off.'

He continued as Pontiff, despite a dramatic decline in health in his later years, exacerbated by the onset of Parkinson's Disease. After his death, he was immediately fast-tracked for sainthood, after he was said to have cured a French nun of Parkinson's.

Elvis Presley

(1935–1977)

Elvis – in the changes he made to the music scene, to popular culture and to many aspects of life, including the changes he made in terms of the relations between us and the United States – was really significant. If he was just a good-looking singer with a good voice he wouldn't be remembered and he wouldn't have made the tremendous impact that he has.

Lord David Trimble (Politician and Nobel Peace Prize winner)

What you hear is this vulnerability in his voice, this way in which he reaches out to an unseen audience that would serve him all of his life. It really is something that can't be taught, that can't be fully analysed.

Peter Guralnick (Biographer)

FROM SLICK-HAIRED teen to cult phenomenon, Elvis Presley was a pioneering, popular and prolific recording star who became larger than life to his adoring fans. The bestselling recording artist in America, he has more gold singles and platinum albums than anyone else before or since. Yet it was not immense record sales but gentle charm and subtle charisma that earned him the title 'the King'. Since his untimely death from an overdose of prescription drugs, every facet of his life has been pored over in minute detail. The result remains the same: he was a boy from the wrong side of the tracks who was catapulted to stardom beyond compare and was ultimately killed by the toxic side effects of immense fame.

Elvis Aaron Presley was born in humble circumstances in Tupelo, Mississippi, with a twin brother who died at birth. When Elvis was 3 years old, his father was jailed for forgery. Despite the misery of a breadline existence, Elvis found considerable comfort in music. He was heavily influenced by (white) church music and (black) rhythm and blues, more so after the family moved to Memphis, Tennessee, when he was 12.

He left school, apparently destined to be an odd job man like his father. In 1953, however, he went to a studio and paid four dollars allegedly to record a song for his mother. He was probably hoping to be noticed by the studio boss, Sam Phillips, but it wasn't until the following year that Phillips took an interest, and Elvis joined his Sun Records label, making five hits. Sam Phillips would later describe him as 'insecure' and that description applies to Elvis in every aspect of his life other than performing music.

There were hiccups at this early stage in his career. He was fired from an early club engagement and told he would never make it. As late as 1956, Elvis told one reporter he could not be sure that rock and roll would last. But with surprising speed he became a celebrity in the American south. 'It all happened so fast it seemed like a dream,' Elvis said later.

Although his influences included ballads, country music and blues, Elvis became the figurehead of rock and roll. This didn't always serve him well.

By the mid 1950s, there was a backlash against the new music, which was blamed for encouraging teenage rebellion and lax morals. Elvis came in for special criticism for the on-stage hip-swinging that earned him the nickname Elvis the Pelvis. 'I'm not trying to be vulgar,' he responded. 'I'm enjoying what I'm doing, I like to make the best of it. I don't like being called Elvis the Pelvis. It is one of the most childish expressions I have ever heard coming from an adult.' Partly to destroy this 'dangerous' image Elvis dressed in tails – and blue suede shoes – and sang his hit 'Hound Dog' to a basset hound on television in 1956.

As well as being a recording artist, Elvis was cast in numerous films, some of which were markedly better than others. With his brooding good looks and melodic voice, he was an obvious candidate for seductive screen star. However, Elvis had higher aspirations than the rom-com musicals with which he became associated, idealising actors like James Dean and Marlon Brando and studying the Stanislavsky method of acting.

In 1958, he was called up for the army. Although he was extremely patriotic and felt he should be treated like other young men his age he privately despaired that his carefully wrought career was abruptly halted. While he was in the army, he trained to expand his vocal range and he returned to civilian life with enormous musical ambition.

Under the guidance of his manager, Colonel Tom Parker, he had been among the first in a generation of stars to benefit from television broadcasting. He did so again, appearing in 1960 on a show with Frank Sinatra designed to reignite Elvis's career. Sinatra had made no secret of the fact he loathed rock and roll, calling it 'the most brutal, ugly, desperate, vicious form of expression it has been my misfortune to hear'. So there was inevitably a frisson between the pair, and show was a hit.

By 1968, however, the movies were tired and the blockbuster records had dried up. One TV station agreed to make an Elvis Christmas special that programme-makers, along with the star himself, hoped would re-launch his flagging career. At the start of the show, his hand trembled nervously as it reached for the microphone. But the distinctive quality in his voice that had won so many fans in the 1950s was unmistakeable.

The following year, he began a demanding schedule which is primarily remembered for the stints in Las Vegas where he played two shows a night for sustained spells. He performed 837 consecutive sold-out shows in front of audiences that totalled 2.5 million. As always, Elvis was passionate about playing and sought the highest professional standards from himself and his musicians. Yet something decayed in that period, not least Elvis's personal dreams. By 1976, when he did his last Vegas engagement, his stage persona was defined by white, studded jumpsuits, extended sideburns and an exaggerated quiff.

Privately, Elvis became difficult and dissolute, pursuing odd hobbies for intense periods. His eating and prescription drug intake was out of control. Always insecure apart from when he was playing, Elvis now seemed dogged by a sense of failure with all his initial aspirations in tatters. His marriage in 1967 to Priscilla, who he'd met as a girl, was also finished. He admitted to a long-time friend, 'I get so tired of being Elvis.'

His body was found on the floor of the bathroom at Graceland, his Memphis home. Initially, his death was said to have been caused by a heart disease. Toxicology reports later highlighted the presence of prescription drugs in his body some of which were given to him for toothache. Afterwards, fans were reluctant to accept his death and the notion that Elvis was still alive gained currency for a number of years.

Sergei Rachmaninoff

(1873–1943)

As a boy I used to hang out at record stores. One day the dealer said, 'I think you are going to enjoy this.' I put on a bit of a recording of the Second Symphony and bought it immediately. From the recordings, what we hear is an extraordinary technique tempered by a wide range of colour and dynamic. I know that if I was going to list five people I would love to have heard live, he would be at the top.

Leonard Slatkin (Conductor)

The compositions that he left are increasing in popularity. Over the last thirty or so years we have come to know practically all his output.

Geoffrey Norris (Biographer)

SERGEI RACHMANINOFF WAS an embodiment of contradiction. He was lauded as a pianist when he wanted to compose. He lived in America when he preferred his Russian homeland, and he worked during the twentieth century in a definitively nineteenth-century style. Perhaps for all these reasons, he was thought to be morose and world-weary.

He wasn't always that way. As a boy, he was known for being skittish with studies, preferring skating to lessons. He was the son of Russian aristocrats who were amateur musicians and lived in comparative luxury in Novgorod, north-west Russia. Yet his childhood wasn't easy. His father Vasily was such a spendthrift the family estate ultimately had to be sold to settle his debts.

Initially, his family went to St Petersburg where Rachmaninoff won a scholarship to study music at the conservatory there. His carefree days came to an end when his sister Sophia died in a diphtheria outbreak and his parents' marriage broke up. Subsequently, his mother Lubov dispatched him to Moscow, where the discipline was greater – and Rachmaninoff responded by producing some memorable works including Prelude in C Sharp Minor. The runaway popularity of this single piece dogged him in later life. He once wrote to a fan to assure him there was no hidden meaning behind it and declared he was tired of being asked the same question. He could not understand how a piece of music written when he was 19 could continue to loom so large in his career. (Having failed to take international copyright, his earnings from it were negligible.)

Rachmaninoff cut quite a figure. He was six feet six inches tall and possessed enormous hands with unusually long fingers, with which he was able to perform astonishing feats of dexterity on a piano keyboard. For this reason, his teacher in Moscow was determined to keep him a piano player. However, Rachmaninoff was at least as keen on composing as he was on playing and he had to fight for the right to undertake composition classes. However, an early setback nearly ended his writing days before they had properly begun.

On 27 March 1897, his first symphony received cruel criticism when it premiered under conductor Alexander Glazunov. Rachmaninoff was so nervous he left the performance building to ride city street cars rather than listen. Inside there was general derision, if not for the music then for the way it was interpreted by Glazunov, who was suspected of being drunk. Rachmaninoff was so scarred by the experience he refused to write for several years and sought counselling to overcome the affecting trauma of the episode.

Fortunately he returned to the public eye as one of the last composer-performers of the age to begin a hugely fertile period that ended only with the Russian Revolution in 1917. However, he did not revisit the first symphony again, and it was only resurrected after his death.

In 1902, he married his first cousin Natalia Satina. The service was conducted by an Army cleric because the Eastern Orthodox Church objected to the close family relationship. The couple went on to have two daughters and enjoyed a happy family life. Rachmaninoff was a devoted father and there's ample evidence the dour mask of the concert pianist was dropped behind closed doors at home, where he laughed and played with his family. At a family home in Switzerland on the banks of Lake Lucerne, he enjoyed fast cars and boats. His wife accompanied him on foreign tours.

Seven years later, he visited America for the first time, which he found too frenetic for his tastes. However, it was to America he finally headed via Copenhagen after the 1917 revolution in Russia when his property was seized. Rachmaninoff never lost a passionate love of his homeland and aching nostalgia is often evident in his music. He was among many Russians making a new life in the USA. He established a household in which Russian servants served Russian food, with plenty of fellow countrymen dropping by to observe familiar customs. There were a number of Russian musicians already established in California, where he chose to live. Once again, his output stalled as he struggled to come to terms with his new existence. Compelled to perform to support his family, he had less time to compose and felt his inspiration was lacking. His heyday was already behind him.

In Russia, public performance of his music was banned for some time in response to his departure, although it wasn't until 1931 that he directly criticised the Soviet government. He was a signatory to a letter that appeared in the *New York Times* condemning the extremes of Stalin's rule. Consequently, he was declared an enemy of the people and forbidden from ever returning.

He now knew beyond doubt that he would never see Russia again, and he became swamped in melancholy. Yet it wasn't enough to silence him completely. In 1934, he produced his most famous work, *Rhapsody on a Theme of Paganini*. He also mastered the diversity of the orchestra better than ever before, and became a major recording artist, producing numerous albums especially with RCA Victor. As an old romantic, he benefitted from new technology in a way his predecessors never did.

Rachmaninoff died of cancer believing he was 'hunting three hares' with composing, conducting and playing. He worried whether or not he had caught any of them. Critics considered him a relic of a bygone age, with his stoic refusal to embrace modern music. However, fans who rued the passing of the melodic age of symphony music ensured he remained at the top of the pile.

Rembrandt

(1606–1669)

Art is made by people and it is made for people. I chose Rembrandt because he embraces the whole of life in the most generous, gutsy way. He is for everybody, his humanity is universal, and you don't have to be taught anything [about art] to look at it. I always refer to him as Ronnie Rembrandt which raises a few eyebrows but makes him more of a pal.

Maggi Hambling (Artist)

For all his ground-breaking and originality, he is very much like Shakespeare – he shows us ourselves. You look at one of his paintings or etchings or drawings and you get a strong sense of the inner person. You feel all these centuries melt away and you think, 'That person could be me.' That is what draws people to his work, that is what makes him a genius. Everybody recognises something in his subjects. And he felt everything in nature was worthy of depiction.

Sarah Emily Miano (Novelist)

WITH EXTRAORDINARY CLARITY, Rembrandt painted the seventeenth-century world bathed in haunting light and furnished with minute detail. He also painted, drew or etched himself more than seventy times, leaving ample evidence of the penetrating gaze which once lingered on subjects and objects that now hang on the walls of the world's finest galleries. Today, Rembrandt is recognised as the finest painter in a generation. He was fashionable for a while during his lifetime, with contemporary Swiss monk Gabriel Bucelimis dubbing him 'the miracle of our age'. But his popularity diminished as trends changed.

The contrast of light and shadow that dominated Rembrandt's early works, a style imported from the Italian Renaissance, fell from grace. Later people also judged his paintings too dark, not realising that was the result of the dull tones of varnish layered onto the canvases down the years. It was only when twentieth-century art restoration techniques were applied to his paintings that Rembrandt's true genius as painter and colourist shone out.

Details of his life are sketchy. Rembrandt Harmenszoon van Rijn was the son of a miller, born in Leiden, the Netherlands. Although his family was not wealthy, he was educated first at the Latin School and later at university. But it was soon clear that he was destined not for an academic future, but an artistic one. He began working with an artist in Leiden then, for a short while, for one in Amsterdam. Then he returned to Leiden as an independent artist.

Previously, European artists were assured of a good living in commissions from the wealthy Catholic Church. Following the Reformation in Holland, this source of income vanished. Rembrandt was capable enough to attract the business of wealthy Leiden residents who wanted portraits of themselves or their families. But when times were quiet he turned to life on the streets for inspiration. Throughout his career he used prostitutes, street sellers and servants as subjects, as well as the rich and locally famous.

Eventually, he returned to Amsterdam with the intention of becoming a court painter and, in 1632, he produced his first group portrait, *The*

Anatomy Lesson of Dr Nicolaes Tulp. Rembrandt was under pressure to earn well, as he was a big spender. Regardless of his income, he bought paintings, sculptures and artefacts he could use as props in paintings and eventually he ran into financial difficulties.

The effects of his extravagance were offset for a while by his marriage to Saskia van Uylenburgh in 1634. Although he was by this time one of the most eminent artists in Amsterdam, her family was still concerned he spent too much of her money on art. She was painted and drawn by him on numerous occasions, so the presumption is the marriage was happy. They had three children but only one, a son named Titus, survived. The union was also brief, as she died in 1642, aged only 29.

In the same year, Rembrandt produced the canvas familiarly known as *The Night Watch*. It has been an accepted truth that the picture was poorly received, although there's no evidence for this. (It may have been perpetuated because some of the subjects felt they were not sufficiently prominent or because the picture was later cut down before being moved to Amsterdam's town hall.) However, Rembrandt did pause in his volley of portrait painting – either through a determined decision or a lack of commission – and experimented with his style after this date, soon using a palette knife to pile on paint on some occasions. The end results were designed to be viewed from a distance and he urged visitors to stand back because 'the smell of the colours' would bother them.

Following Saskia's death, a housekeeper, Geertje Dircx, moved in to care for Rembrandt and his son, and became the artist's mistress. The couple parted acrimoniously when another woman, Hendrickje Stoffels, arrived as a servant. Rembrandt and Stoffels fell in love, and Dircx was ultimately institutionalised for theft on Rembrandt's say-so. A will left by first wife Saskia rendered the couple unable to marry without incurring a huge financial penalty, but once again Rembrandt seems to have been in love. In 1654, the couple had a daughter, Cornelia.

Rembrandt continued to live beyond his means which, against the backdrop of a general economic downturn and a plague epidemic, brought him to bankruptcy. His collection of art and antiquities was sold off in 1656 to satisfy creditors, and his financial affairs were taken over by Stoffels and Titus, with the artist effectively becoming their employee. When they could no longer afford the mortgage repayments, they moved from a grand home that now houses a museum devoted to Rembrandt to a much smaller place. Before his own death, Rembrandt mourned the passing of both Titus, who died shortly after his marriage and six months before the birth of his daughter, and Stoffels.

Subsequently Rembrandt's work was the subject of criticism, particularly as art fashion bobbed and weaved down the centuries. But some people have always kept the faith, like seventeenth-century Dutch artist and admirer Gérard de Lairesse, who declared: 'Everything that art and the brush can achieve was possible for him and he was the greatest painter of the time and is still unsurpassed. For, they say, was there ever a painter who by means of colour came as close to nature by his beautiful light, lovely harmony, and unique, unusual thoughts and so forth?'

Paul Robeson

(1898–1976)

He was a man of enormous stature. The son of a runaway slave, he was a gifted athlete, a great orator. He sang, he acted but he also fought very hard against segregation, against the lynching of black Americans and for African Americans and eventually for the common people all over the world. He could have just hunkered down and made the most of his absolutely beautiful voice. But he decided to be a prophet in his own time and was without honour in his own country.

Anna Ford (Journalist and former newsreader)

There is not a civil rights movement in the way we think of it from the 1950s, but there has never been a point at which African Americans haven't been trying to advance the cause of the race. One of the dominant models is 'the talented tenth'. It meant that if you can excel you will rise to the top and become a black leader. So you must embody all the potential of the race. It is a standard to live up to, to become the embodiment of all that is excellent. Robeson carries that burden as well.

Brian Ward (Professor of American Studies
at the University of Manchester)

ON PAPER, PAUL Robeson was the real deal. He was a gifted athlete, possessed a powerful intellect, was a persuasive orator and had a haunting bass voice. He was both a distinguished actor and a lifelong scholar. But he was a black man living in America when racism was rife. More than that, he spoke loud and long in favour of civil rights and the class struggle, lodging himself firmly on the political left. As a result, he was targeted by the authorities and thrust to the margins of a society that learned to fear rather than fête him. Only decades after his death is it possible to sift through state propaganda and assess the contribution he made to the fight for equality across America.

Paul Robeson was the youngest of seven children born to a minister and his Quaker wife. His father had escaped from slavery in North Carolina in the wake of the American Civil War. After his mother's death in a fire when he was 6, Robeson came increasingly subject to the influence of his father for whom 'good' was not good enough as far as school grades were concerned. Only perfect would do. Robeson inherited this drive and self-discipline, learning to lead by example.

At 17, he won a scholarship to Rutgers University, being only the third black student to attend. He excelled in football, basketball and baseball, as well as in studies. Yet his towering accomplishments were overshadowed by overt intolerance. For example, if a player on an opposing football team refused to play because he was black then he was dropped. Later, he studied law at Columbia University and worked for a New York law firm until a stenographer told him: 'I don't take dictation from a n*****.'

Realising his career would be pegged back by his skin colour, he switched to acting where he could use his rich vocals to maximum effect. He sought roles on stage and in the fledgling film industry that would enhance the image of African Americans among white society. Few were available, and some roles he took were naively stereotypical. On one occasion a woman co-star blacked up so audiences wouldn't be offended by a black man and a paler woman together on stage.

Only when he played Shakespeare's *Othello* from 1930 did he find the dignified role he yearned for – and even then he could still sense hostility inspired by his colour in some audiences. He was the first black Othello in an otherwise white cast to appear in America. But he is popularly remembered for his role as Joe in the 1936 film *Show Boat*, in which he sang his signature tune 'Ol' Man River'.

He married Eslander Goode in 1921, although he conducted numerous affairs afterwards. With remarkable fortitude, she stayed married, bore him a son and managed his career until her death in 1965.

In tandem with his career in the arts, Robeson became a committed socialist. In the 1920s, Robeson learned about the class struggle by talking to miners in Wales, with whom he developed a strong affinity. In 1934, he went to the Soviet Union where he saw no evidence of racial prejudice. (He remained unaware that he was being comprehensively wooed by Russian authorities while he was there.) Later he sang for the republicans fighting Fascism in Spain. In 1937, he co-founded the Council on African Affairs, which campaigned against colonialism and fed news from the continent to the American people. He and Eslander lived in the UK for a number of years until the outbreak of the Second World War.

By the early 1940s, Robeson was at the height of his fame, dubiously referred to in one newspaper as 'America's number one negro'. But already the heady combination of his left-leaning politics and outspoken attacks on colonialism and segregation was attracting the attention of the Federal Bureau of Investigation. While America was allied with the Soviet Union during the Second World War, Robeson's pro-Stalin sentiments caused only mild anxiety. But after 1945, when the cold war began to crank up, his support for the Communist regime rang alarm bells in conservative America. Soon he was deliberately discredited as a threat to American democracy.

When his passport was taken from him in 1950, Robeson was incandescent with rage. He was effectively told he should have kept his criticism of the USA to himself. Like many prominent artists of the era, he was called before the House of Un-American Activities Committee to be quizzed about his political affiliations. The orchestrated campaign carried out during the Red Scare in America neutered people like Robeson. Unofficially blacklisted, TV and film bosses refused to employ him. He might have fared better if he had lashed out against Stalin alongside other Soviet luminaries after the dictator's death. Although he wasn't a member of the Communist Party, he spoke freely in favour of it, never acknowledging gulags, anti-Semitism, corruption or purges. He felt his repudiation of the dictator would be a gift for the right wing that would undermine the politics of the left.

Justifiably, Robeson continued with eloquent attacks on prejudicial policies too. He singled out the USA for failing to stop lynchings by white mobs, in which black people were killed, usually by hanging. He won the support of scientist Albert Einstein in this campaign, but he also garnered powerful enemies.

By the time his travel ban ended in 1958, he had been effectively sidelined in the USA. Robeson went back on the road in Europe and the Soviet Union but he was plagued with ill health. One theory is that he was poisoned by the Central Intelligence Agency.

He returned to America in the mid 1960s to retire. He lived in self-imposed seclusion, although statements he issued revealed he still held left-wing causes close to his heart. He lived with his sister in Philadelphia until he died of a stroke.

Eleanor Roosevelt

(1884–1962)

I started looking at her life because of my interest in the Universal Declaration of Human Rights and she was absolutely at the heart of that incredible document. She was quite formidable, extraordinary, a great political activist and campaigner, very important in the business of dealing with racial segregation in the United States but also [carrying out] an incredible range of activity on welfare, on improving the lot of the poor and the disadvantaged.

Helena Kennedy (Barrister and Peer)

Annually she would visit a women's prison called Alderson Prison. She'd come back and write notes like, 'I could have been any one of the women on the inside.'

Professor Blanche Wiesen Cook (Biographer)

A S AMERICA'S FIRST Lady, Eleanor Roosevelt used the position's associated prestige to speak out for the oppressed and the poor in a manner that was hitherto alien in US politics. She had empathy aplenty, yet this was not even her finest hour. Her White House days were behind her by the time she went to work at the United Nations to help formulate a Universal Declaration of Human Rights. Although she wasn't a scholar or a statesman, she was chosen to chair the committee which drew up this landmark document. She hoped her presumed mediocrity would stand her in good stead: 'I used to tell my husband that, if he could make me understand something, it would be clear to all other people in the country, and perhaps that will be my real value on this drafting commission.' Nor was that the extent of her contribution. Throughout her public life she wrote a daily column that became required reading across America. She was an international ambassador and an American idol. While she may have been too modest to admit it, she was without doubt the most powerful woman in the world for about three decades.

Curiously, she had no ambitions to live such a celebrated existence. Although she was born into a wealthy family – her uncle Theodore was the twenty-sixth US President – her childhood was miserable. Her beautiful mother and aunts could not hide their disappointment at the young, weak-chinned Eleanor who was told she was 'an ugly duckling'. From this developed a paralysing shyness that took years to overcome. Her mother, Anna, died aged 28 from diphtheria, while her father was just 32 when he was killed by alcohol, after which orphaned Eleanor was sent to boarding school in England. It was here she found friends among fellow pupils and inspiration among the teachers, who took time to nurture her self-esteem. Later she said the happiest year of her life was when she made the first team for field hockey. From this short spell of schooling she carried a cut-glass English accent with her for the rest of her life.

She returned to the USA for her debut into society, while simultaneously launching herself into working with immigrants, helping to smooth their path into American society. She met fifth cousin once removed Franklin Delano Roosevelt and they married in 1905. She was an elegant six feet in height, with a narrow frame and sparkling eyes; he was six foot two inches tall and harboured an admiration for her limitless compassion for those in America's underbelly. While her husband worked up a life in politics she had six children quickfire, with one dying in infancy. Living next door was Franklin's demanding and possessive mother, Sara. The marriage came under severe strain during the First World War when Eleanor discovered her husband's affair with her own social secretary, Lucy Mercer. Eleanor was prepared to divorce but Franklin's mother, concerned about the scandal, threatened to cut him off from the family funds.

The Roosevelts worked together as a partnership afterwards but didn't regain the intimacy of a couple. Nonetheless Eleanor nursed Franklin when he was paralysed following an illness in 1921. She embarked on a life that largely centred on public service, initially in lieu of her husband during his recovery. As her confidence grew, Franklin and others in his Democratic camp realised what an asset she was, as he was elected governor of New York in 1928 and thirty-second US President in 1933.

At home, her concern was with women, many of whom were trapped in domestic isolation. She used her newspaper column, magazine articles and press conferences to reach out to them. She was perplexed by segregation, which she worked tirelessly to dismantle. And she visited workers who were reeling from the effects of the sluggish economy following the Depression, fighting for better housing and health. In terms of condemning corporate greed, concern for conservation and equality and other issues she was way ahead of the game. Although she was politically astute, she walked a careful line, being unelected and yet influencing the mood of the day. About particularly problematic issues, her husband would say to her: 'If you can warm it up, I'll run with it.' During the Second World War, she visited wounded troops and revealed remarkable stamina and good humour during long international trips.

Marked down as a suspected communist for her egalitarian leanings, she was the subject of a weighty FBI file.

Her outlook was not always sunny. She confessed to having 'Griselda' moods that would envelop her for days, making her feel inadequate and worthless. Much later, she mastered some psychology which helped eliminate depression. 'No one can make you feel inferior without your consent,' she declared. She developed close relationships with journalist Lorena Hicock and also with bodyguard Earl Miller, who taught her new sports. There's speculation that both were her lovers.

Mercer rather than Eleanor was with Franklin when he died on 12 April 1945 in Georgia. The same year, Eleanor was dispatched by Roosevelt's successor, Harry S Truman, as a delegate at the United Nations General Assembly. Later, she became chair of the Commission on Human Rights with a brief to draw up a modern Magna Carta that would protect the vulnerable and sidestep future conflicts. Introducing the declaration containing thirty articles in 1948 were the historic words: 'This Universal declaration of human rights, as a common standard of achievement for all peoples and all nations, to the end that every individual and every organ of society, keeping this Declaration constantly in mind, shall strive by teaching and education to promote respect for these rights and freedoms and by progressive measures, national and international, to secure their universal and effective recognition and observance, both among the peoples of Member States themselves and among the peoples of territories under their jurisdiction.'

A decade later, Roosevelt marked the declaration's anniversary with a speech that characteristically focused on ordinary folk. She summed up her life's mission statement when she asked the question, where do human rights begin?

> In small places, close to home – so close and so small that they cannot be seen on any maps of the world. Yet they are the world

of the individual person; the neighbourhood he lives in; the school or college he attends; the factory, farm, or office where he works. Such are the places where every man, woman, and child seeks equal justice, equal opportunity, equal dignity without discrimination. Unless these rights have meaning there, they have little meaning anywhere. Without concerted citizen action to uphold them close to home, we shall look in vain for progress in the larger world.

George Sand

(1804–1876)

If you were to compose a roll call of famous French women, she would have to figure very highly. Certainly people in France would be very aware of her not being just a writer but an icon, like Joan of Arc, a female figure who represents something and is a metaphor for ideas. She represents the woman trying to be free, the free spirit, the romantic.

Mary Kenny (Writer and journalist)

She was a remarkable woman. It was an astonishingly full life. Her openness particularly about female sexuality, mattered greatly historically. A great many other women writers were inspired to recognise their feelings and articulate them thanks to George Sand.

Belinda Jack (Biographer)

B Y COMMON CONSENT, sexual liberation for women came with the 1960s on a tie-dye tide of flower power and recreational drugs. If she were alive today, author George Sand would beg to differ. She threw off the bondage of a loveless marriage back in the 1830s to search for love and like-minded people. The list of her lovers includes poet and playwright Alfred de Musset, composer Frederic Chopin and lawyer Michel de Bourges.

Supporters of this prolific writer believe she was not promiscuous but in pursuit of a great love story that would define her life, although, with her idealistic outlook, she was unlikely to find a lasting relationship. Detractors had different ideas. Poet Charles Baudelaire said: 'Her ideas on morals have the same depth of judgement and delicacy of feeling as those of janitresses and kept women ... The fact that there are men who could become enamoured of this slut is indeed a proof of the abasement of the men of this generation.' Her own view reflects a love of love but also a strong desire for independence. 'Don't walk in front of me, I may not follow,' she wrote. 'Don't walk behind me, I may not lead. There is only one happiness in life, to love and be loved.'

Apart from her lively love life, Sand is remembered for cross-dressing in Paris to see a different side of life. Ostensibly, she adopted male garb because it was more durable and comfortable than women's clothing and footwear. In doing so, she saw a different side of life, visiting streets and places that were not frequented by women. She heard conversations between men that might otherwise have been unknown to her. There were more insights too when a woman began flirting with her. She poured the results into novels under her (male) pseudonym:

> I was no longer a woman nor was I a man. I was jostled on the pavements like a thing, an impediment to busy passers-by. It didn't matter to me. I had no business. No one knew me, no one looked at me. No one stopped me. I was an atom lost in that immense crowd. In Paris there was no need to hurry on to avoid

banal comment. I could invent an entire novel without meeting a single person who would say, what in heaven's name are you thinking of?

Her unusual outlook on life had been fashioned in childhood. She was born Amantine-Aurore-Lucile Dupin; her father was a dashing soldier related to the Polish royal family, while her mother had been a prostitute. In 1843, she wrote frankly about her mother Sophie:

'My mother did not come from the hardworking conscientious class. She belonged to that degraded vagabond race, to the bohemians of the world. She was a dancer – no, less than a dancer – an extra in one of the humblest theatres in Paris and rich men removed her from this degradation only to subject her to worse. My father met her when she was already 30 and living amid who knows what debaucheries. But he had a kind heart. He saw that this beautiful creature could still love and he married her against the wishes, under the curses even, of his family.'

After his death, when she was 4 years old, Aurore was brought up by both Sophie and her austere paternal grandmother. She spent her teenage years at an English convent in Paris and then at Nohant, the rural manoir owned by her grandmother. At 19, she married Casimir Dudevant, whose father was a baron and whose mother was a servant, and they had two children. Before long, Aurore inherited Nohant. However, the marriage lacked the romance and intimacy that she yearned for so, aged 27, she left for Paris. A marital separation initiated by a woman was a subject for scandal at the time. It certainly would have been sufficient grounds to robustly question her morals, as her male critics soon did.

In the French capital she fell in love almost immediately with young writer Jules Sandeau. Together they produced a novel which was published with the penname Jules Sand. For her first solo novel in 1832, Aurore kept the name Sand but replaced Jules with George. The book was called *Indiana*, and its theme was a heartfelt plea for marriage based on love rather than expediency. Given its popularity, the novel's message seemed timely. Her motivation for writing was initially to get money to support herself and her children. She was very disciplined, producing a set number of pages each day.

In 1848, France, along with other European countries, was engulfed by revolution. For a while there was universal male suffrage for the first time – although women didn't get the vote – and political efforts were made to help the poor. Sand worked as a minister for propaganda and was in touch with Karl Marx, the writer espousing left-wing theories that created an undertow in Europe at the time. However, the revolution lacked a spine, and there was little structural or strategic opposition when Napoleon III seized power. Disillusioned, Sand spent more time at Nohant, where she found inspiration in her contemplation of rural peace.

She remained frustrated at what she saw as society's double standards. Men of the era commonly took mistresses, while women were lambasted if they shared a bed with anyone other than their husbands. If proof of this were needed, many men in Parisienne society were stricken with syphilis contracted in extramarital relationships. Before the law, women were still chattels and, to her immense irritation, girls rarely received a proper education.

Through her adult life she accommodated faith where it revealed social conscience. There's ample evidence that she took the words of her Jesuit adviser as a motto for life: 'Follow the heart, the heart is never wrong.'

Flora Sandes

(1876–1955)

She was the only British woman to fight and wear uniform officially in the First World War. What I hear in her voice is a woman who was not unusual, weird, bizarre or in any way particularly eccentric. She was commonsensical, practical, she appreciated the world around her and she had an absolutely straightforward approach to the fact that she was in an odd position as a woman. She had neither fantasy nor pretension about it. She looked at it and said, my goodness, this is different.

Kate Adie (Reporter)

Women in that period had to identify themselves, had to almost reinvent themselves, as men in order to do manly things because there were no models for women to go off adventuring. She was one of the women who raised the whole debate about the role of a woman in warfare. She was such a visible symbol. And these women are written out of history, they are not considered important.

Julie Wheelwright (Historian)

IN SERBIA, EVEN today, the mere mention of her name is enough to inspire coos of admiration for a brave-hearted woman who adopted another nation to fight at close quarters against militarism. In Britain she is largely unknown. Flora Sandes was a nurse turned soldier in the First World War, who fought alongside embattled Serbian forces, rose through the ranks on merit and chose to continue a military career at the end of the conflict.

Born in Yorkshire, Flora was the youngest of nine children born to an Irish clergyman and his wife who later moved to Suffolk. Photos from childhood indicate she was something of a tomboy. As an adult she was by any standards remarkable. She enjoyed shooting and riding – and loved motor racing so much she bought a car of her own to drive in competitions. As a young woman, she cycled across South America to visit a brother while he was helping to build the Panama Canal. When she discovered he was struggling to care for an infant son after the death of his wife, she took back her young nephew in the bicycle's front basket.

When the First World War broke out in 1914, she joined the First Aid Nursing Yeomanry (FANYs). Associated with the Red Cross, they were principally ambulance drivers but also helped to deal with battle casualties. With another thirty-six nurses and a case containing hot water bottles, insect powder and a violin, her destination was Serbia, which had been the flashpoint for the conflict, being at the hub of skirmishing empires. Soon the Serbian forces were overrun by invading German and Austro-Hungarian armies, and she found herself in retreat, heading for Kosovo. Travelling on a white horse called Diana, she became separated from her fellow nurses and in the midst of the Fourth Company of the Serbian army's Second Infantry Regiment, also known as the Iron Regiment.

In Serbia the concept of women fighters was not anathema as it was in Britain. Before Sandes joined up, there were peasant women armed and in uniform fighting alongside men. After learning to use a rifle, she enlisted in the Serbian army, an ambition that some fellow nurses believe was long held. She was not mollycoddled by her new comrades nor did she seek to be so. Initially they assigned her a hay wagon as a bed, but she soon realised she would be dangerously cold if she slept alone so she huddled up alongside the men to take advantage of their warmth.

In 1916, she published her story in a book called *An English Woman-Sergeant in the Serbian Army*, not to inflate her reputation but to raise money for the Serbian cause, which had struck a chord among English people. It contains many of her recollections of army life:

> I seem to have just naturally drifted by successive stages from a nurse into a soldier. When the brigade ... began slowly to retreat towards Albania where there were no roads and we could not take ambulances to carry the sick I took the Red Cross off my arms and said, very well, I would join the second infantry regiment as a private.
>
> ... After that we spread our blankets on spruce boughs around the fire and rolled up in them. It was a most glorious moonlit night with the ground covered with white frost and it looked perfectly lovely with all the camp fires twinkling every few yards over the hillside among the pine trees. I lay on my back looking up at the stars and, when one of them asked me what I was thinking about, I told him that when I was old and decrepit and done for and had to stay in a house and not go about any more I should remember my first night with the 4th company on the top of [the mountain].

Although she had no army training, she proved herself in close quarter combat. She was swiftly promoted through the ranks after becoming an adept leader of men. She needed hospital treatment several times after being injured. Ishobel Ross of the Scottish Women's Hospital Unit recalls in her diary of 29 September 1916: 'She is quite tall with brown eyes and a strong yet pretty face. She is a sergeant in the fourth company and talked to us for a long time about her experiences and the fierce fighting she and the men of her company had to face. We felt so proud of her and her bravery.'

Eventually Sandes sustained more serious injuries, about which she remained stoic and matter-of-fact as one letter home reveals: 'I daresay you have heard that I got knocked out by a Bulgur hand bomb, but I've had a very good run for my money all the same as I had three months incessant fighting without a scratch. The Serbs are fine comrades. We've thought once we should all be taken but they wouldn't leave me. I had ever so many cards from them asking when I'm coming back but as I have 24 wounds and a broken arm the doctors seem to think I should wait a bit.'

Sandes was awarded Serbia's highest-ranking medal, equivalent to a Victoria Cross, for her bravery. After the conflict, she stayed in the Serbian army, in which she finally became a captain. She left the military in 1922. It was not the easy option: 'I cannot attempt to describe what it felt like trying to get accustomed to a woman's life and woman's clothes again, and also to ordinary society having lived entirely with men for so many years. Turning from a woman to a private soldier was nothing compared to turning back from a soldier to ordinary woman.'

In 1927, she married a former Russian white army general, Yuri Yudenich. She worked as a matron for the Tiller Girls in Paris at the Folies Bergère and also as a taxi driver. At the start of the Second World War, she was recalled by the Serbian Army Reserve. Her continued preference for men's clothes proved its worth after she was interned by the Germans and escaped by wearing women's clothes, fooling guards who had previously only ever seen her dressed like a man.

Her husband died during the war, at the end of which she decided to return to Suffolk, England, where she'd lived as a child, and find the same quiet lifestyle she'd left some thirty years previously. Although her name has slipped through the pages of English history she still looms large as a Serbian folk hero.

Captain Robert Falcon Scott

(1868–1912)

Think how [Scott and his men] struggled with all that equipment; their feet rotting, a dreadful diet. No, they were great, courageous men. Did [Scott] really want to come back if he hadn't got to the Pole first? It was 1912 when they died, 1913 when they were found and a year later it was the Great War and I don't think anything was ever the same again. Nobody was going to talk about patriotism, the flag or the honour of our country in the same way.

Beryl Bainbridge (Author)

The expedition did achieve the South Pole. The expedition made major scientific discoveries including indications that once it was almost tropical in that frozen region. ... There was much accomplished. [Before they left] the conditions and circumstances were essentially unknown.

Robert Headland (Archivist, Scott Polar Institute
at Cambridge University)

ACURIOUSLY BRITISH hero, Robert Falcon Scott failed to win a race to the South Pole and died in the attempt. Yet still he is better and more fondly remembered than the victor, Roald Amundsen. Accusations that he was foolhardy tend to be trumped with adjectives like daring and stout-hearted.

Scott was born to middle-class parents in Plymouth along with three sisters and a brother. An unremarkable child, one biographer calls him 'shy and diffident, small and weakly for his age, lethargic, backwards and above all dreamy'. Like many Plymouth-born boys, he joined the Royal Navy. Aged 13, he was a midshipman on HMS *Boadicea* and was quickly promoted through the ranks. While he was in the navy, the family home was sold after his father, a brewer, retired and fell on hard times. Following his father's subsequent death, Scott sent most of his wages home to help keep his mother and sisters, forgoing social occasions with fellow officers for lack of cash. This is thought to explain the remoteness that is often associated with Scott.

At the time, Antarctica was the largest remaining unknown tract in the world. Already Africa, Asia and even the Arctic had been mapped. When an expedition there was announced, a restless Scott was attracted by the idea of this distinguished distraction which would etch his name in history books for ever – although he admitted he had no predilection for snow and ice. He became commander of HMS *Discovery*, a survey ship purchased in 1901 for the expedition organised jointly by the Royal Society and the Royal Geographic Society. Its aim was to determine coastlines, to penetrate inland and to survey the region but it was also significant in terms of the whaling and sealing industries in the vicinity.

Scott already had a reputation for being difficult, and the project was skewed by politics from the outset as the two sponsors vied for supremacy. When he reached Antarctica in 1902, he led two ice-floe outings, neither of which was straightforward, before being recalled by the Admiralty. Colleague Ernest Shackleton was carried back to base on a stretcher during one of them. The mission was exciting but not exhaustive, achieving record-breaking latitudes while experiencing difficulties with dog sleds and scurvy. Explorers from Scandinavian countries who had bountiful expertise in dog sled handling were already ahead in the game.

Nonetheless, back in England, Scott was lauded as a hero. He wrote a book, gave lectures about his findings from Antarctica and rubbed shoulders with royalty while taking some naval postings as well. He was, though, itching to get under way with another expedition, this time intended to claim the South Pole for his beloved country. He was frustrated when he discovered Shackleton was fostering similar plans. Convinced he had moral rights over the territory visited in the *Discovery*, Scott insisted Shackleton made his explorations elsewhere in a stance that amply reflected the British Empire's attitude of ownership at the time. (Shackleton made an undertaking to Scott, but he was unable to keep his word and veered into a region Scott saw as his own, although he failed to reached the South Pole.)

In 1907, Scott met bohemian sculptress Kathleen Bruce and, after a tempestuous courtship, they married a year later at Hampton Court. Together they had a son, Peter Markham Scott, to whom *Peter Pan* author J. M. Barrie was godfather. Peter was just months old when his father embarked on the first leg of his second, doomed Antarctic expedition.

Only when Scott reached Melbourne on his way to the extreme south did he receive a telegram telling him the Norwegian Amundsen was heading for the same destination. The race was on.

Accompanying Scott were men from the previous expedition and others drawn from civilian and naval life. He also took Siberian ponies, two mechanical sledges and dog teams. The first two options proved useless in the relentlessly poor weather that now enveloped Antarctica. And it seems Scott was reluctant to use dogs, although they were proven and effective, for fear of having to kill them.

One of the men with him, geologist Frank Debenham, later recalled Scott: 'There were certain very sentimental things about him; his care for dogs, his horror of killing dogs. On the other hand as a naval officer he was bound to exact discipline and see that things went right and sometimes he was in rather too much of a hurry. He only once really unbent to me. Partly due to naval upbringing, he was abrupt, he wanted things spoken clearly and completely. And yet he had a wonderful ear and mind for science. He was really a scientist gone wrong.'

With cautious planning, Scott and his party laid supplies for the journey and then set off in October 1911. Eventually hauling sledges across the icy wastes in the face of unseasonably poor weather, Scott and his men reached the South Pole to find a Norwegian flag fluttering from a cairn. With heavy hearts they turned around, bowed by exhaustion and frostbite. Two men, Edgar Evans and Laurence Oates, died before Scott and two other survivors, 'Birdie' Bowers and Dr 'Bill' Wilson, entered their tent for the last time. They were only twelve miles from a rejuvenating supplies depot but harsh conditions made the trek impossible.

Months later when the tent and the frozen bodies within were eventually discovered, a noise like a pistol shot rang out as Scott's arm was raised to release the journal and letters tucked beneath. In a final letter he urged his wife to marry again. To Dr Wilson's wife he wrote: 'If this letter reaches you Bill and I will have gone out together. We are very near it now. And I should like you to know how splendid he was at the end, everlastingly cheerful and ready to sacrifice himself for others. His eyes have a comfortable blue look of hope and his mind is peaceful with the satisfaction of his faith, regarding himself as part of the great scheme of the Almighty. And I can do no more to comfort you than to tell you that he died as he lived, a brave true man, the best of comrades and staunchest of friends.'

The snow doesn't melt in Antarctica so the tent with its three bodies is now covered with metres of snow and will eventually push down into the Southern Ocean.

Ernest Shackleton

(1874–1922)

He inspired in people a loyalty that is very rare. On his ill-fated
expedition he had to leave behind a large part of his party and set sail
on an incredibly small boat across probably the most dangerous sea in
the world [with men] already weakened and at end of their tether. Yet
the people left behind never, ever thought they would be abandoned.
He has lots of lessons for all of us in terms of the humility, the courage,
the leadership qualities, the lack of selfishness, the guts and optimism.

Rosie Boycott (Writer)

He was appealing to men as well as women. He had what they
call charisma. Though he didn't achieve what he set out to do, the
way he brought triumph from disaster [make him] one of the great
historical figures.

Alexandra Shackleton (Granddaughter)

GROANING AND CREAKING, a high-masted ship, the *Endurance*, was eaten by Antarctic ice in 1915 before the eyes of its marooned crew. Each day they watched as its bow, beams and deck boards were slowly consumed by relentless nature. They were now condemned to live on a drifting ice floe exposed to bone-chilling polar winds on an uncertain journey dictated by the currents of the Southern Ocean.

For expedition leader Sir Ernest Shackleton, it was not the end but the beginning. If his ship was crushed by gathering ice, his spirit was not. He now tasked himself to save his men – who knew him as 'the boss' – from doom in this remote and barren land. Short on options, he was abundant with charisma and his leadership skills were such that none of the men stranded by the loss of the ship ever believed they would be lost while he was in command.

Fifty-five years later, one of the men, Lionel Greenstreet, gave an insight into the Shackleton effect: 'What a wonderful leader he was. You always felt when he was there that you were going to get out. In fact I think the whole expedition had that feeling. With the boss there, well, we'll get out some time.'

Shackleton was born in Ireland soon after the potato famine. His doctor father brought his family to England, where the young Shackleton was educated. But he lacked the necessary concentration for academia. Instead, he determined to join the merchant navy, ultimately qualifying as a ship's master in 1898.

Despite sailing all over the globe his thirst for adventure wasn't satisfied and he seized the chance to join Captain Robert Scott on the 1901 Discovery Expedition heading to Antarctica. His own words reveal the love affair with Antarctica that then began:

> How splendid the western mountains look today. Tongue or pen or pencil would sadly fail were they to attempt to describe the magic of the colouring. Later on in the afternoon the very

clouds light and fleecy were of rainbow hue, iridescent and opaline in their many tints. Days like these stand out amongst the grey ones that are so common here. The sunset was a poem. The change of twilight into night that was lighted by the crescent moon was weirdly beautiful. The cliffs of white gave no part of their colour away and the rocks beside them did not part with their blackness so it was a curious effect of the deepening shadow over these contrasts.

Another love affair was beginning as well, with wife-to-be Emily. As an explorer, Shackleton gained extra kudos with her family. So when Shackleton was invalided home from the Discovery Expedition, it was a bitter disappointment to him on all fronts, although the pair eventually married in 1904.

He set about organising his own expedition, with conquering the South Pole at the top of the agenda. The subsequent Nimrod Expedition came closer to the South Pole than anyone before, but Shackleton retreated from his goal, believing 'a live donkey is better than a dead lion.' He summed up the achievements of the Nimrod Expedition like this: 'On 3 March a party ascended that mountain encountering severe blizzards and for the first time in human history the great mountain Erebus, 13,350 ft high, was ascended by men. And on January 9 1909 the British flag was hoisted at latitude 8823 South and 162 East.'

No one else had seen these sights and, when Shackleton returned, he was fêted for the (failed) attempt. Deeply in debt despite receiving backing, Shackleton was now compelled to lecture, write and embark on business ventures. He also waited with interest to see the results of Scott's South Pole expedition in 1912.

Early promises made to his wife about never returning to Antarctica came to nothing though, after he confessed, 'I think I'm not much good at anything but exploring.' With the South Pole accomplished by Roald Amundsen, the prospect of a transcontinental expedition remained an alluring challenge. Emily proved more understanding than most, declaring, 'One must not try to chain an eagle in a barnyard.' After getting generous sponsorship and more than 5,000 applicants for the team, Shackleton engineered the Endurance Expedition, which left England five days after the outbreak of the First World War.

When the *Endurance* arrived in the Weddell Sea, it was quickly ice-bound and the men moved from ship to floe. Hopes that a thaw would free the ship were dashed in October 1915 when it was slowly consumed by pack ice. Then it became clear the ice floe upon which the men were now based would not pass close enough to land to enable safe passage and indeed was fracturing. Shackleton realised the only chance the men had was to seek land. Using three open lifeboats liberated from the *Endurance*, the fifty-six-man crew had a dicey five-day journey before they landed on Elephant Island.

The island was remote and inhospitable, offering little by way of shelter or food. Ten days later, Shackleton and selected others took a twenty-three-foot lifeboat, named *James Caird* after an expedition backer, to raise the alarm in South Georgia, 800 miles distant, heading across the roughest water on the planet. Against the odds, Shackleton's team survived tumultuous waves on the voyage, avoided being dashed on rocks at their destination and marched thirty miles in thirty-six hours to a whaling station.

Shackleton borrowed a ship and rescued the stranded men. He found them as he had left them, extremely fatigued but in good spirits, following a strict routine and organising sports and shows to pass the time. There were injuries, even amputations, but still their faith in Shackleton was unshakeable. When the group returned to Britain in May 1917, some of the men enlisted immediately and, having survived these tough conditions, died almost immediately on the Western Front.

In 1922, on a fourth expedition with circumnavigation of Antarctica in mind, Shackleton succumbed to a heart attack, probably exacerbated by the extreme conditions he had undergone during the days of the *Endurance* adventure. His body was buried on South Georgia, in accordance with his wife's wishes.

George Bernard Shaw

(1856–1950)

The difficulty with [Shaw] being a satirist and a campaigner is that you are not sure when to take him seriously. But he was exemplary in putting forward reasoned argument and that's what I want from our politicians today. If he was here now he would continue to fight for social justice. You would see him on every blogspot, on YouTube and Myspace. He'd be writing under fifty pseudonyms, popping out all over the place.

Dr Phil Hammond (Comedian and former NHS doctor)

Anybody who uses the phrase 'he who can does, he who can't teaches' is quoting Shaw, and Churchill called him the greatest living master of letters in the English speaking language. Shaw went on to write a quarter of a million letters and all the time we are quoting him. We are just not aware of it.

Ivan Wise (Shaw Society)

'*I LIKE FLOWERS. I also like children but I do not chop off their heads
and keep them in bowls around the house.*'

Wit and acid wisdom like this were the hallmarks of writer George
Bernard Shaw, who used his spare, smart way with words to break the
mould in theatre productions and communicate radical politics. He used
words like rapiers, deftly thrusting into the heart of an argument with a
dexterity normally associated with a high-flying university graduate. In
fact GBS, as he is fondly known, had such a horror of education he barely
completed normal schooling let alone a degree. His skills were self-taught,
his humour instinctive. He seemed to have ink rather than blood running
through his veins.

In 1937, he told a group of sixth-formers: 'To me there is nothing in
writing a play. Anyone can write one if he has the necessary natural turn for
it. And if he hasn't, he can't and that's all there is to it. I have another trick
for imposing on the young. I am old, over 80 in fact. Also, I have a white
beard and these two facts are somehow associated in people's minds with
wisdom. That's a mistake. If a person is a born fool the folly will get worse
not better by a long life's practice.'

Shaw was the youngest of three children born to his father George, an
alcoholic, and his mother Lucinda, who was a singer and music teacher.
After attending a succession of schools, one of which he dubbed 'a futile boys
prison', he worked as a clerk in both Dublin and London. He found the work
dull and uninspiring, resolving instead to become a writer. Spending hours in
the British Library, he knocked out four novels in quick succession without
getting any published. It was his parents who stepped into the breach, to
support him in this period of poverty. 'I did not throw myself into the struggle
for life, I threw my mother into it,' he said. 'I was not a staff to my father's
old age, I hung on to his coat tails. People wondered at my heartlessness. My
mother worked for my living instead of preaching that it was my duty to
work for hers. Therefore take off your hat to her and blush.'

He was remarkably self-deprecating throughout his life. Conversely, he was known for having an outsized ego. Humorist Israel Zangwill once said: 'The way Bernard Shaw believes in himself is very refreshing in these atheistic days when so many people believe in no god at all.'

At first he forged a career as a critic and essayist – and when the play he was reviewing bored him he turned his attentions to the audience, on one occasion focusing his piece on one would-be trendsetter who came with 'a pitiable corpse of a bird on her head'.

In 1884, inspired by left-looking politics, Shaw joined the Fabian Society, which was one of the forerunners of the Labour Party. As a member, he supported pivotal issues of the day, including women's rights. After suffragettes were force-fed in prison, he invited Prime Minister William Gladstone to a Society dinner on the condition he enjoyed the fine wines and gourmet food through a nasal tube. Shaw once spoke for ninety minutes at Speaker's Corner in London in the pouring rain to an audience of only six policemen. Many of the pamphlets issued by the Society came from his hand.

An immensely charming and compelling character, Shaw had no shortage of female admirers. Many were seduced by letter. He eventually married Charlotte Payne-Townshend in 1898, although at least one biographer claims the marriage was never consummated.

Undeterred by a generally low-key reception for socialism in Britain, he continued to foster ambitions for social change, and by 1897 he had become a municipal councillor in St Pancras. He improved the lives of people there by instituting a vaccination programme to stamp out smallpox and the installation of new sewage pipes. Much later, he said it was the part of his life he looked back on with most pride.

After the dawn of the twentieth century, he began writing plays that also served as vehicles for his views, so much so that some critics feel the characters are merely animated opinions. The cleverness of the scripts ensured their popularity, but Shaw fell into a trough of unpopularity when he adopted the unpatriotic view that Britain should not be fighting the First World War, outlined in a pamphlet entitled 'Commonsense about the War', published in 1914 with the *New Statesman*. He saw it as a clash between two equally culpable powers, with the infantry soldiers as the main losers. One politician called for him to be shot.

His reputation was restored with five plays he wrote after the war, all of which received a rapturous welcome – he was awarded the Nobel Prize for Literature in 1925, having done much to expand theatre art beyond melodramatic whodunits. But controversy dogged him again after he visited the USSR in 1931 as a personal guest of dictator Stalin. Already an old man, he failed to look beyond the carefully tailored tour he was given and proceeded to harry Americans in a radio interview about their anti-Soviet stance:

> Hello all you dear boobs who have been saying for a month past that I have gone dotty about Russia. If the latest news from your side is true you can hardly be saying that now. Russia has the laugh of us. She has us fooled, beaten, shamed, shown up, out pointed and all but knocked out. We have rebuked her ungodliness and now the sun shines on Russia as on a country with which God is well pleased whilst his wrath is heavy on us and we don't know where to turn for comfort or approval.

He even proposed Stalin for the Nobel Peace Prize. He was not, however, the only significant figure to be hoodwinked by Stalin, and his naivety does not diminish his commitment to Socialism or his writing skills.

Characteristically, he condemned British participation in the Second World War. He died from complications after falling while pruning trees in his garden aged 93. When he died, Broadway dimmed its lights in recognition of its loss and the Indian cabinet adjourned to mourn.

Nevil Shute

(1899–1960)

He had a very clever way of talking about how ordinary people think and feel and what makes them care for one another and for things. That's very strong and it is quite difficult to get through to teenagers with that sort of emotional stuff – and he did. He hooked me in with the engineering and splatted me with the emotional material. I found that very powerful.

Adam Hart-Davis (Writer and television presenter)

He was a very methodical man. He got up around 7.30 a.m., had breakfast at 8.15 a.m., then about 9 would disappear into his study. He would stay there until about 1 p.m. We lived on a farm in Australia, a couple of hundred acres, and he would go off to see everything was all right. He loved the pigs. In the evening after dinner, he would go into his workshop and build little engines. He needed all these different things as a counterpoint to one another. He never, except maybe at the very end, considered himself a writer. He considered himself an engineer.

Heather Mayfield (Nevil Shute's eldest daughter)

NOVELIST NEVIL SHUTE combined a passion for engineering with a flair for writing to produce some of the best-read books of the twentieth century.

Nevil Shute Norway was born in Ealing, West London, the son of a Cornishman who worked his way up the Post Office hierarchy. Aged 5, Shute developed a stammer which made him the focus of teasing by fellow pupils and teachers alike. As a result, he often played truant from his first preparatory school, finding his way to London's Science Museum where he wandered among the exhibits marvelling at their mechanics. Eventually, he went to Shrewsbury School where he wrote poetry and short stories. His father was a writer, and his grandmother was a Barbara Cartland equivalent in her era.

Although Shute was too young to enlist at the outbreak of the First World War, his older brother Fred went off to fight in France and died in 1915 after a shell landed in his trench. It was a blow for Shute, who idolised his brother. Much later he wrote: 'If Fred had lived we might have had some real books one day, not the sort of stuff that I turn out. For he had more literature in his little finger than I have in my whole body. He was only 19 when he died and after 40 years it still seems strange to me that I should be older than Fred.' All attempts Shute made to join the forces and avenge his brother's death were frustrated by his stammer.

In the meantime, he continued schooling and spent holidays in Ireland, where his father was now in charge of Dublin's post office in Sackville Street. During the Easter Uprising in 1916, it was seized by rebels fighting for Irish independence. Within moments, the teenaged Shute was on the scene and he wrote about what he saw in his diary, as British forces cautiously approached the occupied post office:

> Then, in tense silence, they came on down the far side of the wide street. The rebels in the post office held their fire until the soldiers were opposite them and then opened up with a ragged

volley. Four of the lancers fell from their saddles, killed instantly
I think, and one or two horses went down. Crowds scattered in
alarm, myself with them. But in two or three minutes we were
back again. These were the first men I had seen killed.

As the conflict continued, Shute acted as a stretcher-bearer, winning a
commendation from the British Army in Ireland for gallant conduct.

Later, after gaining a degree at Oxford, Shute embarked on a career in
the burgeoning aircraft industry. In 1924, he became chief calculator at
Vickers, working on the rigid airship R100 with Barnes Wallis, the inventor
who would later be famous for the bouncing bomb of 'Dambusters' fame.

R100 – a massive balloon-style craft capable of transatlantic travel –
was being pioneered in the private sector, while R101 was a rival project
that was publicly funded. Not only did the civil servants running R101
have apparently limitless cash, they also had the right to see the blueprints
drawn up by Vickers. Still, the advantages did not put the team behind
R101 on the front foot. In October 1930, the government's airship crashed
in France, killing forty-eight people. It effectively put an end to hopes for
airship viability in Britain.

Shute was convinced design incompetence had caused the crash, and the
disaster instilled in him a lifelong distrust of governments and the public
sector. For him, it ended a project where he enjoyed both commitment and
camaraderie. Before Vickers abandoned R100, he had travelled with it to
Canada, on the way enjoying meals of soup, stewed beef, peas, potatoes,
greengages and custard, beer, cheese and coffee. He recalled how it was
possible to walk outside the airship while it was in flight:

> R100 had a little cockpit on top at the extreme bow, forward
> of the gas bag. The slope of the hull was about 45 degrees
> which made the first part a bit tricky to climb. When the ship
> was cruising at about 60 mph, as soon as you got to the top of

the horizontal part of the hull, you were in calm air crawling on your hands and knees. If you knelt up you felt a breeze on your head and shoulders. If you stood up the wind was strong. It was pleasant up there, sitting by the fins on a fine sunny day and whenever I went up there I would usually find two or three men sitting and gossiping. The riggers got so used to it that they would walk upright along this little catwalk with their hands in their pockets, leaning against the wind and stepping over my recumbent body as I crawled on hands and knees.

In 1931, he married Frances, a doctor at York Hospital, while still involved in aviation. However, as his writing began to make money he quit: 'When my writing became profitable I was glad to leave the office for the wider life of the office of the novelist though I have little respect for writers as a class. I think that the man or woman who does nothing else in the world but writes novels is a poor fish.' During the Second World War he returned to work on secret weapons projects. But at the end of the conflict he knew he wanted to leave England, unhappy at the nation's socialist tendencies.

After a six-month investigation into the prospects for him and his family in Australia, Shute moved down under and found inspiration for numerous novels. Among the most famous was *On the Beach*, published in 1957 but set in 1962. It's bleak post-apocalyptic storyline struck a chord in a world transfixed by the cold war being conducted between East and West. *On the Beach* was seized upon by Hollywood and filmed in 1959 with Gregory Peck and Ava Gardner in the lead roles. However, Shute so disliked the film version that it may even have hastened his death. In the book, the two main characters had no more than a single kiss, while in the film the relationship was unquestionably physical. Shute suffered immense stress when this plotline was changed.

Although he had suffered his first heart attack when he was in his thirties, he had a succession of strokes and heart attacks after moving to Australia, and one finally killed him a year after the popular film was released.

Joe Slovo

(1926–1995)

Anyone who goes from being a 10-year-old Yiddish-speaking Lithuanian refugee to a hero for tens of thousands of South Africans at the heart of a defining liberation struggle is indeed a great life.
David Milliband (Former Foreign Secretary)

That generation really had a feeling they had worked for a cause and they had won. They are quite a hard act to follow.
Gillian Slovo (Writer and Joe Slovo's daughter)

THERE WERE FEW white men in the 1960s in South Africa who could call Nelson Mandela a friend. Joe Slovo was so close to the man who became an international icon during his imprisonment by the apartheid regime that, on his release in 1990, Mandela paid special tribute to him. Slovo was, according to Mandela, one of the country's finest patriots. Known variously as Comrade Joe or the Teddy Bear Terrorist, Joe Slovo was among the most eminent activists against apartheid. His quest to bring down the South African government lasted more than fifty years, during which time he and others abandoned peaceful protest in favour of armed insurrection. Revelling in the part he played in the downfall of apartheid, Slovo considered himself one of the luckiest men alive because he helped to change the world for the better. Yet it was from unpromising beginnings that he arrived in this pre-eminent role.

Born in Lithuania in 1926 when anti-Semitism was in the ascendancy, Yossel Mashel Slovo arrived in South Africa aged 8, his hair shorn against lice and his only possession a bag of rotten fruit. Soon afterwards, his mother Ann died in childbirth. His father, Woolf, worked as a street vendor, baker, grocer and driver. However, if his father's aim was that his son should escape persecution then the cross-continent trek to a new life was a failure. At school, Slovo was influenced by an Irish teacher who was fervently anti-imperialist. Together they went to political meetings where on one occasion a young Joe found himself sitting next to a black man. Having spent the entire evening thinking himself remarkable for doing so, he emerged to ponder what kind of world it was that he could not concentrate on the speaker because he was so amazed at the proximity of a man with a different skin colour.

After he left school in 1941, Slovo worked as a dispatch clerk and quickly joined the South African Communist Party, one of the few anti-apartheid groups that wasn't solely black and a perpetual target of repression. Inspired by the sacrifices made by Stalin's Red Army, he volunteered to fight for the Allies during the Second World War. However, it was the inequality at home that kept Slovo loyal to the South African Communist Party, rather than admiration for Stalin and Soviet Russia or antagonism towards the capitalist West, despite the fact its nations shored up the apartheid system.

When Slovo was discharged from the army, he completed a law degree at the University of Witwatersrand, where he encountered Nelson Mandela for the first time. Together, and with others, they began a series of political protests against the apartheid regime and soon became targets for governmental oppression. One protest against the pass laws – which forced black men to keep papers with them for spot checks by the police – held at Sharpeville in 1960 ended in the deaths of sixty-nine people after the police opened fire on unarmed marchers. The government then declared a state of emergency and ordered hundreds of arrests. Although Slovo ended up behind bars, he knew he was receiving better treatment than his black counterparts. And it was now painfully apparent that peaceful demonstrations would not persuade the hardline government to change course.

The decision to take up arms was not lightly taken, however. Until the slaughter at Sharpeville, government opponents – including Slovo – had been inspired by Mahatma Gandhi, who beckoned in an independent India with *satyagraha*, passive defiance. Afterwards, they reluctantly decided that no amount of peaceful protest would bring a just system to South Africa. In a major policy shift, it was agreed violence was the only answer. Consequently, Slovo was a founder of Umkhonto we Sizwe ('Spear of the Nation'), the armed wing of the African National Congress. By definition he was a terrorist, but by inclination he was a guerrilla fighter. Lacking the resources to fight a war, Slovo and his associates initially blew up empty buildings, deserted railway stations and communication lines without incurring casualties.

In 1963, he was dispatched into exile by the South African Communist Party and the African National Congress, spending time in Angola, Mozambique, Zambia and the UK where he gained a further degree at the London School of Economics. He and his wife Ruth remained targets, however, and in 1982 she was finally killed by a parcel bomb sent to her office in Mozambique. Much later, the two men responsible – both policemen in South Africa – applied for amnesty after admitting her murder.

When change belatedly swept across South Africa, Slovo arrived back to help in talks that would fashion the nation's new future. An accomplished writer, he surprised many with his 1989 pamphlet 'Has Socialism Failed?' It signalled a departure by degrees from his lifelong devotion to radical politics. And, along with other equally committed figures in the movement, he pressed for compromise in its approach to whites for the sake of South Africa's long-term future.

Later, the Truth and Reconciliation Commission – although the target of some criticism – apparently did much to heal the wounds left by decades of bigotry. In the new government, Slovo became housing minister and immediately began talks with business leaders to bring forward funds for public housing. One day in a restaurant he was approached by a white man on the verge of tears who thanked him for what he had done, having illustrated that not all white people were as cowardly as the stranger considered himself to be.

After his death in January 1995, there were high-level discussions about Slovo's funeral. His family had hoped it would be held in Johannesburg City Hall, where Slovo had spent many hours enjoying classical music. Gently, someone pointed out the venue was probably not big enough. In the end, the ceremony was held in Soweto's Alexander Stadium in front of some 100,000 people.

His body was held in a simple wooden coffin and it began an unlikely trend. Previously, black people who were buried spent big money on an ornate coffin, money that they couldn't afford. Afterwards, they started using the more economical 'Joe Slovo coffin', perhaps a suitable epitaph for someone who thought of himself not as a white but as a South African man of the people.

Benedict de Spinoza

(1632–1677)

Spinoza was a philosopher of science who has a lot of interesting things to say and who a lot of scientists have studied. I came to [Spinoza] through Einstein who was asked if he believed in God. He said: 'I believe in Spinoza's God who reveals himself in the orderly harmony of what exists, not in a God who concerns himself with the fates and actions of human beings.'

Sir Harry Kroto

(Chemist, professor, humanist and Nobel Prize winner)

Spinoza has a particular view of human beings, that they are at the centre of a natural system and that they respond to the world in ways that are sometimes functional, sometimes rather badly adapted for their own good. What we have to do is to understand ourselves and the environment we live in so as to improve our capacity to live in ways that are fruitful for us and, as Spinoza puts it, to enhance our freedom. For him that is an inherently political exercise as well; it is something we can only do together.

Professor Susan James

(Professor of Philosophy, Birkbeck College)

D URING AN AGE when science and philosophy were in their infancy it could be lethal to express new and different ideas. God loomed large in a world of narrow-gauge thinking and the punishment for breaking out from accepted Biblical wisdom was frequently death. Despite the risks, Benedict de Spinoza articulated groundbreaking ideas that would influence the opinions of future generations. In seventeenth-century Holland, Spinoza was condemned by fellow Jews and the ruling Protestant church for espousing his considered beliefs, which were outside the accepted margins of faith. Still, he produced some of the most wide-ranging rational and radical examinations of religion and philosophy, although his most important work was thought so dangerous it did not appear until after his death.

Spinoza was born into a Jewish family that had been hounded out of the Iberian peninsula and finally settled in comparatively tolerant Holland. As a boy his able mind was applauded by teachers at the Talmud Torah Academy, where he was largely occupied with religious study. Eventually he left to become a merchant like his father. Now, as he went about his business, he met dissenting Protestants for the first time who were embracing the work of French philosopher René Descartes (1596–1650). Furthermore, Spinoza became the pupil of an ex-Jesuit and medical doctor at a Latin school in Amsterdam which further broadened his outlook.

His home nation also had a role to play in his intellectual development. There was a diverse and lively community in the Netherlands generally and in Amsterdam in particular, where people flocked to find the freedom to philosophise. But his growing unorthodoxy wasn't welcomed by those he had once worshipped alongside. In 1656, when he was 24, he was excommunicated by the Jewish community for his so-called heretical beliefs amid a volley of curses:

> The Lord will not spare him but in the anger of the Lord and his
> jealousy shall lie upon him and the Lord shall blot out his name

from under heaven. We order that nobody should communicate with him neither in writing nor accord him any favour nor stay with him under the same roof not within four cubits in his vicinity. Nor shall they read any treatise composed or written by him.

Synagogues often chose to control by excommunication but they rarely used such ferocious terms. After paying a penance, the religiously outlawed were frequently permitted to return. But Spinoza did not seek to do so:

They do not force me to anything that I would not have done of my own accord if I did not dread scandal. But since they want it that way I enter gladly on the path that is open to me with the consolation that my departure will be more innocent than was the exodus of the early Hebrews from Egypt although my subsistence is no better secured than was theirs. I take away nothing from anybody and whatever injustice may be done to me I can boast that people have nothing to reproach me with.

With his brother now at the helm of the family business, Spinoza learned to grind lenses, a new and flourishing trade. At the same time, he began cautiously to publish his ideas. But if they excited fellow thinkers, the response from the buttoned-down world of Calvinism was positively hostile. Spinoza's thoughts were deemed heretical and 'a work forged in hell by a renegade Jew and a devil.'

The ideas that Spinoza produced are still being debated today. Some people insist his pantheism mirrors atheism with God, nature, the universe and so forth all being an expression for the same thing. It is true that he possibly uses the language of religion to convey a more secular viewpoint. For others, he offers a traditional view drawn from the inner reaches of Christianity and Judaism that reflect his lifelong fascination with faith. Out of it he fashions a religion that provides a moral doctrine through which people can live a good life. What is certain is that his work provides a bridge between orthodox religious life of centuries past and modern, secular thinking. Here are some of Spinoza's views:

> God is one, that is, only one substance can be granted in the universe. Whatsoever is, is in God, and without God nothing can be or be conceived. God is the indwelling and not the transient cause of all things ... there can be nothing in itself external to God.

> God is without passions, neither is he affected by emotions of pleasure or pain. Strictly speaking God does not love anyone. He who loves God cannot endeavour that God should love him in return.

> Be not astonished at new ideas; for it is well known to you that a thing does not therefore cease to be true because it is not accepted by many.

> Peace is not an absence of war, it is a virtue, a state of mind, a disposition for benevolence, confidence, justice.

> Happiness is a virtue, not its reward.'

He died from respiratory illness, perhaps a by-product of a life spent lens-grinding. His greatest work, *Ethics*, appeared a year later, suggesting clerics should be stripped of power and that states should be secular, with all faiths tolerated. The message trickled down the centuries to find a warm welcome, particularly among today's atheist and humanist movements.

Tom Spring

(1795–1851)

Boxing started with Cain and Abel. It is the most primitive sport and also arguably the best organised. There are rules, and fighters stick to them. The Tom Spring era founded not only organised legitimate boxing but it also founded sports writing.

Frank Keating (Sportswriter)

There were some fairly strict rules: there had to be two referees; when a fighter went down, he was allowed to be rescued; and they were given half a minute intermission between rounds. It was life or death in the ring. Spring's hands were very weak, so he boxed rather than slugged. He avoided punishment and no one likes that except the true boxing fan. He had a very classical English style.

John Hurley (Biographer)

B ARE-KNUCKLE BOXING has a history that extends to the ancient Greeks. However, it was in Britain in the nineteenth century that unruly bouts became popular in both cities and the countryside, and the object of feverish betting among aristocrats and the working classes. Among the most popular fighters was Tom Spring, who was arguably the first world heavyweight champion. Having established himself at the pinnacle of the sport, Spring did more than anyone to take it from an illegal dust-up to an organised and respected feat of athleticism.

Spring was the youngest of five children born to a butcher in Hereford, although the family name was in fact Winter. His name change was dispensed by an ebullient referee in an early bout. Both his father and grandfather were enthusiastic amateur boxers, and he was trained to fight from childhood. From them, he learned the classic upright pose that defined British boxing at the time. Like them he also enjoyed gambling.

Young Spring's talents were first spotted by the Marquis of Worcester, who would stage sparring contests among local fighters to entertain visiting lords and earls. The Duke of Norfolk likened the young Spring to a Greek god. While most of the well-heeled crowd that gathered to watch were drawn by the possibilities of making some ready cash through gaming, there's a suggestion that it was also a smokescreen for predatory homosexuals.

It was events like this that attracted existing prize fighters and one, Tom Cribb, noticed the potential exhibited by Spring. He invited the young man to London where he could further his fighting career. At first, Spring turned down the offer. His father went to prison as punishment for the non-payment of a loan, and he stayed home to keep the family business afloat. In 1816, however, Spring made his way to the Union Arms in London, where Cribb lived and worked. Soon he had a job in the bar and a training schedule. In the twilight of his own career, Cribb was keen to pass the mantle to his protégé and he was confident Spring would do well, so much so he took out an advertisement for potential opponents:

To all England. The Championship Tom Crib [sic] having been called to the bar, which now so completely occupies his time ... has in consequence, entirely resigned the whole of his practice in the ring to Tom Spring, his adopted boy ... anxiously seeking the path of glory informs all those heroes whom it may concern that for three months he is open to all England, for 100 to 200 guineas a side.

It was, of course, an appeal for an opponent to fight Spring with generous prize money provided by backers. The advertisement ran for three months with no takers. Eventually, Spring fought for a 40 guinea purse against an experienced Yorkshireman. With superior speed and agility, Spring won the fight. He also, though, revealed certain inherent weaknesses to would-be opponents. He did not possess a killer instinct – for this reason his fights would last for fifty, seventy or even more than a hundred rounds – and his hands were brittle, so his punch was weak. Consequently he was known as 'the Light Tapper'. But his prowess was sufficient to attract two wealthy patrons, who would help organise future fights.

The sport was not the same as boxing today. There were no gloves and few rules, so fighters would brawl as much as box, and even resorted to wrestling if it offered an advantage. Men were thrown down or even out of the ring. Rounds were not set by time but ended when a man buckled in the face of extraordinary brutality. The match was stopped until he 'toed the line' or 'came up to scratch' and was ready to fight again. Usually, it ended with a knockout or submission through sheer exhaustion.

Although there were two referees, they were frequently not able to stop the crowds encroaching on the ring. Fights often broke out between bystanders as well, making it a frantic occasion. If they felt minded, local magistrates who got to hear about planned boxing fights would ban them, causing chaos among the crowds. When bare-knuckle boxers like Spring had no fights lined up, they would make extra money by modelling bare-chested for artists or sculptors.

An early defeat stalled his career, but Spring vowed to get back in shape. On 4 May 1819, Spring fought Jack Carter on Crawley Down in Sussex for a 50 guinea purse, winning in the sixty-fifth round after nearly two hours. His reputation was further enhanced by winning some more brutal bouts, gaining sufficient money to buy a London pub in 1821. The same year he was employed at the coronation of George IV as one of eighteen ushers. Their chief role was to keep the unpopular Queen Caroline, who was detested by her husband the king, at bay.

By now, he was winning as much as £200 a fight and also received income from the betting operation. He had seen off the most likely competition in England. It wasn't until 1824, when he fought Irish champion John Langan, that he could legitimately describe himself as world titleholder. He won in a mammoth seventy-seven rounds.

Langan pressed for a rematch and this time it lasted for 108 rounds. Spring was undisputed champion but also a physical wreck and vowed he would never fight again. He did enter the ring once more, to help raise money for his old sponsor Cribb, who had fallen on hard times. Spring was by this time a popular hero of colossal proportions.

His departure from the sport signalled a lull in its fortunes, and boxing became closely associated with fixed matches and shady characters. It wasn't until fifteen years after Spring's death that the Queensbury rules were introduced, codifying boxing etiquette.

Although the verse written to honour Spring by one E. Hodges is far from lyrical, it helps put into context his life and times.

We once had a champion, his name was Winter Spring
A man both upright and kind, by high and low esteemed
He was loyal to his queen, so brave and noble was his mind

Poor Tom Spring was never bought, all his battles well were fought
In his praise old England would ring
All classes far and near so delightfully would cheer
And their motto was: Victory and Spring.

Lady Hester Stanhope

(1776–1839)

[She] navigated her way through an extremely difficult childhood, found herself at the centre of British politics alongside her uncle William Pitt. When she lost her power base because he died, she then went off and carved her own life and found her own place of power. She ended up in the East. She wasn't just a traveller. She got involved in the politics and the allegiances of the area. She eventually found herself crowned as queen of the Arabs by the Bedouins.

Deborah Meaden (Businesswoman)

When she was asked what sort of man she would be, she would say she was born to be a general. She was the same age as Jane Austen, but she could ride like a demon, she could swordfight and was also a tomb raider as she led what was in effect the first archaeological dig in the Holy Land.

Kirsten Ellis (Biographer)

GEORGIAN ENGLAND WAS a man's world, in which women were seen but rarely heard. Lady Hester Stanhope was a much-needed antidote to a patriarchal society in which she was more demonic than demure.

Her childhood was chaotic after her mother's untimely death when Stanhope was aged only 4 but was already the eldest of three sisters. In this era of turmoil, her father Charles, 3rd Earl Stanhope, chose to embrace the principles of the French Revolution, calling himself Citizen Stanhope and denying his children privileges. He married again and fathered three sons.

Young Hester went to live first with her maternal grandmother, then her uncle, William Pitt the Younger, an outstanding politician who admired her greatly. She kept house for her unmarried uncle, acting as his hostess and secretary while he was Prime Minister for a second time. She forthrightly discussed major issues of the day with him and his Tory party colleagues, giving her an intimate window on the political landscape. Speaking her mind, she often won enemies as well as friends and admirers. One visitor remarked: 'She will never marry until she finds someone of superior intelligence'. Pitt replied, correctly as it turned out, that meant she would never marry.

By her own admission, she was an attractive woman: 'At 20 my complexion was like alabaster and at five paces distance the sharpest eye could not discover my pearl necklace from my skin. My lips were of such a beautiful carnation that without vanity I assure you very few women had the like. A dark blue under the eyes and the blue veins were observable through the transparent skin heightened the brilliancy of my features. Nor were the roses wanting in my cheeks and to all this was added a permanency to my looks that no fatigue could impair.'

She didn't mention her nose, which was large, or her height – she was far taller than average.

When Pitt died in 1806, Stanhope found herself homeless, although she had an income from the government secured by him on his deathbed.

She enjoyed a number of romances but, after one suitor was killed in the war in Spain in the same battle that killed her brother, she decided to leave England. She headed east on a trail followed by few before her, especially not women from influential and wealthy families. With an entourage including a doctor and a lover, she went to Greece and Turkey and, after being shipwrecked at Rhodes, adopted something approximating traditional male attire from the region which she stuck with for the rest of her life.

Then she visited Egypt, the Lebanon and Syria, particularly perilous for Christians. Despite this, Stanhope decided to ostentatiously process into the notoriously dangerous city of Damascus where she insisted on lodging in the Turkish rather than the Christian quarter. She wrote about the welcome she received in a letter home, mistaking obligatory Islamic hospitality for something approaching idolatry:

> All I can say about myself sounds like a conceit but others could tell you I am the oracle of the place and the darling of all the troops who seemed to think I am a deity because I can ride and I wear arms. And all the fanatics all bow down before me because the dervishes think me a wonder and have given me a piece of Mohammed's tomb and I have won the heart of the Pasha. I was even admitted into the library of the famous mosque and fumbled over the books at leisure, books that no Christian dare touch or even cast their eyes upon. Although sometimes followed by over 2,000 people to my own door not a soul insults me. The women treat me with the greatest kindness. How different they are from English women. What surprises me so much is the extreme civility of the Turks to a Christian, which they detest so much more here than in any other part of the Sultan's dominions. A woman in man's clothes, a woman on horseback, everything directly in

opposition to their strongest prejudices yet never a smile of impertinence. They let me go where I will.

Having in her own view conquered Syria, her aim was now to visit Palmyra, the first western woman to do so, where Queen Zenobia once ruled. In 1813, she set off with twenty-two camels carrying her luggage. Striking up a relationship with Bedouin tribesmen in the desert, she claimed she was crowned an Arab queen:

> To have spent a month with some thousand Bedouin Arabs is no common thing. When the world becomes more corrupt, when civilised people become still more brutal and still more incisive it is a pleasure to reflect there is a spot on earth inhabited by what we call barbarians who have at least some sense of honour and feeling and where one is sure never to be bored with stupidity or gabble. For they are the most brilliant and eloquent people I ever knew.

There was by now some confusion about her mission on behalf of Britain. Having once believed herself a powerbroker and bridge-builder she became more remote from the British. Exotic and eccentric, she had shaped for herself a remarkable role that wasn't repeated for a century, until the advent of Lawrence of Arabia. But English eyes were on France rather than Arabia, and her achievement went largely unrecognised.

At any rate her political potential was ended by illness. After a poorly planned archaeological expedition, she moved to an abandoned monastery at Djoun in the Lebanon, where she gave shelter to numerous refugees from tribal clashes in the region. As people sought her out in the belief she possessed mystical powers, so she believed she was destined to be the bride of a powerful Islamic leader sent by God to rule the Middle East. As a result she studied philosophy and the stars as her debts accrued. When her generous government pension was stopped, she shut herself away at Djoun to die.

She became something of a cautionary tale for Victorians, but for Stanhope there were no regrets: 'I believe in my duty, the duty of everyone of every religion. I have no reproaches to make of myself but that I went rather too far. But such is my nature.'

Robert Louis Stevenson

(1850–1894)

Treasure Island *was the first sustained novel I ever read, with the result that I became addicted to books which had maps in them. It is Stevenson's struggle with his sense of identity that I identify with myself, alongside his aspiration to be honest to his imagination and experience. He made a gallant effort to live life to the full as if he knew he did have a deadline, which I always find affecting.*

Douglas Dunn OBE (Poet and professor)

He was a feverish child in the literal sense, but also there was that concentration of love on the one and only child, who might die at any time. He was the focus of a lot of fretful love and it is clear that he struggled against the bad effects of that.

Claire Harman (Biographer)

A S A CHILD, Robert Louis Stevenson defied the doctors, who declared he was so sickly it was unlikely he would see adulthood. As an adult, RLS defied convention, turning away from established professions to pursue the precarious path of a writer pursuing immortality through print. His sharply curtailed life was marked by the creation of some of the most compelling literature ever produced, including *Treasure Island*, *Strange Case of Dr Jekyll and Mr Hyde* and *Kidnapped*.

He was born to a middle-class family in Edinburgh: his mother Isabella was from a distinguished line of lawyers, while his father Thomas was an engineer responsible for securing lighthouses to some of Scotland's most notoriously treacherous coasts. An only child, RLS was afflicted with weak lungs, which made his parents and beloved nurse overprotective. His mother spent much of his childhood in her bed, suffering what is presumed to be depression. Later he recalled his family life as 'a picnic on a volcano'.

As the focus of abundant, anxious love, RLS escaped into the fantasy world of books powered by his own imagination. Hopes that he would follow his father into engineering were soon dashed by his poor state of health. RLS did qualify as an advocate but never practised in the Scottish legal system. Fortunate to have the financial support of his father for many years, he set about establishing a career as a writer at the same time as seeking a climate that would improve his frail health.

He worked hard to improve his writing skills: 'Nobody had ever such pains to learn a trade as I had but I slogged at it day in, day out and I frankly believed that thanks to my dire industry I have done more with smaller gifts than almost any man of letters in the world.' His published works at this time were primarily essays. Meanwhile he also enjoyed a life marked by extravagant high living and pranks, as he pointedly refused to conform to the strictures of Scottish Victorian and Calvinist living. He wore a velvet smoking jacket over his painfully thin body, had long hair and was known for having a mesmeric appeal. Periodic bouts of ill-health took him to France where he recuperated then travelled at his father's expense.

At an artist's retreat at Grez, outside Paris, he met Fanny Osbourne, a mother of two, eleven years his senior, and escaping from an unhappy marriage. Stevenson fell for her despite the fact she was independently described as having 'the build and character of Napoleon'. In 1879, he followed her back to America, although the gruelling trip was a risk to his health. The following year they married and honeymooned in a disused Californian silver mine. At around this time he wrote a description of himself to fellow author J. M. Barrie:

> Exceedingly lean, dark, rather ruddy – black eyes ... crow's footed, beginning to be grizzled, general appearance of a blasted boy – or blighted youth – or to borrow Carlyle on De Quincy 'child that has been in hell'. Past – eccentric, obscure and oh, we never mention it. Present – industrious, respectable and fatuously contented. Hopelessly entangled in apron strings. Drinks plenty, curses some, temper unstable.

It was thanks to his marriage that the seeds of *Treasure Island* – his first novel and one of the most successful books of all time – were sown. On a rainy holiday in Scotland, he drew a treasure map to amuse his stepson and a plot quickly took shape. RLS knew it had promising beginnings:

> If this don't fetch the kids, why, they have gone rotten since my day. Will you be surprised to learn ... that it begins in the Admiral Benbow public house on [the] Devon coast, that it's all about a map and a treasure and a mutiny and a derelict ship and a current and a fine old Squire Trelawney ... and a doctor and another doctor, and a Sea Cook with one leg, and a sea song with the chorus 'Yo-ho-ho and a bottle of rum' ...

Treasure Island was sold in instalments to a boys' paper even before the story was completed. It was followed by two others, which didn't possess the magic of the first. However, his fourth novel, appearing in 1886, was the enduring *Strange Case of Dr Jekyll and Mr Hyde*, a study in good and evil that reflected society's fears about the rampant advance of chemistry. In the same year, *Kidnapped* was published, with its sequel *Catriona* coming some seven years later. In addition he co-wrote novels with his stepson. RLS was also an accomplished poet and was lauded for his short stories, too, which were admired by writer Sir Arthur Conan Doyle.

In 1888, a year after his father's death, RLS and his family took a cruise from San Francisco to the South Seas, visiting islands including Hawaii, New Zealand and Tahiti. He found the sea air, the native cultures and the warmth restored his general health and spirits.

When finances dictated that his maritime adventures came to an end, he eventually fetched up on Samoa, where he bought a large plot and built a substantial villa. Considerable respect sprang up between him and the Samoans. However, he disliked European politicians who he felt were making a poor job of administering the island. His anti-imperialist stance was courageous for the era.

In Samoa he embarked on a frenzied purple patch of creativity, which left him exhausted. Once again, his health appeared in jeopardy and he resolved to die 'with his boots on' rather than linger as an invalid. In fact, he got his way, keeling over as he strained to open a bottle of wine. The likely cause of death was a brain haemorrhage.

His body was borne shoulder-high by Samoans to its final resting place at the top of Mount Vaea. His tomb bore an inscription written by Stevenson in California some fourteen years before his death, at a time when his demise had seemed imminent:

> *Under the wide and starry sky*
> *Dig the grave and let me lie:*

Glad did I live and gladly die,
And I laid me down with a will.
This be the verse you grave for me:
Here he lies where he longed to be:
Home is the sailor home from sea,
And the hunter home from the hill.

Alfred, Lord Tennyson

(1809–1892)

He wrote two brilliant public poems. That famous physique – the famous hat, the famous cloak – set an idea in the public mind about what a poet might be like and look like. Yet almost everything that is best about his poems has to do with a sense of inwardness, a sense of isolatedness. He is an elegiac poet who found himself having to shoulder all kinds of public burdens and he does it absolutely marvellously.

Sir Andrew Motion (Former Poet Laureate)

He was incredibly famous in a way that we can hardly believe now for a writer. He worried about money even when he was earning masses. Also he worried about his health right through his life. He is tremendously memorable.

Ann Thwaite (Biographer of Tennyson's wife, Emily Sellwood)

ALFRED, LORD TENNYSON'S words have helped to define a generation. Imbued with noble sentiment and picturesque detail, the works of this Poet Laureate, who was born in the same year as William Gladstone and Charles Darwin, put the very essence of Victorian England onto the page. But there is nothing mawkish or corny about his well-remembered works. He adopted a journalistic tenor when he wrote about the Crimean War and the death of British stalwart the Duke of Wellington. 'The Charge of the Light Brigade' was so current because it was rooted in a report published by *The Times* and even included criticism of the government.

In verse, Tennyson drew a searing portrait of suffering and sorrow that has endured through generations. However, his lyrical dexterity blossomed after he was born into what would today be branded a dysfunctional family. He was one of eight sons and four daughters born to Reverend George Clayton Tennyson and his wife Elizabeth in the village of Somersby, Lincolnshire. Although his father was an eldest son, he'd been overlooked by his own landowner father, also called George, in favour of a younger brother and compelled to become a clergyman. The comparatively small inheritance from George after his death caused bitterness in Alfred's family for years.

Prone to depression and bouts of drunkenness, Dr Tennyson intimidated his wife and on at least one occasion took up a knife and fought with one of his sons. Three of the poet's brothers suffered from mental illness in adulthood and were duly hospitalised. Dr Tennyson himself described his children as 'strangely brought up'. In lucid moments, however, the scholarly Dr Tennyson taught his children at home, which was fortunate for Alfred, who hated his spell at a local grammar school.

In 1827, he and another brother went to Trinity College, Cambridge, where he continued a home-grown habit of writing poetry. There he joined a group known as 'the Apostles', where he debated issues of the day. The face of England was changing with the passage of the industrial revolution accompanied by a generous measure of social upheaval. In the passions aroused by talk of democracy and demographics, Tennyson formed some close friendships particularly with fellow student and poet Arthur Hallam. In 1831 upon the death of his father Tennyson left Cambridge without a degree. But this trauma was as nothing compared to the grief he experienced two years later after Hallam's unexpected demise from a brain haemorrhage. At the time Hallam was engaged to one of Tennyson's sisters.

Hallam's death coincided with some of Tennyson's poems receiving hostile reviews from the combative critics of the day. For a decade Tennyson licked his wounds and published nothing. During this reflective period he fell in love with Emily Sellwood, a family friend, but his plans to marry her were shelved after he lost his inheritance by investing in an ecclesiastical woodwork business that failed. He found the sudden uncertainty surrounding his income disconcerting and it sparked a life-long concern about financial security.

In 1842, Tennyson began to publish his output again compelled perhaps by a necessity to make ends meet and became increasingly prodigious. By 1850 he had succeeded William Wordsworth as Poet Laureate, published *In Memoriam*, an elegy to his friend Hallam, and married Emily in the wake of his newfound success. For Emily's part, she had loved him since childhood and pays tribute to his immense physical presence: 'I can scarcely imagine anything more glorious in human form.' She praised his strength, spirituality and tenderness.

Sales of his poetry began to exceed other writers of the day by a considerable margin, although plays that he wrote failed to capture the public imagination in the same way. Still, he seemed an unlikely star of the literary world. Wearing a distinctive hat and cloak, he was shrouded with clouds of cheap, dry tobacco and body odour – in an era when baths were a weekly rather than a daily event, Tennyson still avoided washing. He was also terrified that he had inherited his family's predisposition towards epilepsy, which perhaps accounts for why Emily was his first and only romantic involvement. He was by turns gloomy and funny. For a while he lived with his family on the Isle of Wight where, among his callers, came Prince Albert, the husband of Queen Victoria. After the prince's death Victoria was said to keep *In Memoriam* at her bedside for solace.

Tennyson later moved to Surrey and, when he was knighted in 1883, he became the 1st Baron Tennyson of Aldworth and Freshwater. After some persuasion he took up a seat in the House of Lords. He was still Poet Laureate upon his death, completing a record-breaking tenure of forty-two years.

Recurring influences in his work included Arthurian legend, the myths of classical times, the uncertain fate of Christianity and the frailties of Victorian society. Although he fell from popular favour in the early twentieth century, Tennyson's attention to detail has endured, with critics praising his extraordinary eye and ear. He has remained one of the most quoted of poets. Among the phrases that still pepper everyday life that come originally from Tennyson are: 'Tis better to have loved and lost/Than never to have loved at all', 'Knowledge comes but wisdom lingers' and 'Theirs not to reason why/ Theirs but to do and die.'

Having feared ill health all his life he died aged 83 and was buried in Westminster Abbey. Years after his death he was described by his great-grandson Hallam Tennyson as 'an awesome and slightly ludicrous figure'.

Mother Teresa

(1910–1997)

A lady like Mother Teresa will bring you nearer to religion, [she was] a wonderful person. All she had was what she stood up in which wasn't much. [She was] holding children with all sorts of diseases and malnutrition; loving them, kissing them and caring for them. That is my kind of person.

Bernard Manning (Comedian)

She was there to demonstrate Christ's love in action. On many occasions she said, 'You won't change the situation of the poor. The poor are there in order that we can do our work.' A lot of people didn't understand that. They treated her like a social worker.

Anne Sebba (Biographer)

S HE'S LAUDED AS a saint in our time. Armed with faith and hope, Mother Teresa hauled the dying out of the gutter and into her refuge so that their weakened bodies were lovingly embraced as they slipped towards inevitable death. Initially, Mother Teresa focused the single-minded simplicity of her mission on the mean streets of Calcutta. Eventually, her brand of charity spread across the globe, attracting fame and fortune. Although she displayed few outward symbols of a newfound celebrity status, she did find herself rubbing shoulders with some of the most powerful people of her era.

Life in the media spotlight was a world away from her humble beginnings. She was born Agnes Gonxha Bojaxhiu at a time when the Ottoman Empire still held sway in Eastern Europe. Although she was born in present-day Macedonia, her parents were of Albanian descent. As a child she was fascinated by the work of missionaries, and from the age of 12 she was sure she had a religious calling. Consequently, aged 18, she moved first to Ireland to join the Sisters of Loreto and then to Calcutta where she took her vows as a nun.

Between 1931 and 1948, she worked as a teacher then a headmistress at an Indian convent school. But outside the convent walls, India was being assailed by the unrest that accompanied independence. Hindus and Muslims clashed as Pakistan sheered away from India during Independence from the British Empire in August 1947. For many people, this meant still more distress and misery piling up in a country already renowned for its appalling poverty. Struck by the suffering she witnessed, Mother Teresa won permission to begin working in the slums – at first alone and without funds. She started an open-air school and was soon joined by volunteers and a trickle of cash. She and her fellow sisters wore a simple white sari with a blue border.

In 1950, the Vatican gave its blessing for Mother Teresa to head up her own order, the Missionaries of Charity. The aim was to care for people at the margins of society who lived without the benefit of health, a home, regular food or a loving family. These were people who were generally shunned by society and were considered a burden upon it. This was the launch pad for a group that had grown to a million workers in forty countries by the time of Mother Teresa's death.

Her fame began to grow exponentially after a 1969 television documentary hosted by Malcolm Muggeridge focusing on her work, called *Something Beautiful for God*, later followed by a book. In it, her success in saving unwanted babies from being thrown into dustbins was highlighted. Muggeridge not only hailed her achievements in the gutter but also hinted that he'd seen a divine light emanating from Mother Teresa, which perhaps had more to do with his own spiritual journey than hers.

For her, the perimeters of her charitable works were clear. She helped the poor, often in death. It was never her ambition to resolve the overarching problem of poverty. In the speech she gave after winning the Nobel Peace Prize in 1979, she gave an insight into the nature of her work:

> I have never forgotten bringing a man in from the streets. He was covered with maggots. His face was the only place that was clean. And yet that man, when we brought him to our room for the dying, said just one sentence. 'I have lived like an animal in the streets but I am going to die like an angel [with] love and care.' And he died beautifully. He went home to God.

Indeed, Mother Teresa believed the poor were in some ways fortunate in modern society as the remedy for their ills was relatively straightforward. She reserved special sympathy for the wealthy: 'Being unwanted, unloved, uncared for, forgotten by everybody, I think that is a much greater hunger, a much greater poverty than the person who has nothing to eat.'

But her brand of charity was not to everyone's taste. Her mission ultimately attracted a lot of cash and plenty of medical equipment. None of it was used to help prolong life or even to provide comfort for people in their death throes. Modern X-ray machines lay idle and unused, while liquidisers were rejected as luxury items. Not only were babies and adults left on hard floors during their suffering, they were also observed by touring parties as Mother Teresa was keen to show Christ's care in action. There were even accusations of deathbed baptisms. It was, said some, a cult of suffering that had no place in the modern world.

Moreover, Mother Teresa kept company with some of the more unsavoury characters of the times, including the Duvalier family who cruelly ruled in Haiti and disgraced businessmen including Charles Keating and Robert Maxwell. Unintentionally, she is also thought to have fed prejudice with the notion that India was a barbarous society that could only be remedied with white-faced intervention. Her fierce opposition to contraception and abortion – which also featured in her Nobel acceptance speech – attracted further condemnation. Despite this volley of concerns, the public's perception of her goodness largely remained undented. Mother Teresa was consistently voted the most widely admired person by the US public in annual polls.

The Nobel Prize was by no means the sole accolade awarded to Mother Teresa. She was given numerous degrees, prizes and orders of merit worldwide and stood on podiums alongside the highest-ranked politicians of the late twentieth century to receive them. Her lined face and diminutive figure became familiar on newspaper front pages around the world.

After her death, it came as no surprise to discover the Vatican were fast-tracking her passage to sainthood, although her detractors continued to make themselves heard. She was beatified by Pope John Paul II in 2003 in record time, and is known as Blessed Teresa of Calcutta.

Leon Trotsky

(1879–1940)

I didn't pick him just for his revolutionary career, remarkable though that was. I chose him as a man of action who was also a man of ideas, an intellectual and a tremendous foreign and war correspondent. And perhaps also as the exemplar of the non-fatalist Jew, of the Jew who won't be pushed around and who fights back – and he also demonstrates military genius. [It was] quite an amazing life. He is the only person of the twentieth-century revolutionary generation who hasn't vanished into complete and possibly deserved obscurity as a result of the defeat which may have been inevitable, as Trotsky was concluding at the end of the whole enterprise.

Christopher Hitchens (Journalist)

The man was an orator of genius, had the full range of tones. He was taller than most Russians and he was a very fine-looking man. Some of the original photographs are in the vein of a matinee idol. He was very vain with it and went to the best photographers, to the best suit-makers. He was very egotistical as well as charismatic. He did have absolute commitment to the use of state terror. Because he was so charismatic, because he wrote so well, that tends to coat what we think about Trotsky.

Robert Service (Professor and biographer)

A T THE START of the twentieth century, it seemed like revolution was poised to sweep away age-old institutions in favour of new, radical ideas of government. In fact, most of the European-wide aspirations for social transformation were swallowed up by the all-engulfing imperialist First World War – except in Russia, the bastion of feudal rule where insurgency had been sparking for decades. There was a revolution in Russia – in fact there was more than one – and one of the architects was Leon Trotsky.

More intelligent than Stalin, less dogmatic than Lenin, he nonetheless fared the worst out of the trio who were the headline names of the 1917 Russian Revolution. He famously died after his skull was cleaved by an ice pick. It is less well known that he had spent months leading up to his death questioning whether proletarian revolution was in fact unwinnable and if his life's mission had been futile.

Trotsky was born Lev Davidovich Bronstein, into a Jewish farming household that had moved from northern to southern Russia to escape state-sponsored anti-Semitism. Two years later, Tsar Alexander II was assassinated by young subversives from the 'People's Will' movement.

As a teenager, the young Bronstein latched on to Marxist ideas that were circulating underground in Russia among people weary of the iniquities in Russian society. He was exiled even before the failed 1905 revolution, although the Tsar scaled down his autocracy to stem the chaos. Trotsky escaped and returned to St Petersburg via London to help lead the city's newly wrought Soviet, or political council. En route, he used the false name of a prison guard at a border crossing and was thereafter known as Leon Trotsky.

Tsar Nicholas II regretted making concessions in 1905 in the face of bloodshed and bitterness, and clawed them back as soon as he was able. If the revolution had been a success or had more lasting consequences, the First World War might have been averted. Nor was there harmony among the revolutionaries in Russia who split into two camps. Trotsky was at odds with former comrades, having decided to support the Menshevik movement, an equivalent perhaps to the British Labour Party, rather than the more strident Bolsheviks. At the heart of Menshevik policy was working-class democracy.

Trotsky continued agitating for political change and was exiled several more times before the 1917 February Revolution. During this time, he wrote for the Menshevik newspaper *Iskra* and, through charisma, tended to dominate socialist meetings that he attended. He finally joined Lenin and other Bolsheviks in 1917 in time to help secure Communist rule by the end of the year. An apparent talent, he was immediately made foreign commissar, charged with suing for peace with Germany. Trotsky was then made war commissar, with the new regime under threat from 'the Whites' who supported the old order. His response was to create the Red Army, which he did with characteristic single-mindedness.

Soon he won a reputation for toughness that he justified like this: 'An army cannot be built without reprisals. Masses of men cannot be led to death unless the army command has the death penalty within its arsenal. So long as these malicious tail-less apes that are so proud of their technical achievements, the animals that we call men, will build armies and wage wars the command will always be obliged to place soldiers between the possible death in the front and the inevitable one in the rear.'

It fell to Trotsky to suppress the 1921 Kronstadt rebellion, in which sailors confronted the Bolsheviks on numerous issues including lack of political freedom. Sailors like these had been at the forefront in previous insurrections against the Tsar, but now they showed ruthless brutality to naval officers loyal to the Bolshevik regime. Hundreds were killed when the Red Army arrived to settle the uprising. It was an ethical quagmire for a socialist like Trotsky and something that haunted him for the rest of his life. In reality his choices were limited. Later he insisted: 'The end may justify the means as long as there is something that justifies the end.'

The future seemed assured for Trotsky, who was much admired by Lenin for the way he fashioned an effective fighting force out of the hungry and dispossessed who typically volunteered for the Red Army. Before Lenin's death in 1924, Trotsky was poised to become his successor. But Stalin was canny enough to see what lay ahead and used deft political manoeuvring to assure his own rise to the top. Stalin was supported by Bolsheviks who wanted a period of retrenchment after war, revolution and the associated hardships including starvation. But Trotsky felt the USSR would remain in a state of siege if the socialist revolution did not spread overseas. By 1927 he had been thrown out of the party he helped shape, portrayed as a troublemaker and a threat.

During the following years of exile he continued to criticise Stalin who was responsible for millions of deaths through disastrous rural policies and then widespread purges. Yet Trotsky was reviled through the USSR and elsewhere, with Winston Churchill calling him 'an ogre of international subversion'.

He and his family were finally welcomed by Mexico, and in 1937 he said: 'When monstrous and absurd accusations were hurled at me and my family, the Mexican government opened the doors of this magnificent country and said to us, "Here you can freely defend your right and your honour."'

Still Stalin could not let their rivalry rest, although he knew the chances of Trotsky returning to seize power were nil. In 1940, he dispatched Ramón Mercader to kill Trotsky, who knew he was a target following the suspicious deaths of two of his children. It wasn't until 1987 under glasnost, the political antidote to Stalinism, that he was finally accepted as 'a hero and a martyr'.

Swami Vivekananda

(1863–1902)

I caught religion when I was at Oxford. I'd been a Marxist, and then I felt as though I'd been at a kind of bazaar of spirituality with everybody advertising their own brand. I got indigestion with all of them, as they are all based on rather insecure history. In this bewilderment, by chance, I came across Vivekananda who more or less said, 'Include them all in [your belief system].' One of the problems with western religions is that we all live in little ghettoes and we just don't see each other. He was inclusive.

Rabbi Lionel Blue

He sensed very powerfully there was a change taking place in the world order. He lived in Calcutta, which was a city built by the British, he was very aware of the power of the British Empire. When he travelled to America, he saw a world that was changing and he was trying to sense where India's place would be. He is also seen as an architect of, not the nationalist movement, but the revival of Hinduism that fed into nationalism. He was one of the most significant shapers of what we now know as modern Hinduism.

Gwilym Beckerlegge (Chair, World Religions course,
Open University)

PATRIOT, SAINT AND scholar Swami Vivekananda was one of many who searched for earthly enlightenment on questions of gods, heaven and the afterlife. Most travel from the materialistic West to the ascetic East. He distinguished himself by doing the journey in reverse, changing outlooks and opinions en route.

His career was defined by one eureka moment. Nervously, he stood before 7,000 people at the Parliament of Religions held in Chicago in 1903 as a humble Hindu monk, before addressing the meeting: 'Sisters and Brothers of America.' This typically genial and encompassing greeting alone evoked two minutes of thunderous applause. When he resumed, his message was one of tolerance and universal acceptance for all faiths: 'The Christian is not to become a Hindu or a Buddhist, nor a Hindu or a Buddhist to become a Christian. But each must assimilate the spirit of the others and yet preserve his individuality and grow according to his own law of growth.'

'Vivekananda is undoubtedly the greatest figure in the Parliament of Religions,' said the *New York Herald*. 'After hearing him we feel how foolish it is to send missionaries to this learned nation.'

Vivekananda was born in Calcutta to a rational and pragmatic father, who was a lawyer, and a devoutly Hindu mother. He was educated in the British system and, being a keen reader, learned about different philosophies and faiths when he was a teenager. At around the time his father died, he met spiritual leader Ramakrishna and became drawn to a monastic life. As a result, he spent five years wandering in India with the barest comforts in a quest for greater understanding.

After the death of Ramakrishna, he led the remaining devotee monks, and it was in this context he went to the faith-based conference in Chicago. At first, his aim was to raise money for the poor in India while he was overseas. He soon realised he was something of a celebrity himself and, as a guru, began to question western values.

His charm and intelligence won him many followers. French writer Romain Rolland was one of them, claiming his words 'are great music, phrases in the style of Beethoven, stirring rhythms like the march of Handel choruses.' Describing Vivekananda he said:

> He had an olive complexion, a full face, vast forehead, strong jaw, a pair of magnificent eyes; large, dark and rather prominent with heavy lids whose shape record the classic comparison to a lotus petal. Nothing escapes the magic of his glance, capable equally of embracing with its irresistible charm or of sparkling with wit, irony or kindness, of losing itself in ecstasy or plunging imperiously to the very depths of consciousness and of withering with its fury. But his preeminent characteristic was kingliness. He was a born king, and nobody ever came near him either in India or America without paying homage to his majesty.

At times, Vivekananda had short, sharp rebukes for the West: 'National prosperity is another name for death and degradation to millions of other races.'

As a curious blend of the practical and the divine, he sometimes acted against expectation trying to match the two different worlds of the East and the secular, seductive West. If he drew criticism it was because he enjoyed fine food, snuff and smoking, embracing the metropolitan lifestyle that he condemned. Often, he was readily forgiven. One American woman recalled him at the Chicago conference: 'Seven thousand people rose to their feet as a tribute to something, they knew not what. When it was over, I saw scores of women walking over to the benches to get near him and I said to myself, well, my lad, if you can resist that you are indeed a god.'

After Chicago he travelled to Europe where he discovered unexpected depravation: 'There are three civilised nations in Europe; the French, the Germans and the English. The rest are almost as badly off as we are. The majority of them are so uncivilised that you can find no race in Asia so degraded. Throughout Serbia and Bulgaria you find the same mud houses and people dressed in tattered rags and heaps of filth and I was almost inclined to think I was back in India.'

For many, his words were inspirational. Much later, Mahatma Gandhi said: 'My patriotism increased a hundred times after reading the teachings of Swami Vivekananda.' Yet Vivekananda did not blindly idolise India and, frustrated by his countrymen's passive acceptance of their lot, made passionate rallying calls:

> If you have faith in the 330 million of your mythological gods and in all the gods which foreigners have introduced into your midsts and you have no faith in yourselves there is no salvation for you. Have faith in yourselves and stand up on that faith. Why is it that we millions of people have been ruled by any and every handful of foreigners? Because they had faith in themselves and we had not.

In spite of a splendid physique he was troubled by ill health all his life. He suffered from diabetes, asthma and circulatory problems and was physically exhausted by the exertions of travelling. Still, no one expected his death when it came so prematurely. English writer Christopher Isherwood described the circumstances of his passing:

> His departure from this life had all the marks of a premeditated act. For some months he had been quietly releasing himself from his various responsibilities and making final arrangements. His health gave no particular cause for alarm. He had been ill and now seemed better.
>
> He ate his midday meal with relish, talked philosophy with his brother swamis and went for a walk. In the evening he sat down to meditate, giving instructions that he was not to be

disturbed. Presently he lapsed into samadhi [deep meditation] and the heart stopped beating. It all happened so quietly that nobody could believe this was the end. For hours they tried to rouse him. But his mother's work was done. And Ramakrishna had set him free at last.

Today about 130 centres across the world to help the poor and spread spirituality exist in his name.

George Washington

(1732–1799)

He is someone who had a tremendous influence not only in our history but in world history. He was an insurgent. He could have become a radical who wanted to tip all the known laws of civilisation on their heads and he would have spread the wrong message around the world. As it was he still insisted on maintaining the norms and standards of civilisation.

General Sir Michael Rose

He wanted to make a bold strike and to win [the War of American Independence]. On the other hand, he certainly knew he was fighting a war of attrition, both sides were. It was a matter of who could stay the longest. He did change tactics over time but I don't think success was a guaranteed outcome for the Americans. In fact, many times the army was on the verge of disbanding.

Frank E. Grizzard (Biographer)

A S A SOLDIER, he defeated the English army when its redcoats were the best in the world. As a statesman, he shaped a government that was in essence fair and just. He did not act for personal gain, refusing a crown that would have made him King of America. Generations of Americans had no better example to mirror than the high integrity demonstrated by the country's first President – George Washington.

Washington was a third-generation settler in Virginia, whose father died when he was 11. He trained himself to be a surveyor and as a young man spent some time mapping the Shenandoah Valley.

Initially, he fought alongside the British as a member of the Virginia militia against the combined forces of the French and Indians, as colonists sought to push into new territories, and he distinguished himself with acts of extraordinary or even foolhardy bravery. On at least one occasion, he was saved from certain death by the blade of a tomahawk thanks to the timely intervention of a British soldier. After one defeat at the hands of the French, he wrote to his brother: 'I can with truth assure you I heard bullets whistle and believe me there was something charming in the sound.' Later, King George II, who was the last English king to lead troops into battle, remarked: 'These are the words of a man who has not seen battle.'

After these wars, Washington retired to Virginia to manage his family plantation. He was elected to Virginia's governing body in 1758 and married widow Martha Custis the following year. But unfolding events put an end to relaxed country living. Americans including Washington were aggrieved by excessive taxation levied by the ruling British. With feelings running high, Washington was recalled to lead the American army in 1775, although he readily confessed he did not feel equal to the task.

The men fighting for America were fervent but ill-disciplined and inexperienced. Opposing them after America declared independence were the world's most competent and seasoned forces, albeit fighting a long way from home. Washington soon realised that conventional warfare would not bring about results for the Americans, so he resolved on a policy of harassment, the precursor of guerrilla warfare. Thomas Jefferson described Washington, the military commander, as a man 'incapable of fear':

> Certainly no general ever planned his battles more judiciously but if deranged during the course of the action if any member of his plan was dislocated by sudden circumstances he was slow in readjustment. Perhaps the strongest feature in his character was prudence, never acting until every circumstance, every consideration was maturely weighed, refraining if he saw doubt but when once decided going through with this purpose whatever obstacles opposed. His integrity was most pure, his justice the most inflexible I have ever known. No motives of interest or consanguinity of friendship or hatred being able to bias his decision. He was indeed in every sense of the word a wise, a good and a great man.

For a while, Washington struggled to mould a fighting force out of the men before him. His problems were compounded when officers began to drift back to their homes and farms after defeats inflicted by the British. Finally, with persistence, sound planning and a few inspired appointments, Washington overcame the occupying force by 1781.

Now he saw a role for himself in the all-new political arena and he had very certain ideas which way America should be administratively organised. 'It is clear to me as a, b, c that an extension of federal powers would make us one of the most happy, wealthy, respectable and powerful nations that ever inhabited the terrestrial globe. Without them we shall soon be everything which is the direct reverse. I predict the worse consequences from a half starved limping government always moving upon crutches and tottering at every step.'

Thus the federal model was born. In 1789, Washington, who represented no political party, was unanimously elected first President by the government operating within the new constitution and saluted a flag that featured just 13 stars, representing the number of states under his jurisdiction. (Five more would be added during his eight-year tenure.)

Filling a blank page, Washington felt responsible for every major appointment himself. He made himself accountable for bookkeeping. He attempted to reply to every letter sent to government. A strong moral code prevented him from feather-bedding by siphoning off cash benefits for himself and he bent over backwards not to put his friends and relatives in high office unless he genuinely thought they were the best applicants for the job. Against his better judgement, the two-party system took root in the USA. At the end of two terms in office, he was exhausted and even disillusioned but at the time he did not appreciate the far-reaching effects of his presidency. Intuitively, in his farewell address he warned America against getting too close to any other nation. Underlying his behaviour was a devout faith that was also confident and tolerant. Speaking to a Jewish congregation in Newport in August 1790, he underlined American achievement in an age frequently pockmarked by persecution:

> The citizens of the United States of America have a right to applaud themselves for having given to mankind examples of an enlarged and liberal policy, a policy worthy of imitation. All possess alike liberty of conscience and immunities of citizenship. It is now no more that toleration is spoken of as if it was by the indulgence of one class of people that another enjoyed the exercise of their inherent natural rights. For happily the government of the United States which gives to bigotry no sanction, to persecution no assistance, requires only that they who live under its protection should demean themselves as good citizens in giving it on all occasions their effectual support while everyone shall sit in safety under his own vine and fig tree and there shall be none to make him afraid.

Duke of Wellington

(1769–1852)

First of all he was a man whose achievements changed the whole face of the continent in which we live. The effects of what he did are probably still with us. I thought also that he was remarkable because he was ahead of his time in many of his attitudes. He made it [to the top] by sheer talent.

Frederick Forsyth (Author)

He was far and away the greatest commander that the allies had at the time. He had never lost a battle in all of the sixty-two battles he fought in his career and never lost a single gun. Pretty much any other general would have fared worse [at Waterloo] and it was a pretty close battle even then.

Andrew Roberts (Biographer)

ARTHUR WELLESLEY WAS an idle schoolboy, talented musician, skilful general, 'the saviour of nations', a failed prime minister, class enemy and public hero. He was acknowledged as an equal by Napoleon abroad and he was hated by the mob at home. For him, sturdy rubber boots were named. Although the title was hereditary and still exists today, the term Duke of Wellington only brings one man to mind.

Arthur Wesley was the fourth son born in Ireland to an aristocratic family – the spelling of his surname changed in 1798. Although he went to Eton, he was an undistinguished scholar. After his father died, the family were short of money and Wesley abandoned hopes of a musical career to join the army. A fellow officer described him like this: 'In person he was about 5ft 7ins with a long pale face, a remarkably large, aquiline nose, a clear blue eye and the blackest beard I ever saw. I have known him shave twice in one day which I believe was his constant practice. He was remarkably clean in his person. He spoke at this time remarkably quickly with a very, very slight lisp. He had a particular way when pleased of pursing up his mouth. I have often observed it when he's been thinking abstractedly.'

Aged 24, he went to the Netherlands as a lieutenant colonel to fight for the Duke of York. The campaign was unsuccessful and Wesley returned home mildly grateful for having witnessed the wrong way to run a battle, a lesson learned. He was then dispatched to India where he embarked on a career as a commander that was barely blemished by defeat. Struck by the importance of the correct tactics, his approach was marked by painstaking reconnaissance, the appropriate positioning of men before battle, strict discipline, the supply of adequate provisions and shelter for soldiers, flanking manoeuvres and timed rifle firing from two lines of men. Consequently he shone as an efficient commander in an era where incompetents were commonplace, and for exhibiting a degree of concern for his men that was also rarely found.

His success in India brought promotion to field marshal, a considerable personal fortune and a knighthood, and he finally returned home in 1805, the year Nelson set about French naval forces at Trafalgar. Two years later, he entered Parliament as MP for Rye, not for any great political desire but for personal advancement. Two of his brothers were already in Parliament. In 1806, he finally married Catherine or Kitty Pakenham, thirteen years after his first proposal was dismissed by her family because he appeared a poor prospect. Although she adored him, he found her tedious company and was well known for taking numerous mistresses.

Two years later, he set off for Portugal heading an expeditionary force intended to spike the French guns in occupied Iberia. The Peninsular Wars raged for six years. Wellesley created a coalition with the Spanish and Portuguese and worked hard to keep it intact, ensuring local support by stopping his men robbing local people. Using fewer soldiers than usual, he found his army quicker on its feet and easier to feed than their more numerous French opponents. If he felt it necessary he retreated rather than risk his men in a hopeless battle. Before the war was over, he defeated six Napoleonic marshals with his superior strategies.

He was then made the Duke of Wellington and sent as British ambassador to France after Napoleon was exiled, where he was so unpopular he was even the target of an assassination attempt. After 100 days, Napoleon escaped from Elba, gathered a volunteer army and shaped up for the Battle of Waterloo. Wellington was so relaxed he even attended a ball the night before hostilities. Victory was his, but it was a narrow margin after support troops led by Prussian ally Gebhard Leberecht von Blücher turned up late. MP Thomas Creevey later noted Wellington's cool response:

> 'It has been a damned serious business,' he said. 'Blücher and I have lost 30,000 men. It has been a damned nice thing, the nearest run thing you ever saw in your life.' As he walked about he praised greatly those guards who had kept the farm against the repeated attacks of the French. And then he praised all our

troops uttering repeated phrases of astonishment at our men's courage. He repeated so often: 'It's been so nice a thing, so nearly run a thing'. Then he said: 'By God, I don't think it would have been done if I had not been there.'

Blücher wanted to shoot the captured Napoleon but Wellington had a more humane approach, realising the French ruler's career was finished. He was surprisingly downbeat after the triumph, writing to his brother: 'Nothing except a battle lost can be half as melancholy as a battle won.'

When he returned to England, Wellington was bathed in glory before he turned his attentions to politics once more, finally becoming Prime Minister in 1828. Unfortunately his shine was soon dimmed as he proved immoveable in his reactionary views. After his first cabinet meeting, he muttered: 'An extraordinary affair. I gave them their orders and they wanted to stay and discuss them.' His administration made some unpopular moves, particularly with regard to extending rights for Catholics.

Diarist Charles Greville wrote about Wellington and his short-lived time in office in the following terms: 'Confident, presumptuous and dictatorial, but frank, open and good humoured, he contrived to rule in the cabinet without mortifying his colleagues and he has brought it to ruin without forfeiting their regard. Choosing with a very slender stock of knowledge to take upon himself the sole direction of every department of government he completely sank under the burden. He has not been thoroughly true to any principle or any party. He contrived to disgust and alienate his old friends and adherents without conciliating or attaching those whose measures at the eleventh hour he undertook to carry into execution.'

He and the Tory party continued to block reform of the outdated voting laws, using their might in the House of Lords to prevent Liberal proposals. He put iron shutters in front of his house to deter protestors, thus earning the title 'the Iron Duke'. When he finally retired from public life in 1846 he was seen as a hero with feet of clay. Yet upon his death, his body lay in state in Chelsea hospital and an estimated million and a half people watched the funeral procession, grateful for the prolonged period of peace that his military achievements had given them.

Mae West

(1893–1980)

She makes every writer want to impale themselves on her pen because she is so talented. She has this minestrone mix of talent which made her a successful comedian, singer, dancer, playwright, director, actress, scriptwriter, producer, sex goddess and novelist. She was also a feminist who made Madonna look like Julie Andrews, an intellectual who rubbed shoulders with Roosevelt, a civil libertarian and a brilliant businesswoman. She did all this in an era when women did not have the vote.

Kathy Lette (Author)

She had a great singing voice, she sang ragtime and she had a large bosom. Everyone commented on that because it was unusual at the time for a performer. The men loved it and the women loved her independence, so she had it both ways. She developed this sassy persona on the fly.

Simon Louvish (Biographer)

'BETWEEN TWO EVILS, I always pick the one I never tried before.' It's swift, suggestive and one of many wisecracks that made Mae West the darling of stage and silver screen between two world wars. Bold, blonde and bosomy, it seemed West was sufficiently well-endowed with natural assets to keep her star soaring for years. During the Second World War, lifejackets used by servicemen at sea were called Mae Wests, for the way they inflated around the chest. But there was more to West than just curves and quips. She worked ceaselessly on jokes, scripts and plays to elevate her act from the norm. Moreover, she confronted censors of the age with dignity and courage, risking her career to do so.

Mary Jane West was one of three children born to a prize fighter known as 'Battling Jack' and a former corset model called Matilda or Tillie. As a child she began entertaining at church socials and got hooked on adulation. 'I always wanted to be admired,' she confessed later. 'I was crazy about admiration.' After school she appeared in vaudeville shows, cashing in as much on her ready wit as her good looks. Indeed, her hourglass figure was unfashionable at a time when a boyish look was more in vogue.

After shows, she went back to her room to write new material. She spent hours meticulously collating and refining gags from books, magazines and other performers. With her husky delivery, she could wring new mileage from the oldest jokes. And while she made the most of her dissolute image, she was in fact virtually teetotal, didn't smoke or take drugs. She ate well, exercised and worked long hours, sometimes through the night.

But she also nurtured a capacity to shock. She shimmied on stage, mimicking the way black people danced. At the time this kind of imitation never happened among white people and it was considered dangerously egalitarian. In 1926, she was the writer, producer and star of a Broadway show called *Sex*. Although the public flocked through the doors, she was asked to close because of the play's racy content. She declined. Ultimately, the theatre was raided by the police and West landed in the dock, charged with corrupting the morals of youth, for which she got a ten-day jail sentence. She was released after eight for good behaviour.

Afterwards, she marketed herself as a figurehead for marginalised groups in society, like prostitutes and homosexuals. 'I realised the problem and devoted my career in the theatre to the education of the masses. I shall boldly continue to do so in spite of criticism, insults and narrow-minded bigots,' she declared. Often it was her refusal to 'redeem' characters, by having them renounce their bad old ways and begin a goodly life, that outraged the censors. In a bid to sidestep their attention, she developed a range of slight movements, like a raised eyebrow or a shrug, to impart innuendo. Her performances were also laden with irony and self deprecation.

In her private life she married as early as 1911, but it didn't last. She also had a few long-term relationships, including one with her agent James Timony and later with bodybuilder Paul Novak, when he was a quarter of a century younger than her. She was brutally honest about her shortcomings as a partner: 'Marriage and one man for life is fine for some people but for me it wasn't any good. Every time I looked at myself I became absorbed in myself and I didn't want to get involved with another person like that. I was my own baby, I had myself to do things for.'

She created the character which ultimately defined her on Broadway and in Hollywood – brothel madam Diamond Lil, a 'tart with a heart' – in April 1928. Then, with the arrival of talkies, she found another outlet for her caustic dialogue and discovered an army of fans hungry for her brand of humour. Although she was 38 before her making her film debut in 1932 she looked much younger and doctored her real age. Starring opposite George Raft in *Night after Night*, she insisted on rewriting her scenes and, according to Raft, 'stole everything but the cameras'. There followed a successful partnership with Cary Grant, and by 1934 she was the highest-paid performer in America.

But her free use of double entendres attracted the attention of the censors, who determined to silence her once and for all. Although the film company Paramount initially fought for her freedom of expression, the release of a film that had a Diamond Lil character discussing religion and hypocrisy was widely deemed beyond the pale. The Hays Code, which controlled Hollywood, was a powerful instrument at the time. However, she continued in character at every opportunity. When her first husband cropped up seeking a divorce and revealing her real age at the end of the thirties, she sashayed into court looking every inch a star.

In the late 1940s and 1950s, she took her show to Broadway and then to Las Vegas, where she surrounded herself with beefcakes while she wore blonde wigs and ball gowns. In a short hop, she was a gay icon, proving that she was nothing if not a survivor. While Mae West was a feminist, she had remarkably few female friends, although she remained close to her sister. It's unlikely her glamour repelled women, since, without make-up and glitter, she could go unnoticed in restaurants. The presumption is that she was too concerned with work to devote time and energy to friendship. Her one-liners have certainly stood the test of time and phrases like 'Come up and see me sometime' and 'I believe it is better to be looked over than overlooked' live on.

There is an argument to say that she paved the way for later stars, including Katharine Hepburn, who was similarly cutting, and Marilyn Monroe. In a 1971 interview with *Playboy*, she revealed that at aged 78 she had lost none of her spark: 'A reporter asked me recently what I wanted to be remembered for. And I told him: everything.'

Edith Wharton

(1862–1937)

She came from a very fine nineteenth-century New York family, and it's not so much a story of rags to riches as from riches to writing. She overcame the social barriers at the top to become an artist and to achieve her life's goals.

Kimberley Fortier (Publisher)

She started her writing career with a novel about eighteenth-century Italy and put up a kind of barrage of scholarship against any question she might face. Her main problem was that the background she came from was deeply philistine. It may have been affluent – but she was an intellectual.

Professor Janet Beer (University Vice Chancellor)

W RITER EDITH WHARTON was born into an unusual dilemma. The daughter of an American 'old money' family, nothing more was expected of the young, auburn-haired Edith than to make a good marriage and to embrace a social life in fashionable society. She wasn't so much born with a silver spoon in her mouth as the entire cutlery set. But Wharton valued education much more highly than the rest of her family. As a child, in the absence of formal schooling and only sporadic tutoring, she hunkered down in her father's library when they were at home and pored over every book she could reach. Much of her childhood was spent overseas, however, as her family travelled around Europe.

Her first challenge as an aspiring writer was to find some paper on which to write among her family's numerous high-spec possessions. The inner conflict between what she wanted and what was expected of her often induced a fog of depression. In old age, her mantelpiece was laden with awards. Wharton received the Légion d'Honneur for her work during the First World War, the 1921 Pulitzer Prize for one of her novels and, two years later, she became the first woman to be awarded an honorary doctorate from Yale. Yet her acclaimed dexterity with words brought her more satisfaction than any number of gongs.

Her first volume of poems was published when she was 16, at her mother's expense. A non-fiction book called *The Decoration of Houses*, co-written with an architect, won some commercial success in 1897. It is, however, novels rather than poetry or interior design for which she is best remembered. She penned various short stories before publishing her first novel, *The Valley of Decision*, in 1902 when she was 40 years old. By this time she was unhappily married to 'Teddy' Wharton, a wealthy Bostonian. Before meeting her husband-to-be, she had lost her heart to lawyer and judge Walter Berry, although her feelings were never returned. She and Berry enjoyed a lifelong friendship while her marriage lacked warmth, intellectual parity and, indeed, fidelity. The same sense of suffocation that at times descended in her youth recurred.

In her forties, Wharton began an affair with Morton Fullerton, an American journalist who worked for the London *Times* in Paris. Both were friends of writer Henry James. Excerpts from the letters she wrote to Fullerton, which came into the public domain some thirty years ago, reveal it was at times a pretty one-sided affair:

> Write or don't write, as you feel the impulse – but hold me long & close in your thoughts. I shall take up so little room, & it's only there that I'm happy!

> And when you spoke of your uncertain future, your longing to break away & do the work you really like, didn't you see how my heart broke with the thought that, if I had been younger & prettier, everything might have been different.

> What you wish, apparently, is to take of my life the inmost & uttermost that a woman – a woman like me – can give, for an hour, now & then, when it suits you; & when the hour is over, to leave me out of your mind & out of your life as a man leaves a companion who has accorded him a transient distraction. I think I am worth more than that.

Her marriage finally ended after her husband, who suffered a long-term mental breakdown, confessed he had embezzled thousands of dollars from her to set up his mistress in a love nest.

Throughout the turmoil, writing wielded curative powers and, in 1905, she published *The House of Mirth*, a rich and ultimately distressing tale of high society. Critic Diana Trilling called it 'one of the most telling indictments of the whole of American society, of a whole social system based on the chance distribution of wealth, that has ever been put on paper.' In 1911, *Ethan Frome* was published, one of her best read works, followed two years later by *The*

Custom of the Country, a satire on American provincial life in her usual punishing style. Wharton was in London when the First World War broke out. Immediately she headed for France where she carried out extensive relief work and even visited the front line. Some of her experiences are chronicled in *Fighting France, From Dunkerque to Belfort*, published in 1915. In a tally of more than forty books, the acknowledged masterpiece is *The Age of Reason*, which won the Pulitzer Prize. Like many of her works, it focuses on the havoc wreaked by social conventions corseting New York society.

A committed Francophile, she returned to America only once after the war and instead made herself at home in Paris and Provence. Here she mixed with artists and writers who loved to talk about her books, which went largely unmentioned by her remaining family in America. Her talents were more broadly recognised in America, though, and in 1930 she became the first woman to be awarded a gold medal by the American Institute for Arts and Letters.

In 1934, her memoirs, *A Backward Glance*, revealed more about how torn she was between the life she was born to and the one she fashioned for herself. She considered herself from 'the most displaced and useless class on earth' and it is this theme centring on the idle rich that recurs time and again in her writing. Finally she managed to pare down her formula for a full and happy life to a few words:

> In spite of illness, in spite even of the arch enemy sorrow, one can remain alive long past the usual date of disintegration if one is unafraid of change, insatiable in intellectual curiosity, interested in the big things and happy in small ways.